# *Life and Vision*
# *of*
# Jawaharlal Nehru

# Life and Vision *of* Jawaharlal Nehru

**Dr. Vivekanand Shukla**
*University Professor, Dept. of History*
*B.R.A. Bihar University, Muzaffarpur*

**ABD PUBLISHERS**
Jaipur ■ New Delhi

**ABD PUBLISHERS**

**Regd. Off.** "Bony Residency", Gate No. 2
Opp. Tilak Public School, Vishweswariya Nagar,
Gopalpura Road, Jaipur - 302018, India
Ph: 0141 - 2761280, Telefax: 2761381
Email: abdpublishersjpr@gmail.com

**Delhi Office:** 102, 1st Floor, Satyam House,
4327/3, Ansari Road, Darya Ganj,
New Delhi - 110002, India
Ph: 011-45652440

visit us: www.oxfordbookcompany.com

Published in India, 2024



ISBN : 9788183762397

Price : ₹ 1625/-



Typeset by Shivangi Computer, Jaipur

Printed and bound in India by Thomson Press Ltd.,
New Delhi

# Preface

After independence Nehru served as India first Prime Minister from 1947 until he died in May, 1964. He was also a great internationalist, and one of the founders of the non-aligned movement.Nehru was a renowned orator. He could give many extemporaneous speeches in a single day. His most famous speech is the "Tryst With Destiny" address to the Constituent Assembly of India in New Delhi on the night of August 14th and 15th, 1947.

In a few moments, India was to become independent after centuries of colonial invasion and rule:

"Long years ago we made a tryst with destiny, and now the time comes when we shall redeem our pledge, not wholly or in full measure, but very substantially. At the stroke of the midnight hour, when the world sleeps, India will awake to life and freedom. A moment comes, which comes but rarely in history, when we step out from the old to the new, when an age ends, and when the soul of a nation, long suppressed, finds utterance. It is fitting that at this solemn moment we take the pledge of dedication to the service of India and her people and to the still larger cause of humanity.""

Jawaharlal Nehru, the man who made a tryst with destiny, was a leader who kept his promise and led India to freedom. The first Prime Minister of India, he came to the forefront of the Indian freedom struggle after Jallianwalah Bagh massacre. Devoted to the cause of freedom, he was a representative of a whole new generation of India. World Peace and all round development of India were the main concerns of this great statesman. 'Chacha Nehru', as he was fondly called by children, was amongst the prominent names behind the establishment of the Non Aligned Movement (NAM).

Though he had a good career record, his last eight-years as the Prime Minister of the country were not very successful. The country was facing both internal and external crisis during these eight years. Some of the economic policies that were set by Pandit Jawaharlal Nehru were not accepted in the country as well as in the foreign countries. It was also believed that he could not control the ongoing procedures in the country and there was anarchy all around. During the tenure of Nehru as the Prime Minister, Five-Year plans were initiated for the development and progress of the nation. The second Five Year Plan was initiated in the year 1956 and it mainly concentrated on the industrial development of the country. The establishment of several heavy engineering industries was emphasized in this Five Year Plan.

However, there was a problem that hampered the growth of these industries completely. Huge finances were required to set up these establishments, but the Government could fund only about one-third part of the total budget. The rest had to be funded by the several international institutions, World Bank and many more financing companies. This clearly depicted that India was greatly dependent on international financial aids and showed a clear picture of the economic conditions in the country. This pushed Jawaharlal Nehru into back gear. Within a year of the inception of the Second Five Year Plan, the whole plan failed to meet most of the targets that were set. Weather conditions were also unfavorable during this time and this hampered the growth of the nation to a great deal.

Pt Jawaharlal Nehru was not just a man or a Prime Minister, he was a phenomenon who gave shape to the dreams of independent India and permeated the lives of Indians. The present publication included a brief account of the life of Pt. Jawaharlal Nehru and his religious, political , economic, social and educational thoughts. It is hoped that the publication will be of great value not only to the religious and political thinkers, social scientists, educationists and students but also to the general reader.

—*Dr. Vivekanand Shukla*

# Contents

# 1 Introduction

Pandit Jawaharlal Nehru (November 14,1889–May 27, 1964) was a major political leader of the Congress Party, a pivotal figure in the Indian independence movement and the first Prime Minister of independent India. He was also a key figure in international politics in the post-war period (in which he was considered the leader of third world interests) and patriarch of the Nehru-Gandhi family, one of the most influential forces in Indian politics. He is popularly referred to as Panditji (*Scholar*) and Pandit Nehru.

The son of the wealthy Indian barrister and politician Motilal Nehru, Nehru became a leader of the left-wing of the Indian National Congress at a remarkably young age. Rising to Congress President under the mentorship of Mahatma Gandhi, Nehru was a charismatic, radical leader, advocating complete independence from the British Empire, and was eventually recognised as Gandhi's political heir. A life-long liberal intellectually, Nehru was also an advocate for Fabian socialism and the public sector as the means by which long-standing challenges of economic development could be addressed.

Serving as Congress President, Nehru raised the flag of independent India in New Delhi on August 15, 1947, and served as Prime Minister. His daughter Indira and grandson Rajiv would both also serve as Prime Minister and President of the Indian National Congress, as would Rajiv's wife Sonia. His long tenure was instrumental in shaping the traditions and structures of independent India.

## Early Life

Jawaharlal Nehru was born in the city of Allahabad, situated along the banks of the Ganges River (now in the state of Uttar Pradesh). He was the eldest child of Swarup Rani, the wife of wealthy barrister Motilal Nehru. The Nehru family descended from Kashmiri heritage and belonged to the Saraswat Brahmin caste of Hindus. Training as a lawyer, Motilal had moved to Allahabad and developed a successful practise and had become active in India's largest political party, the Indian National Congress. Nehru and his sisters – Vijaya Lakshmi and Krishna – lived in a large mansion called Anand Bhavan and were raised with English customs, mannerisms and dress. While learning Hindi and Sanskrit, the Nehru children would be trained to converse fluently and regularly in English.

### *Jawaharlal and Kamala at their Wedding*

After being tutored at home and attending some of the most modern schools in India, Nehru travelled to England at the age of 15 to attend Harrow. Nicknamed "Joe" while there, he proceeded to study natural sciences at Trinity College, Cambridge before choosing to train as a barrister at the Inner Temple in London. Frequenting the theatres, museums and opera houses of London, he would spend his vacations travelling across Europe. Observers later described him as an elegant, charming young intellectual and socialite. Nehru also actively participated in the political activities of the Indian student community, growing increasingly attracted to socialism and liberalism, which were beginning to influence the politics and economies of Europe.

Upon his return to India, Nehru's marriage was arranged with Kamala Kaul. Married on February 8, 1916, Nehru was 27 and his bride was 17 years old, at the time. The first few years of their marriage were hampered by the cultural gulf between the anglicized Nehru and Kamala, who observed Hindu traditions and focused on family affairs. The following year Kamala gave birth to their only child, their daughter Indira Priyadarshini. Having made few attempts to establish himself in a legal practise, Nehru was immediately attracted to Indian political life, which at the time was emerging from divisions over World War I. The moderate and extremist factions of the Congress had reunited in its 1916 session in Lucknow, and Indian politicians had demanded *Home Rule* and dominion status for India. Joining the Congress under the patronage of his father, Nehru grew increasingly disillusioned with the liberal and anglicized nature of Congress politicians, which included his father. Although frequently hailed as a future leader of the Congress and India, Nehru's political rise did not begin until the arrival of Mahatma Gandhi on India's political arena.

## Young Leader

Nehru was very strongly attracted to Gandhi's philosophy and leadership. Gandhi had led a successful rebellion on behalf of indentured Indian workers while a lawyer in South Africa. Upon his return to India, Gandhi organised the peasants and farmers of Champaran and Kheda in successful rebellions against oppressive tax policies levied by the British. Gandhi espoused what he termed as *satyagraha* – mass civil disobedience governed by *ahimsa,* or complete non-violence. A forceful exponent of Indian self-reliance, Gandhi's success electrified Indians, who had been divided in their approach to contesting British rule. Having met Gandhi and learning his ideas, Nehru assisted him during the Champaran agitation.

The family of Motilal Nehru, with Jawaharlal, his wife Kamala and daughter Indira.

Following Gandhi's example, Nehru and his family abandoned their Western-style clothes, possessions and wealthy lifestyle. Wearing clothes spun out of *khadi,* Nehru emerged as one of the most energetic supporters of Gandhi. Under Gandhi's influence, Nehru began studying the *Bhagavad Gita* and practiced yoga throughout his life. He would increasingly look to Gandhi for advice and guidance in his personal life, and would spend a lot of time travelling and living with Gandhi. Nehru travelled across India delivering political speeches aimed at recruiting India's masses, especially its youth into the agitation launched in 1919 against the Rowlatt Acts and the Khilafat struggle. He spoke passionately and forcefully to encourage Hindu-Muslim unity, spread education and self-reliance and the need to eradicate social evils such as untouchability, poverty, ignorance and unemployment.

*The Young Nehru*

Emerging as a key orator and prominent organiser, Nehru became one of the most popular political leaders in northern India, especially with the people of the United Provinces, Bihar and the Central Provinces. His youth and passion for social justice and equality attracted India's Muslims, women and other minorities. Nehru's role grew especially important following the arrest of senior leaders such as Gandhi and his father, and he was also imprisoned along with his mother and sisters for many months. Alarmed by growing violence in the conduct of mass agitations, Gandhi suspended the struggle after the killing of 22 state policemen by a mob at Chauri Chaura on February 4, 1922. This sudden move disillusioned some, including Nehru's father Motilal, who joined the newly formed Swaraj Party in 1923. However, Nehru remained loyal to Gandhi and publicly supported him.

A lull in nationalist activities enabled Nehru to turn his attention to social causes and local government. In 1924, he was elected president of the municipal corporation of Allahabad, serving as the city's chief executive for two years. Nehru launched ambitious schemes to promote education, sanitation, expand water and electricity supply and reduce unemployment – his ideas and experience proved valuable to him when he would assume charge of India's government in 1947. Achieving some success, Nehru was dissatisfied and angered by the obstruction of British officials and corruption amongst civil servants. He resigned from his position within two years.

In the early part of the decade, his marriage and family life had suffered owing to the constant activity on his part and that of his father. Although facing domestic pressures and tensions in the absence of her husband, Kamala would increasingly travel with Nehru, address public meetings and seek to sponsor and encourage nationalist activities in her hometown. In the late 1920s, the initial marital gulf between the two disappeared and the couple grew closer to each other and their daughter. In 1926 Nehru took his wife and daughter to Europe so that Kamala could receive special medical care. The family travelled and lived in England, Switzerland, France and Germany. Continuing his political work, Nehru was deeply impressed by the rising currents of radical socialism in Europe, and delivered fervent speeches in condemnation of imperialism. On a visit to the Soviet Union, Nehru was favourably impressed by the command economy, but grew critical of Stalin's totalitarianism.

## Congress President

### *Nehru and Gandhi*

In the 1920s, Nehru was elected president of the All India Trade Unions Congress. He and Subhash Chandra Bose had become the most prominent youth leaders, and both demanded outright political independence of India. In 1927, he became a member of the League against Imperialism created in Brussels. Nehru criticised the Nehru Report prepared by his father in 1928, which called for dominion status for India within the British Empire.

The radicalism of Nehru and Bose would provoke intense debates during the 1928 Congress session in Guwahati. Arguing that India would deliver an ultimatum to the British and prepare for mass struggle, Nehru and Bose won the hearts of many young Indians. To resolve the issue, Gandhi said that the British would be given two years to grant India dominion status. If they did not, the Indian National Congress (INC) would launch a national struggle for full political independence. Nehru and Bose succeeded in reducing the statutory deadline to one year.

The failure of talks with the British caused the December 1929 session in Lahore to be held in an atmosphere charged with anti-Empire sentiment. Preparing for the declaration of independence, the AICC elected Jawaharlal Nehru as Congress President at the encouragement of Gandhi. Nehru himself recalled that he was sensible of the fact that it was considered somewhat surprising:

> *"I have seldom felt quite so annoyed and humiliated... It is not that I was not sensible of the honour... But I did not come to it by the main entrance or even the side entrance: I appeared*

*suddenly from a trap door and bewildered the audience into acceptance."*

On December 31, 1929 President Nehru hoisted the flag of independence before a massive public gathering along the banks of the Ravi River. The Congress would promulgate the *Purna Swaraj* (*Complete Independence*) declaration on January 26, 1930. With the launching of the Salt Satyagraha in 1930, Nehru travelled across Gujarat and other parts of the country participating and encouraging in the mass rebellion against the salt tax. Despite his father's death in 1931, Nehru and his family remained at the forefront of the struggle. Arrested with his wife and sisters, Nehru was imprisoned for all but four months between 1931 and 1935. During that same period, however, his popularity grew enormously. According to John Gunther, Nehru was both "distrustful of it, while simultaneously unable to control being somewhat " exhilarated and impressed".

His family quickly chastened him with raillery; his wife and sisters, and even his small daughter, began to call him in the home the names he was given by the crowd. They would say, "Oh Jewel of India, what time is it?" or "Oh Embodiment of Sacrifice, please pass the bread."

***Nehru and Gandhi at the 1942 Congress in Bombay***

Nehru was released by the British and he traveled with his family once again to Europe in 1935, where his ailing wife Kamala would remain bed-ridden. Torn between the freedom struggle and tending to his wife, Nehru would travel back and forth between India and Europe. Kamala Nehru died on February 28, 1936. Deeply saddened, Nehru nevertheless continued to maintain a hectic schedule. In her memory, he wore a fresh rose on his coat for the rest of his life.

His popularity continued to grow, and his personal discomfort with that popularity rose with it. In the November, 1937 issue of the Calcutta-based journal *Modern Review*, an article entitled 'The Rashtrapati' severely criticized him. The anonymous author acknowledged Nehru's initiative and innate drive but also pointed out glaring streaks of autocracy, saying that his character was marked by "intolerance of others and a certain contempt for the weak and inefficient". The author, who signed himself "*Chanakya*", added that Nehru's conceit was "already formidable", and worried that soon "Jawaharlal might fancy himself as a Caesar". It was not suspected at the time that *Chanakya* was Nehru himself. This publication is a significantly important example of autocritique.

Nehru had been re-elected Indian National Congress(INC) President in 1936, and had presided over its session in Lucknow. Here he participated in a fierce debate with Gandhi, Patel and other Congress leaders over the adoption of socialism as the official goal of the party. Younger socialists such as Jaya Prakash Narayan, Mridula Sarabhai, Narendra Dev and Asoka Mehta began to see Nehru as leader of Congress socialists. Under their pressure, the Congress passed the *Avadi Resolution* proclaiming socialism as the model for India's future government. Nehru was re-elected the following year, and oversaw the Congress national campaign for the 1937 elections. Largely leaving political organisation work to others, Nehru travelled the length and breadth of the country, exhorting the masses on behalf of the Congress, which would win an outright majority in the central and most of the provincial legislatures. Although he did not contest elections himself, Nehru was seen by the national media as the leader of the Congress.

Jawaharlal Nehru sitting next to Mahatma Gandhi at the AICC General Session, 1942.

### *Maulana Azad and Nehru*

At the outbreak of World War II, the Assemblies were informed that the Viceroy had unilaterally declared war on the Axis on behalf of India, without consulting the people's representatives. Outraged at the viceroy's arbitrary decision, all elected Congressmen resigned from their offices at the instigation of Subhash Bose and Nehru. But even as Bose would call for an outright revolt and would proceed to seek the aid of Nazi Germany and Japan, Nehru remained sympathetic to the British cause. He joined Maulana Azad, Chakravarthi Rajagopalachari and Patel in offering Congress support for the war effort in return for a commitment from the British to grant independence after the war.

In doing so, Nehru broke ranks with Gandhi, who had resisted in supporting war and remained suspicious of the British. The failure of negotiations and Britain's refusal to concede independence outraged the nationalist movement. Gandhi and Patel called for an all-out rebellion, a demand that was opposed by Rajagopalachari and resisted by Nehru and Azad. After intensive debates and heated discussions, the Congress leaders called for the British to *Quit India* – to transfer power to Indian hands immediately or face a mass rebellion.

Despite his skepticism, Nehru travelled the country to exhort India's masses into rebellion. He was arrested with the entire Congress Working Committee on August 9, 1942 and transported to a maximum security prison at a fort in Ahmednagar. Here he remained incarcerated with his colleagues till June 1945. His daughter Indira and her husband Feroze Gandhi were also imprisoned for a few months. Nehru's first grandchild, Rajiv Gandhi was born in 1944.

After his release from prison at the end of the Second World War, Nehru immediately resumed his political work and toured through India preparing grounds for the elections that had been promised for 1946. In October 1945, with the decisions to carry on with the INA trials announced, Nehru was instrumental in announcing the formation of the INA Defence Committee for the defence of the officers of the Indian National Army who faced court Martial in Delhi. Nehru chaired the INA Defence Committee and the legal defence team, while at the same time carrying on with his political work.

## India's First Prime Minister

Nehru and his colleagues had been released as the British Cabinet Mission arrived to propose plans for transfer of power. The Congress held a presidential election in the knowledge that its chosen leader would become India's head of government.

Once elected, Nehru headed an interim government, which was impaired by outbreaks of communal violence and political disorder, and the opposition of the Muslim League led by Muhammad Ali Jinnah, who were demanding a separate Muslim state of Pakistan. After failed bids to form coalitions, Nehru reluctantly supported the partition of India as per a plan released by the British on June 3, 1947. He would take office as the Prime Minister of India on August 15, and delivered his inaugural address titled "A Tryst With Destiny:"

"Long years ago we made a tryst with destiny, and now the time comes when we shall redeem our pledge, not wholly or in full measure, but very substantially. At the stroke of the midnight hour, when the world sleeps, India will awake to life and freedom. A moment comes, which comes but rarely in history, when we step out from the old to the new, when an age ends, and when the soul of a nation, long suppressed, finds utterance.

It is fitting that at this solemn moment we take the pledge of dedication to the service of India and her people and to the still larger cause of humanity."

However, this period was marked with intense communal violence. This violence swept across the Punjab region, Delhi, Bengal and other parts of India. Nehru conducted joint tours with Pakistani leaders to encourage peace and calm angry and disillusioned refugees. Nehru would work with Maulana Azad and other Muslim leaders to safeguard and encourage Muslims to remain in India.

The violence of the time deeply affected Nehru, who called for a ceasefire and UN intervention to stop the Indo-Pakistani War of 1947. Fearing communal reprisals, Nehru also hesitated in supporting the annexation of Hyderabad State, and clashed with Patel on the Kashmir dispute and relations with Pakistan. Nehru asserted his own control over Kashmir policy while Patel objected to Nehru sidelining his Home Ministry's officials.

Nehru felt offended by Patel's decision-making regarding the states' integration without consulting either him or the Cabinet. Patel asked Gandhi to relieve him of his obligation to serve. He knew that he lacked Nehru's youth and popularity, and believed that an open political battle would hurt India. After much personal deliberation and contrary to Patel's prediction, Gandhi on January 30, 1948 told Patel not to leave the Government, and to stay by Nehru's side in joint leadership. A free India, according to Gandhi, desperately needed both Patel and Nehru's joint leadership.

Nehru climbs atop the gate at Birla House to announce the death of Gandhi to the crowd outside. This photograph by Henri Cartier-Bresson is one of the most famous images of the 1940s.

Gandhi was assassinated on January 30, 1948. At Gandhi's wake, Nehru and Patel embraced each other and addressed the nation together. Despite working together, the two leaders would clash on various issues. Nehru declined Patel's counsel on sending assistance to Tibet in 1950 with the disputed entrance of the People's Republic of China and ejecting the Portuguese from Goa by military force.

When Nehru pressured Dr. Rajendra Prasad to decline a nomination to become the first President of India in 1950 in favour of Rajagopalachari, he thus angered the party, which felt Nehru was attempting to impose his will. Nehru sought Patel's help in winning the party over, but Patel declined, and Prasad was duly elected. When Nehru opposed the 1950 Congress presidential candidacy of Purushottam Das Tandon, a conservative Hindu leader, he endorsed Jivatram Kripalani and threatened to resign if Tandon was elected. Patel rejected Nehru's views and endorsed Tandon in Gujarat, in a disputed election where Kripalani received not one vote despite hailing from that state himself.

In the years following independence, Nehru frequently turned to his daughter Indira to look after him and manage his personal affairs. Following Patel's death in 1950, Nehru became the most popular and powerful Indian politician. Under his leadership, the Congress won an overwhelming majority in the elections of 1952, in which his son-in-law Feroze Gandhi was also elected. Indira moved into Nehru's official residence to attend to him, inadvertently estranging her husband, who would become a critic of Nehru's government. Nevertheless, Indira would virtually become Nehru's chief of staff and constant companion in his travels across India and the world.

## Economic Policies

### *Nehru's Study in Teen Murti Bhavan*

Nehru presided over the introduction of a modified, "Indian" version of state planning and control over the economy. Creating the Planning commission of India, Nehru drew up the first Five-Year Plan in 1951, which charted the government's investments in industries and agriculture. Increasing business and income taxes, Nehru envisaged a mixed economy in which the government would manage strategic industries such as mining, electricity and heavy industries, serving public interest and a check to private enterprise.

Nehru pursued land redistribution and launched programmes to build irrigation canals, dams and spread the use of fertilizers to increase agricultural production. He also pioneered a series of *community development programs* aimed at spreading diverse cottage industries and increasing efficiency into rural India. While encouraging the construction of large dams, irrigation works and the generation of hydroelectricity, Nehru also launched India's programme to harness nuclear energy.

For most of Nehru's term as prime minister, India would continue to face serious food shortages despite progress and increases in agricultural production. Nehru's industrial policies encouraged the growth of diverse manufacturing and heavy industries, yet state planning, controls and regulations began to impair productivity, quality and profitability. Although the Indian economy enjoyed a steady rate of growth, chronic unemployment amidst entrenched poverty continued to plague the population. Nehru's popularity remained unaffected, and his government succeeded to an extent in extending water and electricity supply, health care, roads and infrastructure for India's vast rural population.

## Education and Social Reform

Jawaharlal Nehru was a passionate advocate of education for India's children and youth, believing it essential for India's future progress. His government oversaw the establishment of many institutions of higher learning, including the All India Institute of Medical Sciences, the Indian Institutes of Technology and the Indian Institutes of Management.

Nehru also outlined a commitment in his five-year plans to guarantee free and compulsory primary education to all of India's children. For this purpose, Nehru oversaw the creation of mass village enrollment programmes and the construction of thousands of schools. Nehru also launched initiatives such as the provision of free milk and meals to children in order to fight malnutrition. Adult education centres, vocational and technical schools were also organised for adults, especially in the rural areas.

Under Nehru, the Indian Parliament enacted many changes to Hindu law to criminalize caste discrimination and increase the legal rights and social freedoms of women. A system of reservations in government services and educational institutions was created to eradicate the social inequalities and disadvantages faced by peoples of the scheduled castes and scheduled tribes. Nehru also championed secularism and religious harmony, increasing the representation of minorities in government.

The founding leaders of the Non-Aligned states meet in New York in October 1960. From left: Nehru, representing India; Kwame Nkrumah (Ghana); Gamal Abdel Nasser (Egypt); Sukarno (Indonesia); and Josip Broz Tito (Yugoslavia).

## National Security and Foreign Policy

Although having promised in 1948 to hold a plebiscite in Kashmir under the auspices of the U.N., Nehru grew increasingly wary of the U.N. and declined to hold a plebiscite in 1953. He ordered the arrest of the Kashmiri politician Sheikh Abdullah, whom he had previously supported but now suspected of harbouring separatist ambitions; Bakshi Ghulam Mohammad replaced him.

On the international scene, Nehru was a champion of pacifism and a strong supporter of the United Nations. He pioneered the policy of non-alignment and co-founded the Non-Aligned Movement of nations professing neutrality between the rival blocs of nations led by the U.S. and the U.S.S.R. Recognising the People's Republic of China soon after its founding (while most of the Western bloc continued relations with the Republic of China), Nehru sought to establish warm and friendly relations with it despite the invasion of Tibet in 1950, and hoped to act as an intermediary to bridge the gulf and tensions between the communist states and the Western bloc. This policy of pacifism and appeasement with respect to China soon came unraveled when China annexed Aksai Chin, the region of Kashmir adjoining Tibet in 1962 that led to the Sino-Indian war.

Jawaharlal Nehru declined a United States offer for India to occupy a permanent seat on the United Nations Security Council around 1953. Nehru instead suggested that the seat be given to China. Jawaharlal Nehru talks to Pakistan prime minister Muhammad Ali Bogra during his 1953 visit to Karachi.

Nehru was hailed by many for working to defuse global tensions and the threat of nuclear weapons. He commissioned the first study of the human effects of nuclear explosions, and campaigned ceaselessly for the abolition of what he called "these frightful engines of destruction." He also had pragmatic reasons for promoting de-nuclearisation, fearing that a nuclear arms race would lead to over-militarisation that would be unaffordable for developing countries such as his own.

In 1956 he had criticised the joint invasion of the Suez Canal by the British, French and Israelis. Suspicion and distrust cooled relations between India and the U.S., which suspected Nehru of tactily supporting the Soviet Union. Accepting the arbitration of the UK and World Bank, Nehru signed the Indus Water Treaty in 1960 with Pakistani ruler Ayub Khan to resolve long-standing disputes about sharing the resources of the major rivers of the Punjab region.

## Final Years

Mr. Nehru had led the Congress to a major victory in the 1957 elections, but his government was facing rising problems and criticism. Disillusioned by intra-party corruption and bickering, Nehru contemplated resigning but continued to serve. The election of his daughter Indira as Congress President in 1959 aroused criticism for alleged nepotism, although Nehru disapproved of her election, partly because he considered it smacked of "dynastism"; he said, indeed it was "wholly undemocratic and an undesirable thing", and refused her a position in his cabinet. Indira herself was at loggerheads with her father over policy; most notably, she used his oft-stated personal deference to the Congress Working Committee to push through the dismissal of the Communist Party of India government in the state of Kerala, over his own objections. Nehru began to be frequently embarrassed by her ruthlessness and disregard for parliamentary tradition, and was "hurt" by what he saw as an assertiveness with no purpose other than to stake out an identity independent of her father.

Although the Pancha Sila (Five Principles of Peaceful Coexistence) was the basis of the 1954 Sino-Indian treaty over Tibet, in later years, Nehru's foreign policy suffered through increasing Chinese antagonism over border disputes and Nehru's decision to grant asylum to the Dalai Lama. After years of failed negotiations, Nehru authorized the Indian Army to annex Goa from Portugal in 1961.See liberation of Goa. While increasing his popularity, Nehru received criticism for opting for military action.

In the 1962 elections, Nehru led the Congress to victory yet with a diminished majority. Opposition parties ranging from the right-wing Bharatiya Jana Sangh and Swatantra Party, socialists and the Communist Party of India performed well.

In a matter of months, the border disputes with China turned into open conflict. Nehru assumed that as former victims of imperialism (India being a colony itself) they shared a sense of solidarity, as expressed in the phrase "Hindi-Chini bhai bhai" (Indians and Chinese are brothers). He was dedicated to the ideals of brotherhood and solidarity among developing nations. Nehru, naively, did not believe that one fellow Socialist country would attack another; and in any event, he felt secure behind the impregnable wall of ice that is the Himalayas. Both proved to be severe miscalculations of China's intentions and military capabilities. Following reports of his intention to confront Chinese occupation of the disputed areas-summarised in a memorable statement that he had asked the Army to "throw them (Chinese) out"-China launched a pre-emptive attack.

In a matter of months, a Chinese invasion of northeastern India exposed the weaknesses of India's military as Chinese forces came as far as Assam. Widely criticised for his government's insufficient attention to defence, Nehru was forced to sack the defence minister Krishna Menon and accept U.S. military aid. Nehru's health began declining steadily, and he was forced to spend months recuperating in Kashmir through 1963. Upon his return from Kashmir in May 1964, Nehru suffered a stroke and later a heart attack.

He died in the early hours of May 27, 1964. Nehru was cremated in accordance with Hindu rites at the Shantivana on the banks of the Yamuna River, witnessed by hundreds of thousands of mourners who had flocked into the streets of Delhi and the cremation grounds.

# 2 Political Career of Nehru

## *Early Years*

Nehru came from a family of Kashmiri Brahmins, who had migrated to the plains early in the eighteenth century. He was the son of Motilal Nehru, a renowned lawyer and one of Mahatma Gandhi's prominent lieutenants. Jawaharlal was the eldest of four children, two of whom were daughters. His sister, Vijaya Lakshmi Pandit, later became the first woman president of the UN General Assembly.

Until the age of 16, Nehru was educated at home by a series of English governesses and tutors. Only one of these, a part-Irish, part-Belgian theosophist, Ferdinand T. Brooks, appears to have made any impression on him. Gradually, he developed a taste for writers such as Walter Scott, Charles Dickens, Thackery, H.G. Wells, and Mark Twain, as well as for John Stuart Mill, Gladstone, John Morley, Bertrand Russell, and Bernard Shaw. Jawaharlal also had an Indian tutor who taught him Hindi and Sanskrit. In 1905 he went to Harrow, a leading English school, where he stayed for two years. Nehru's academic career was in no way outstanding.

From Harrow he went to Trinity College, Cambridge, where he spent three years earning an honours degree in natural science. On leaving Cambridge, Nehru joined the Inner Temple in 1910 to read law, where in his own words he passed his examinations "with neither glory nor ignominy". It was here that he also confessed: "In my likes and dislikes, I was perhaps more an

Englishman than an Indian." In London he was drawn to the Fabian socialists, also known as the Bloomsbury group. He returned home in 1912 after seven years of education in England.

Four years after his return to India, in March 1916, Nehru married Kamala Kaul, who came from a Kashmiri family settled in Delhi. Their only child, Indira Priyadarshini, was born in 1917; she would later (under her married name of Indira Gandhi) also serve as prime minister of India.

### *Political Apprenticeship*

On his return to India, Nehru at first tried to settle down as a lawyer. But, unlike his father, he had only a desultory interest in his profession and did not relish either the practice of law or the company of lawyers. At this time he might be described, like many of his generation, as an instinctive nationalist who yearned for his country's freedom, but, like most of his contemporaries, he had not formulated any precise ideas on how it could be achieved.

Nehru's autobiography discloses his lively interest in politics. His letters to his father over the same period reveal their common interest in India's freedom. But not until father and son met Gandhi and were persuaded to follow in his political footsteps did either of them develop any definite ideas on how freedom was to be attained. The quality in Gandhi that impressed the two Nehrus was his insistence on action. A wrong, the Mahatma argued, should not only be condemned, it should be resisted. Earlier, Nehru and his father had been contemptuous of the run of contemporary Indian politicians, whose nationalism, with a few notable exceptions, consisted of interminable speeches and long-winded resolutions. Jawaharlal was also attracted by Gandhi's insistence on fighting Great Britain without fear or hate.

Nehru met Gandhi for the first time in 1916 at the annual meeting of the Indian National Congress in Lucknow. Gandhi was 20 years his senior. Neither seems to have made any initially strong impression on the other. Nehru did not assume a leadership role in Indian politics, however, until his election as Congress president in 1929, when he presided over the historic Lahore session that proclaimed complete independence as India's political goal. Until then the objective had been dominion status.

Nehru had joined the Allahabad High Court Bar in 1916, practising till 1920. But the legal profession did not hold him for long, and he found a meaningful vocation in politics. The year 1917 had seen the Russian Revolution, and it was also the year of agitation for Home Rule, under the leadership of Annie Besant (1847-1933). Expelled from Bombay and then from the Central Provinces, she was finally interned. Jawaharlal signed up as one of the joint secretaries of the Home Rule League in the United Provinces with Motilal Nehru as president. "Home Rule has come and we have to take it if we stand up like men and falter not", so wrote Jawaharlal in a letter to *The Leader*. Nehru's close association with the Congress party dates from 1919 in the immediate aftermath of World War I. This period saw a wave of nationalist activity and governmental repression.

According to his testimony and that of his contemporaries, three events during 1919 and 1920 had a profound influence on Nehru's political career. The first was the Jallianwala Bagh massacre (April 1919), when General Reginald E.H. Dyer, a British officer, ordered his troops to fire on an unarmed crowd of Indians gathered for an anti-British political meeting. By the time the ammunition ran out, nearly 400 civilians were dead and 1,200 wounded. The massacre shook Nehru's faith in the beneficence of British rule.

The second experience was Nehru's first-hand encounter with India's poverty in the countryside in the 1920s, and lastly, Gandhi's emergence during 1919-20, and his call for civil disobedience struck Nehru deeply. In fact, the Non-cooperation Movement (1920-22) of the Congress under Gandhi's leadership seemed to him to answer some of the major challenges of the time. Jawaharlal accepted the non-violent method as the only practical strategy that was then available.

Beginning his political career in the United Provinces (now Uttar Pradesh), during the Non-cooperation Movement, Jawaharlal came in contact with the impoverished peasants whose indomitable spirit defied the crushing economic burden, which an oppressive imperial regime imposed upon them. Nehru left a graphic account of the India which his sojourn in the rural areas opened up before him: "I went (to the rural districts near Allahabad) with some colleagues and we spent three days in the villages far from the railways and even the *pucca* (paved) road. The visit was a revelation to me. We found the whole countryside afire with enthusiasm and full of strange excitement...(The) people would come streaming out or even running as fast as they could.

They were in miserable rags, men and women, but their faces were full of excitement and their eyes glistened and seemed to expect strange happenings which would, as if by a miracle, put an end to their long misery....(A) new picture of India seemed to arise before me." He was, as he records, "filled with shame and sorrow....at the degradation and overpowering poverty of India", and this experience was to shape his later political thinking. The Non-cooperation Movement helped him emerge as a popular leader: "I took to the crowd and the crowd took to me." The movement also widened his political and social perspective.

When, late in 1921, the prominent leaders and workers of the Congress party were outlawed in some provinces, Nehru went to prison for the first time. Over the next 24 years he was to serve another eight periods of detention, the last and longest ending in June 1945, after an imprisonment of almost three years. In all, Nehru spent more than nine years in jail. Characteristically, he described his terms of incarceration as normal interludes in a life of abnormal political activity.

His political apprenticeship with the Congress lasted from 1919 to 1929. In 1923 he became general secretary of the party for two years and again, in 1927, for another two years. His interests and duties took him on journeys over wide areas of India, particularly in his native United Provinces, where his first exposure to the overwhelming poverty and degradation of the peasantry had a profound influence on his basic ideas for solving these vital problems. Though vaguely inclined towards socialism, Nehru's radicalism had set in no definite mould. The watershed in his political and economic thinking was his tour of Europe and the erstwhile Soviet Union.

Nehru's explorations into the socialist theory after his visit to Europe in 1926-27, and his experiences with Nazi Germany marked a turning point in his social and political outlook. In 1927 he, as a representative of the Indian National Congress, attended the International Congress against colonial oppression and imperialism in Brussels. There he met some of the leading leftists of the world including George Lansbury, Ellen Wilkinson, Fenner Brockway, and Harry Pollitt, besides a large number of nationalists from Asia, Africa, and Latin America.

This was followed by his visit to Moscow where he was greeted by the newspaper *Pravda* as a "leader of the left wing of the Congress". There he had a first-hand glimpse of the reconstruction of a major society on the basis of socialism. His experience made him realise the need for an economic revolution, which would redeem India from the backwardness of its agrarian structure and, in fact, from its dependence on agriculture itself. He was convinced that the solution to India's socio-economic problems lay in socialism "not in a vague humanitarian way, but in the scientific economic sense." He thus involved himself with the Trade Union Movement and emerged as a champion of independence and socialism.

Nehru's radicalism came to the fore in 1927 over the debate on the extent and character of *swaraj* or self-government that the Congress was struggling for. In 1927, the British government sent an all-British commission (the Simon Commission), under the terms of the Government of India Act of 1919, to report as to "whether and to what extent it was desirable to establish the principle of responsible government, or to extend, modify, or restrict the degree of responsible government existing therein". The Congress gave a call for the boycott of the Simon Commission in its Madras (now Chennai) session (December 1927), with Nehru and his associates contributing to the success of the boycott.

The Simon Commission thus raised the issue of the type of constitution or the kind of independence that India should obtain for itself. So far *swaraj*, for the Congress leaders, had meant dominion status for India (similar to the position of self-governing Australia, New Zealand, and South Africa) within the ambit of the British Empire. But to Jawaharlal and his associates the acceptance of the dominion status implied recognizing the inevitability of British presence in India, as well as the perpetuation of imperialistic exploitation.

In the Madras session in December 1927, Jawaharlal moved a resolution demanding real independence instead of dominion status. It was, however, at the Congress session at Calcutta (now Kolkata) in December 1928 that he, joined by Subhash Chandra Bose, pressed claim for complete independence as the Congress objective. The actual success of this demand came in the following year when as the newly elected president of the Indian National Congress at the Lahore session, Nehru gave the call for a new goal: *purna swaraj* (complete independence). When the clock struck at midnight on the night of December 31, 1929, Jawaharlal Nehru rose and led a solemn procession on the banks of the Ravi River. It was here that he raised India's national flag.

## Struggle for Indian Independence

After the Lahore session of 1929, Nehru emerged as the leader of the country's intellectuals and youth. Hoping that Nehru would draw India's youth, at that time gravitating towards extreme leftist causes, into the mainstream of the Congress movement, Gandhi had elevated him to the presidency of the Congress party over the heads of some of his seniors. The Mahatma also correctly calculated that, with added responsibility, Nehru himself would be inclined to keep to the middle way.

It was also in these years Nehru and Subhas Chandra Bose were communicating with the people in general and to the youth (through the Youth League, the Hindustani Seva Dal, the Naujawan Bharat Sabha and the Volunteers' Movement), the students (through the students' organizations and conferences), and the workers (mainly through the All India Trade Union Congress whose presidentship was taken over by Jawaharlal in 1929 and Subhas in 1931) in particular.

In 1931, Jawaharlal and his wife Kamala were arrested in connection with the salt *satyagraha*. Jawaharlal clearly defined the kind of independence the Congress must stand for. In his draft of the Fundamental Rights that was adopted in the Karachi session of the Congress (March 1931), he stated: "In order to end the exploitation of the masses, political freedom must include real economic freedom of the starving millions." The Congress, he hoped, could be converted into a real anti-imperialist "joint popular front", and he suggested as a first step "corporate membership" of trade unions and *kisan sabhas*. This indeed was an important step in the march towards Congress socialism and Nehru's emergence as a champion of civil liberties.

After his father's death in 1931, Jawaharlal moved into the inner councils of the Congress party and became closer to the Mahatma. Although Gandhi did not officially designate him his political heir until 1942, the country as early as the mid-1930s saw in Nehru the natural successor to Gandhi. The Gandhi-Irwin Pact of March 1931, signed between Gandhi and the British viceroy, Lord Irwin (later Lord Halifax), signalized a truce between the two. It climaxed one of Gandhi's more effective civil-disobedience movements, launched the year before, in the course of which Nehru had been arrested.

As an ardent anti-imperialist, Nehru was unhappy at the enactment of the Gandhi-Irwin compromise (March 1931), as well at the prospect of the Round Table Conference (September-December 1931) in London to resolve the Indian political question. He also saw no point in the formal withdrawal of the Civil Disobedience Movement (May 1933). In the closing stage of the Civil Disobedience Movement, Nehru had renewed his interest in the agitation of the Uttar Pradesh peasantry His commitment to the youth, the students, and the underprivileged inspired him towards a radical political temper. This eventually facilitated the formation of the Congress Socialist Party (May 1934) within the framework of the Congress organization. Though Nehru did not formally join the party, he drew its support on vital issues. He continued to give importance to the principles of Democratic Socialism in India, as well as a vision of an independent, liberated, and secular India.

After he was elected the Congress president in the Lucknow and the Faizpur sessions in 1936, Nehru offered his socialist ideas with greater clarity. He made significant advances on the agrarian question (by contributing to the formulation of a liberal Faizpur Congress Agrarian Programme), on the issue of constitution, and on the question of civil liberties (by ordering the Congress provincial ministries to release all political prisoners), on responsible government (especially by championing the cause of the *Praja Mandal* (peoples group) movement in the Indian states against the tyranny of their rulers) and on the world-wide campaign against Fascism (by taking the side of "forces of progress" in the Spanish Civil War, by protesting against the Italian attack on Ethiopia, and by organizing relief for China when it was attacked by Japan).

Hopes that the Gandhi-Irwin pact would be the prelude to a more relaxed period of Indo-British relations were not borne out; Lord Willingdon (who replaced Irwin as viceroy in 1931) jailed Gandhi in January 1932, shortly after his return from the Second Round Table Conference in London. He was charged with attempting to mount another civil-disobedience movement; Nehru was also arrested and sentenced to two years' imprisonment.

The Round Table Conferences in London, held to advance India's progress to self-government, eventually resulted in the Government of India Act of 1935, giving the Indian provinces a system of popular autonomous government. Ultimately, it provided for a federal system composed of the autonomous provinces and princely states. Although federation never came into being, provincial autonomy was implemented. During the mid-1930s Nehru was much concerned with developments in Europe, which seemed to be drifting towards another world war. He was in Europe early in 1936, visiting his ailing wife, shortly before she died in a sanitarium in Switzerland. Even at this time he emphasized that in the event of war India's place was alongside the democracies, though he insisted that India could only fight in support of Great Britain and France as a free country.

In the 1936-37 election campaign for the provincial legislatures under the Government of India Act of 1935, Nehru was the principal vote-getter for the Congress and came to occupy a powerful position in the ranks of the Congress party. When the elections following the introduction of provincial autonomy brought the Congress party to power in a majority of the provinces, Nehru was faced with a dilemma. The Muslim League under Mohammed Ali Jinnah (who was to become the creator of Pakistan) had fared badly at the polls. Congress, therefore, unwisely rejected Jinnah's plea for the formation of coalition Congress-Muslim League governments in some of the provinces, a decision on which Nehru had significant influence. The subsequent clash between the Congress and the League hardened into a conflict between Hindus and Muslims that was ultimately to lead to the partition of India and the creation of Pakistan.

## Imprisonment during World War II

When, at the outbreak of World War II in September 1939, the viceroy, Lord Linlithgow, committed India to war without consulting the autonomous provincial ministries, the Congress party's High Command withdrew its provincial ministries as a protest. Congress's action left the political field virtually open to Jinnah and the Muslim League. Nehru's views on the war differed from those of Gandhi. Initially, the Mahatma believed that whatever support was given to the British should be given unconditionally and that it should be of a non-violent character. Nehru held that non-violence had no place in defense against aggression and that India should support Great Britain in a war against Nazism, but only as a free nation. If it could not help, it should not hinder.

In October 1940, Gandhi, abandoning his original stand, decided to launch a limited civil-disobedience campaign in which leading advocates of Indian independence were selected to participate one by one. Nehru was arrested and sentenced to four years' imprisonment. After spending a little more than a year in jail, he was released, along with other Congress prisoners, three days before the bombing of Pearl Harbor in Hawaii. When the Japanese carried their attack through Burma to the borders of India in the spring of 1942, the British government, faced by this new military threat, decided to make some overtures to India.

Prime Minister Winston Churchill dispatched Sir Stafford Cripps, a member of the war Cabinet who was politically close to Nehru and also knew Jinnah, with proposals for a settlement of the constitutional problem. Cripps's mission failed, however, for Gandhi would accept nothing less than independence. Nehru played a significant role in negotiations with Sir Stafford Cripps as well as in the developments leading to the Quit India Movement (1942). Equally memorable is his role during the trial of the three officers of the Indian National Army in the Red Fort in November

1945, when he, along with Bhulabhai Desai and T.B. Sapru fought on behalf of the INA officers. He was also a chief negotiator during the Simla Conference (June 1945), Cabinet Mission (May 16, 1946), and June 3rd Plan (1947).

The initiative in the Congress party now passed to Gandhi, who called on the British to leave India; Nehru, though reluctant to embarrass the war effort, had no alternative but to join Gandhi. Following the Quit India resolution passed by the Congress party in Bombay on August 8, 1942, the entire Congress working committee, including Gandhi and Nehru, was arrested and imprisoned. Nehru emerged from this—his ninth and last detention—only on June 15, 1945.

Though there were perceptible differences between Nehru and Gandhi, they were inseparable. Gandhi's verdict on him also points to Nehru's contribution to India's struggle for freedom: "Jawaharlal is as pure as crystal, he is truthful beyond suspicion. He is knight *sanspeur, sans reproche*. The nation is safe in his hands." The Mahatma regarded him as his political heir. Nehru adopted Gandhi's idea of non-violent struggle for liberating India from British rule, and believed that only the right means could produce right ends.

Within two years India was to be partitioned and free. A final attempt by the viceroy, Lord Wavell, to bring the Congress party and the Muslim League together failed. The Labour government that had meanwhile displaced Churchill's wartime administration dispatched, as one of its first acts, a Cabinet mission to India and later also replaced Lord Wavell with Lord Mountbatten. The question was no longer whether India was to be independent but whether it was to consist of one or more independent states. While Gandhi refused to accept partition, Nehru reluctantly but realistically acquiesced. On August 15, 1947, India and Pakistan emerged as two separate, independent countries. Nehru became independent India's first prime minister.

## Achievements as Prime Minister

In the 35 years from 1929, when Gandhi chose Nehru as president of the Congress session at Lahore, until his death as prime minister in 1964, Nehru remained—despite the Chinese debacle of 1962—the idol of his people.

Nehru imported and imparted modern values and ways of thinking, which he adapted to Indian conditions. Apart from his stress on secularism and on the basic unity of India, despite its racial and religious diversities, Nehru was deeply concerned with carrying India forward into the modern age of scientific discovery and technological development. In addition, he aroused in his people an awareness of the necessity of social concern with the poor and the outcast and of respect for democratic values. One of the achievements of which he was particularly proud was the reform of the ancient Hindu civil code that finally enabled Hindu widows to enjoy equality with men in matters of inheritance and property.

Internationally, Nehru's star was in the ascendant until October 1956, when India's attitude on the Hungarian revolt against the Soviets brought his policy of nonalignment under sharp scrutiny. In the United Nations, India was the only non-aligned country to vote with the erstwhile Soviet Union on the invasion of Hungary, and thereafter it was difficult for Nehru to command credibility in his calls for non-alignment. In the early years after independence, anticolonialism had been the cornerstone of his foreign policy, but, by the time of the Belgrade conference of non-aligned countries in 1961, Nehru had substituted non-alignment for anticolonialism as his pressing concern. In 1962, however, the Chinese threatened to overrun the Brahmaputra River valley as a result of a long-standing border dispute. Nehru called for Western aid, exposing the weakness of his non-alignment policy, and China withdrew.

Kashmir—claimed by both India and Pakistan—remained a perennial problem throughout Nehru's term as prime minister. His tentative efforts to settle the dispute by adjustments along the cease-fire lines having failed, Pakistan, in 1948, made an unsuccessful attempt to seize Kashmir by force. In solving the problem of the Portuguese colony of Goa—the last remaining colony in India—Nehru was more fortunate. Although its military occupation by Indian troops in December 1961 raised a furore in many Western countries, in the hindsight of history, Nehru's action is justifiable. With the withdrawal of the British and the French, the Portuguese colonial presence in India had become an anachronism.

Both the British and the French had withdrawn peacefully. If the Portuguese were not prepared to follow suit, Nehru had to find ways to dislodge them. After first trying persuasion, in August 1955 he had permitted a group of unarmed Indians to march into Portuguese territory in a non-violent demonstration. Even though the Portuguese opened fire on the demonstrators, killing nearly 30, Nehru stayed his hand for six years, appealing meanwhile to Portugal's Western friends to persuade its government to cede the colony. When India finally struck, Nehru could claim that neither he nor the government of India had ever been committed to non-violence as a policy.

Nehru's health showed signs of deteriorating not long after the clash with China. He suffered a slight stroke in 1963, followed by a more debilitating attack in January 1964. He died a few months later from a third and fatal stroke.

### *Assessment*

While assertive in his Indianness, because of his modern political and economic outlook, he attracted the younger intelligentsia of India to Gandhi's movement of non-violent resistance against the British and later to rally them around him after independence. Nehru's Western upbringing and his visits to Europe before independence had acclimatized him to Western ways of thinking. Nehru has been held responsible for Wavell's recall, and his relationship with Mountbatten may have been responsible for smoothing things over during the transfer of power. In free India, Nehru as first prime minister laid the foundations of a democratic and secular India. If Gandhi was India's liberator, Nehru was its modernizer.

Throughout his 17 years in office, he held up democratic socialism as the guiding star. With the help of the overwhelming majority that the Congress party maintained in Parliament during his term of office, he advanced towards that goal. The four pillars of his domestic policies were democracy, socialism, unity, and secularism. He succeeded to a large extent in maintaining the edifice supported by these four pillars during his lifetime.

Even during his lifetime, individual and collective perceptions of his leadership ranged from him being adored as a revolutionary and vibrant personification of the forward-looking spirit of India to being described as a pampered young man who accidentally acquired national leadership owing to the influence of his father and the favouritism of Mahatma Gandhi. Doubtless, Nehru was a leader of the freedom movement, as the founding father of institutional democracy in India and as the architect of India's policy in all its manifestations, and the longest serving prime minister of India (from 1946 to 1964). As an international statesman and as a popular leader, he was second only to Gandhi in this century.

Nehru came to such prominence in the freedom struggle primarily for two reasons. First, the Congressmen made him their leader because of their conviction that he was committed to the cause of freedom and to the service of the people of India. Second, Nehru worked his way up through municipal elections in Allahabad and through mass movements in Pratapgarh of Uttar Pradesh. After that there was no looking back from him.

Though Nehru accepted Gandhi as his mentor, they differed on many points. Gandhi's non-violence stemmed from his religious convictions, while Nehru believed in a liberal conception of ethics. Nehru believed in representative institutions, especially the dominance of the poorer classes in the elected institutions. In other words, he believed in the democratic empowerment of the poorer and lower castes. So if Gandhi was the father of India, Nehru was the principle architect of India's democracy and planning.

Nehru's only child, Indira Gandhi, served as India's prime minister from 1966 to 1977 and from 1980 to 1984. Her son, Rajiv Gandhi, was prime minister from 1984 to 1989.

Nehru wrote extensively, especially during his interminable jail detentions—*Glimpses of World History* (1934-35) in the form of letters to his daughter Indira; his *Autobiography* (1936), largely a story of the nationalist struggle for independence; *Discovery of India* (1946), a foray into India's historical and cultural past; and

*Selected Works* that contain several useful materials pertaining to India's freedom struggle.

## Tryst with Destiny

### *Jawaharlal Nehru's Tryst with Destiny Speech*

Tryst with Destiny was a speech made by Jawaharlal Nehru, the first Prime Minister of the Republic of India. The speech was made to the Indian Constituent Assembly, on the eve of India's independence, towards midnight on August 14, 1947. It focuses on the aspects that transcend India's history.

It is considered in modern India to be a landmark oration that captures the essence of the triumphant culmination of the hundred-year Indian freedom struggle against the British Empire in India.

## Text

Long years ago we made a tryst with destiny, and now the time comes when we shall redeem our pledge, not wholly or in full measure, but very substantially. At the stroke of the midnight hour, when the world sleeps, India will awake to life and freedom. A moment comes, which comes but rarely in history, when we step out from the old to the new, when an age ends, and when the soul of a nation, long suppressed, finds utterance. It is fitting that at this solemn moment we take the pledge of dedication to the service of India and her people and to the still larger cause of humanity.

At the dawn of history India started on her unending quest, and trackless centuries are filled with her striving and the grandeur of her success and her failures. Through good and ill fortune alike she has never lost sight of that quest or forgotten the ideals which gave her strength. We end today a period of ill fortune and India discovers herself again. The achievement we celebrate today is but a step, an opening of opportunity, to the greater triumphs and achievements that await us. Are we brave enough and wise enough to grasp this opportunity and accept the challenge of the future?

That future is not one of ease or resting but of incessant striving so that we may fulfil the pledges we have so often taken and the one we shall take today. The service of India means the service of the millions who suffer. It means the ending of poverty and ignorance and disease and inequality of opportunity. The ambition of the greatest man of our generation has been to wipe every tear from every eye. That may be beyond us, but as long as there are tears and suffering, so long our work will not be over.

And so we have to labour and to work, and work hard, to give reality to our dreams. Those dreams are for India, but they are also for the world, for all the nations and peoples are too closely knit together today for any one of them to imagine that it can live apart Peace has been said to be indivisible; so is freedom, so is prosperity now, and so also is disaster in this One World that can no longer be split into isolated fragments.

We have to build the noble mansion of free India where all her children may dwell. The appointed day has come-the day appointed by destiny-and India stands forth again, after long slumber and struggle, awake, vital, free and independent. The past clings on to us still in some measure and we have to do much before we redeem the pledges we have so often taken. Yet the turning-point is past, and history begins anew for us, the history which we shall live and act and others will write about.

It is a fateful moment for us in India, A new star rises, the star of freedom in the East, a new hope comes into being, a vision long cherished materializes. May the star never set and that hope never be betrayed! We rejoice in that freedom,

The future beckons to us. Whither do we go and what shall be our endeavour? To bring freedom and opportunity to the common man, to the peasants and workers of India; to fight and end poverty and ignorance and disease; to build up a prosperous, democratic and progressive nation, and to create social, economic and political institutions which will ensure justice and fullness of life to every man and woman.

We have hard work ahead. There is no resting for any one of us till we redeem our pledge in full, till we make all the people of India what destiny intended them to be. We are citizens of a great country on the verge of bold advance, and we have to live up to that high standard. All of us, to whatever religion we may belong, are equally the children of India with equal rights, privileges and obligations. We cannot encourage communalism or narrow-mindedness, for no nation can be great whose people are narrow in thought or in action.

To the nations and peoples of the world we send greetings and pledge ourselves to cooperate with them in furthering peace, freedom and democracy. And to India, our much-loved motherland, the ancient, the eternal and the ever-new, we pay our reverent homage and we bind ourselves afresh to her service. Jai Hind.

## Popular Culture

The speech is referenced in the 1998 Hindi film *Earth* directed by Deepa Mehta. The film portrays the main characters listening to the speech on radio, against the backdrop of the Hindu-Muslim riots following the Partition of India. This provides an interesting juxtaposition between the realities of Partition and the optimism that followed Independence.

### *1947, First-hand between Karachi and Delhi*

I shall skip past her delightful account of the Karachi ceremony—which took place on August 13 and 14 within eyeshot of a bronze statue of Mahatma Gandhi in a nearby circle—even though some of her irreverent comments are worth quoting even now ("Jinnah, whose smile muscles seem to be permanently out of order ..."). Karachi was still a Hindu-majority city, and large sections of the population were understandably subdued at the partition of the country.Delhi's mood was altogether more joyous. The Talbots arrived at the Constituent Assembly just in time after a hair-raising journey from Pakistan on the afternoon of August 14. Mildred describes Nehru's famous "tryst with destiny" speech, recounts the now-forgotten exuberance of a delegate who marred the decorum of the occasion by shouting a cheer for the Mahatma, and then tells a story I have not come across elsewhere:

"At the moment when the clock was chiming the [midnight] hour there was a rude interruption which startled everyone. A conch shell was blown long and loudly from the rear of the hall.

Involuntarily every head turned .... It was revealing to witness the [...] relief [...] when they saw that it was one of the most highly respected members of the Assembly, a devout Hindu, simply invoking the gods to witness this ceremony.... I happened to spot Nehru just as he was turning away, trying to hide a smile by covering his mouth with his hand."

Mildred describes the pressure of the throngs outside the Assembly clamouring for a glimpse of their idol, Nehru, whom the police obliged "to slip out by a back entrance". As an American, she was struck by the fact that when the crowds got out of hand it was the VIP who changed his plans. There are numerous fascinating vignettes in her letter of the next morning's Independence Day events: of Nehru's horror at seeing a horse fall (he only turned his attention back to the ceremony when he saw the horse rise again and move); of the U.S.

Ambassador's irritation that President Truman's cable of congratulations had been omitted when other leaders' greetings were read (it turned out that it had been misplaced); of Mountbatten's demeanour of "sincere pleasure", a sharp contrast with his stiffness in Karachi ("Here he was relaxed and at home among friendly companions ... his good wishes were obviously heartfelt.") Mildred's harrowing account of the evening's ceremony, ruined by rain and by 5,00,000 people turning out for an event planned for 25,000, is too long to summarise here, but for one detail: amidst the chaos, Indira Gandhi "looking woebegone and bedraggled. Her sari was torn, her hair straggling, her fingernails ruined. And she was one of the dignitaries!"

### *The Flag Goes up*

But the highlight of Mildred's account is of the morning of August 15, 1947, when the national flag was raised over the Council Hall: "the multitudes had gathered as far as the eye could see in the two-mile long parkway approach to the Secretariat, on tops of buildings, in windows, on cornices, in trees, perched everywhere like so many birds. The raising of that first flag was the single most thrilling experience of the entire celebration .... The first who spotted it pointed like eager childen; others ... looked up and tried to push their way to a vantage point so they too could see this miracle. For a few minutes there was almost a subdued hush over the whole crowd; then a soft bass undertone slowly swelled until, perhaps when the flag reached the top,... there was a breathtaking roar of cheering, shouting, and excited cries which others said penetrated to the hall inside and made their spines tingle. While I was being stirred by the sheer power and grandeur of the spectacle,... the Indians either stood mute, immersed in their own overwhelming thoughts, or were shouting almost uncontrollably. It was a grand emotional experience that left most of us with shaky voices or complete inability to speak."

These are the words not of an Indian nationalist but of a young American woman. Mildred Talbot wrote to her American friend two weeks after witnessing that first flag-raising: "The memory of the feelings that surged up within us as we watched their [i.e. the Indian masses'] excitement and awe still brings tears to my eyes." Fifty-seven years later, the memories of that first Independence Day have faded in all but a tiny percentage of our population. But the power of that magical moment when India became free, and the hopes raised of what we would make of that freedom, must never be forgotten. Today is the day to remember that moment, and to rededicate ourselves to its promise. It is a promise every Indian can do his or her own part to fulfil.

### *Gandhi & Nehru*

They were opposite in nature, but they shared a passion for freedom and justice, and together created a giant of democracy.

The 20th century produced many remarkable leaders, but few nations were blessed with a pair quite like India's Mahatma Gandhi and his protégé Jawaharlal Nehru. Gandhi was idealistic, quirky, quixotic and determined, a cross between a saint and a ward politician; like the best crossbreeds, he managed to distill the qualities of both and yet transcend their contradictions. Nehru was a moody, idealistic intellectual who felt an almost mystical empathy for the toiling peasant masses; an aristocrat who had passionate socialist convictions; a product of Harrow and Cambridge who spent over 10 years in British jails; an agnostic radical who became an unlikely follower of the deeply spiritual Mahatma. Together they brought a nation to freedom and laid the underpinnings for the world's largest democracy. Gandhi was the extraordinary leader of the world's first successful nonviolent movement for independence from colonial rule. To describe his method, he coined the expression *satyagraha*—literally, "holding on to truth" or, as he variously described it, truth force, love force or soul force. He disliked the English term passive resistance because *satyagraha* required activism, not passivity.

If you believed in truth and cared enough to obtain it, Gandhi felt, you could not afford to be passive. You had to be prepared actively to suffer for truth. It was *satyagraha* that first bound Nehru to Gandhi, soon after the latter's return to India in 1915 from a long sojourn in South Africa, where his morally charged leadership of the Indian community against racial discrimination had earned him the sobriquet of Mahatma ("Great Soul," a term he detested).

Gandhi's unique method of resistance through civil disobedience, allied to a talent for organization, gave the Indian nationalist movement both a saint and a strategist. His singular insight was that self-government would never be achieved by the resolutions passed by a self-regarding and unelected élite pursuing the politics of the drawing room. To him, self-government had to involve the empowerment of India's suffering multitudes in whose name the upper classes were clamoring for Home Rule. This position did not go over well with India's political class, which consisted largely of maharajahs and lawyers—men of means who discoursed in English and demanded the rights of Englishmen.

To put his principles into practice, Gandhi lived in near-absolute poverty in an ashram and traveled across the land in third-class railway compartments, campaigning against untouchability, poor sanitation and child marriage, while also preaching an eclectic set of virtues from sexual abstinence and frequent enemas to the weaving of hand-spun cotton cloth. That he was an eccentric was beyond doubt. That he had touched a chord amongst the masses was equally apparent. That he was a potent political force soon became clear. He captured the imagination of the nation by publicly breaking English law in the name of a higher law ("the voice of conscience") and challenging the British to jail him.

Despite differences over both tactics (Nehru wanted independence immediately whereas Gandhi believed Indians had to be made ready for their own freedom) and philosophy (the agnostic Nehru had little patience for the Mahatma's spirituality), the two men proved a formidable combination. Gandhi guided Nehru to the political pinnacle; Nehru in turn proved an inspirational campaigner as President of the Indian National Congress, electrifying the nation with his speeches and tireless travel. Gandhi took the issue of freedom to the masses as one of simple right and wrong and gave them a technique to which the British had no response.

By abstaining from violence Gandhi wrested the moral advantage. By breaking the law nonviolently he demonstrated the injustice of the law. By accepting the punishments imposed on him he confronted his captors with their own brutalization. By voluntarily imposing suffering upon himself in his hunger strikes he demonstrated the lengths to which he was prepared to go in defense of what he considered right. Gandhi's moral rectitude and Nehru's political passion made the perpetuation of British rule an impossibility.

Of course there was much more to Gandhism—physical self-denial, self-reliance, a belief in the human capacity for selfless love, religious ecumenism, idealistic internationalism, and a passionate commitment to equality and social justice. The improvement of his fellow human beings was arguably more important to him than the political goal of ridding India of the British. But it is his central tenet of nonviolence in the pursuit of these ends that represents his most significant original contribution to the world. Martin Luther King in the U.S., Adolfo Pérez Esquivel in Argentina, Nelson Mandela in South Africa and Aung San Suu Kyi in Burma all sought inspiration from the Mahatma's teachings.

Upon Gandhi's assassination in 1948, a year after independence, Nehru, the country's first Prime Minister, became the keeper of the national flame, the most visible embodiment of India's struggle for freedom. Gandhi's death could have led Nehru to assume untrammeled power. Instead, he spent a lifetime trying to instill the habits of democracy in his people—a disdain for dictators, a respect for parliamentary procedures, an abiding faith in the constitutional system. He himself was such a convinced democrat that, at the crest of his rise, he authored an anonymous article warning Indians of the dangers of giving dictatorial temptations to Jawaharlal Nehru. "He must be checked," he wrote of himself. "We want no Caesars." During Nehru's 17 years as Prime Minister, democratic values became so entrenched that when his daughter Indira suspended India's freedoms with a State of Emergency for 21 months, she felt compelled to return to the Indian people for vindication, held an election, and comprehensively lost it.

While the world was disintegrating into fascism, violence and war in the 20th century, Gandhi taught the virtues of truth, nonviolence and peace. The principal pillars of Nehru's legacy—democratic institution-building, staunch pan-Indian secularism, socialist economics at home and a foreign policy of nonalignment—were all integral to a vision of Indianness that sustained the nation for decades. Today, both legacies are fundamentally contested, and many Indians have strayed from the ideals bequeathed to them by Gandhi and Nehru. Yet they, in their very different ways, each represented that rare kind of leader who is not diminished by the inadequacies of his followers.

The American editor Norman Cousins once asked Nehru what he hoped his legacy to India would be. "Four hundred million people capable of governing themselves," Nehru replied. The numbers have grown, but the very fact that each day over a billion Indians govern themselves in a pluralist democracy is testimony to the deeds and words of these two men.

*Nehru Declined offer of Permanent U.N. Seat'*

MUMBAI, JAN. 9. Jawaharlal Nehru "declined a United States offer" to India to "take the permanent seat on the United Nations Security Council" around 1953 and suggested that it be given to China, according to the United Nations Under-Secretary General, Sashi Tharoor.

In his latest book, "Nehru—The Invention of India," Mr. Tharoor writes that Indian diplomats who have seen files swear that Nehru declined the offer about the same time as he turned down "with scorn" John Foster Dulles' support for an Indian Monroe Doctrine.

Nehru had suggested that the seat, till then held by Taiwan, be offered to Beijing instead. He wrote that "the seat was held with scant credibility by Taiwan."

Rafiq Zakaria, historian and scholar, and Murli Deora, MP, highlighted the disclosure at a function organised here to release the book. Manmohan Singh, Leader of Opposition in the Rajya Sabha, handed over the first copy to the Maharashtra Chief Minister, Sushilkumar Shinde.

Later, talking of the book, brought out by Penguin Viking, Mr.Tharoor spoke of Nehru's legacy which included four elements – democratic institution building, socialism, a non-aligned foreign policy and secularism, and said the legacy was far too important not to be re-looked at from the point of view of the 21st century.

In Nehru's time, India had no foreign policy and it was correct to say "Nehru had a foreign policy."

Often, other politicians and the foreign office mandarins came to know about the policy when they heard Nehru speak on the issue, Mr. Tharoor said.

He had been alive, Jawaharlal Nehru would have been 110 years and one month old at the turn of the century. It is 36 years since his moving away from the centrestage of Indian and world politics. With death and with the passage of time, great leaders undergo a process of demystification. Distances in terms of time and the elimination of the physical presence of these larger-than-life figures enable succeeding generations to a assess their lives more objectively, without being afflicted by their charisma and power, whatever the ingredients of that power might have been.

Nehru even during his life-time went through the spectrum of individual and collective reactions to his leadership, from being adored as a revolutionary and vibrant personification of the forward-looking spirit of India to being described as a pampered young man who accidentally acquired national leadership due to the influence of his father and the favouritism of Mahatma Gandhi.

He has been admired as a leader of the freedom movements, as the founding father of institutional democracy in India and as the architect of India's policy in all its manifestations, being the longest serving prime minister of India (from 1946 to 1964).

It would be pertinent to evaluate Nehru as a leader and a statesman because of the decisive and over-arching role that he played in Indian history in the 20th century. Regardless of criticisms, he was one of the most influential leaders of our freedom struggle. He was a pioneering articulator of Asian resurgence and was an unusually idealistic advocate of conscience in international politics. India's parliamentary democracy, free judiciary and media, the apolitical civil servants and armed forces, the commitment to secularism, social justice and equality before law, all originated in the blue print for free India which he worked out.

Nehru had a profound belief in India's destiny as a moral and stabilizing force in inter-state relations. He had faith in the Indian people and an equally strong hope that their maturity and civilisational wisdom would ensure for India an important role in the world. His education in the West, and his exposure to the political movements of Europe in the first three decades of this century, combined with his eclectic sense of history, made him realise that science, technology and economic modernisation and development were essential pre-requisites to fulfill the vision of a free India that he had in mind and to which he devoted three-fourths of his life.

These ingredients and influences, cannot be denied in generic terms but in is necessary to assess Nehru through the prism of India's realities today, and to judge him in the context of criticisms leveled against him as an individual and as a public figure.

This exercise should necessarily be an assessment of him as a leader of the freedom struggle, as a founding ideologue of the Indian Republic, as the prime minister, as an international statesman and as a leader beloved of the people of India, second only to Gandhi in this century. I can do no better than to recall two remarks made by senior members of the Congress over his role as leader of the freedom struggle. Acharya Kripalani, speaking at a seminar of the Gandhi Vichar Parishad in Wardha in 1954, said

Nehru became a prominent leader of the freedom struggle basically because of the colonial mindset of the Indians. "He is an Englishman in Indian clothing." So the respect for him. I was one of the audience to which this remark was made. Though we were very young, we did not accept this assessment. We attributed it to the breaking away of Jayaprakash Narayan and Kriplani from the Congress at the point of time.

The second view was expressed years later by former prime minister P.V. Narasimha Rao when I asked him how Nehru came to such prominence in the freedom struggle. He said Congressmen made him their leader because of their conviction that he was committed to the cause of freedom and to the service of the people of India. But he also reminded me that Nehru had worked his way up through municipal elections in Allahabad and through mass movements in Pratapgarh of Uttar Pradesh.

As the ideologue of the Indian Constitution and the Indian polity, Nehru's contributions cannot be denied. It is his implementation of the doctrine of secularism and his approach to harmonizing the diversities of India which seem flawed in retrospect. The basic reasoning of secularism which he put forward was valid—that a plural, multi-religious, civil society like that of India's could remain harmonious and united only if it is underpinned by religious tolerance and separation of religion from politics. The flaw, however, was that he did not underline the fact that the secular ethos of Indian society was rooted in two factors. That Hindus constituted the majority of the people of the country and that Hindu ethos at the profoundest intellectual and spiritual levels believed deeply in religious tolerance and respect for other religions.

If the majority of people in India were not Hindus, India would not have been a secular country. Instead of emphasising this, Nehru put the Hindu majority somewhat on the defensive, predicating Indian secularism on certification by the minorities, that the majority is secular. This resulted in a certain defensiveness and self-conscious denial of their religious and cultural identity by the Hindu community, which has perhaps made secularism a surface phenomenon in India's socio-political processes.

Similarly, Nehru's decision to reorganise the states on the basis of languages, while being good-intentioned, perhaps germinated the seeds of the present centrifugal territorial demands, affecting the unity of our country. While he was the builder of democratic institutions and conventions, one has to acknowledge that he did not groom a second generation of leadership in the party or the country, nor did he show any awareness of the need for anchoring the Congress in a trained cadre of party workers. He presumed that the commitment and organisational cohesion of the Congress during the freedom struggle would continue which was not to be because the party in a freedom movement is always different from a party in power in terms of ethos and motivations.

It is fashionable now to criticise Nehru's economic policies. He is castigated for making the public sector occupy the commanding heights of Indian economy. He is criticised for not linking up with western market economies.

It has to be remembered that the Indian private sector did not have the resources and motivation to invest in infrastructural sectors of the economy which required long-term investments and gestation periods. More importantly, between 1947 and 1955, all his efforts to get the major western powers involved in infrastructural development did not get a positive response. It was in consequence of this predicament that he entrusted the responsibility of mobilising resources and channelling them to fundamental sectors of the Indian economy to the government and the public sector.

While the decisions that he took seem logical and relevant to those times, the question to be answered is whether he would have continued the same policies had he lived into the '80s. Whatever his faults, he was alert and sensitive to changing domestic and international situations. Who knows, he might have been an equally active participant in the process of economic liberalisation and modernisation?

As an international statesman and foreign minister, there is a questioning of his founding the Non-Aligned Movement and its relevance today. It is true that the movement has not been very effective in safeguarding the interests of its member countries, particularly India. Two facts have to be kept in mind while evaluating Nehru's adherence to the movement. First, he made a distinction between being "non-aligned" and being part of "the Non-Aligned Movement".

He believed in non-alignment as a guiding principle of India's foreign policy so that India is assured of having the freedom of choice in making decisions responsive to its national interests without being subject to external influences. He articulated apprehensions about being part of a movement which in itself could become a bloc of countries. It was Krishna Menon who ultimately persuaded him to make India join the movement, arguing that the parallel interests of the countries of the movement would increase their influence in international transactions.

He did not believe in the non-aligned movement as a dogma. He rightly believed in non-alignment (as distinct from neutrality) as a guiding principle of India's foreign and security policies. Nehru can certainly be faulted for his idealism and belief in the sanctity of international law and agreements, in the light of his decision to go to the United Nations on the Kashmir issue and his faith in morality and goodwill as effective principles in inter-state relations. It was only at the end of 1962 after the military debacle against China that he acknowledged this reality, but it was too late. He can be blamed with Vallabhbhai Patel for the impatience which led to Partition about which Maulana Azad has written. In retrospect, Partition was good. It is preferable to India facing more profound centrifugal alienations than it is facing now.

Nehru was the beloved leader of his people. But when one intermeshes his individual persona with his public persona, one cannot but come to the conclusion that he was for the people, was committed to India's destiny being governed by the people but to a great extent was not "of the people". He was essentially a remote, aristocratic, glamorous and private person. Gandhi, Patel and Ambedkar were perhaps more immersed in the mass identity of Indians.

Regardless of the fault lines, Nehru remains the most important architect of free India. The words of Justice Oliver Wendell Holmes come to mind here. "A great man represents a great ganglion in the nerves of society, or to vary the figure, at a strategic point in the campaign of history and his greatness consists in seizing that opportunity and being there at that particular strategic point."

J.N. Dixit is a former foreign secretary, and the last generation to serve under Nehru as foreign minister. Among others, he is the author of Across Borders: 50 Years of India's Foreign Policy.

## Interim Prime Minister

Nanda was the interim Prime Minister of India twice for thirteen days each: the first time after the death of Prime Minister Jawaharlal Nehru in 1964, and the second time after the death of Prime Minister Lal Bahadur Shastri in 1966. His both terms were uneventful, yet they were important because of potential danger to the country following Nehru's death soon after a war with China in 1962, and Shastri's death after a war with Pakistan in 1965.

## The Pre-independence Era

First session of Indian National Congress, Bombay, 28-31, December, 1885.

Founded in 1885 with the objective of obtaining a greater share in government for educated Indians, the Indian National Congress was initially not opposed to British rule. The Congress met once a year during December. Indeed, it was a Scotsman, Allan Octavian Hume, who brought about its first meeting in Bombay, with the approval of Lord Dufferin, the then-Viceroy.

Womesh Chandra Bonerjee was the first President of the INC. The first meeting was scheduled to be held in Pune, but due to a plague outbreak there, the meeting was later shifted to Bombay. The first Session of INC was held from 28-31 December 1885, and was attended by 72 delegates.

A few years down the line, the demands of INC became more radical in the face of constant opposition from the government, and the party became very active in the independence movement. By 1907 the party was split into two halves: the *Garam Dal* of Bal Gangadhar Tilak, or Extremists (literally "hot faction"), and the

*Naram Dal* of Gopal Krishna Gokhale, or Moderates (literally "soft faction"), distinguished by their attitude towards the British. Under the influence of Bal Gangadhar Tilak, the Congress became the first integrated mass organization in the country, bringing together millions of people against the British.

The official flag of the Congress during the Independence struggle.

In its time as the nation's leader in the freedom struggle, it produced the nation's greatest leaders. Before the Gandhi Era came leaders like Bal Gangadhar Tilak, Bipin Chandra Pal, Lala Lajpat Rai, Gopal Krishna Gokhale, Mohammed Ali Jinnah (later leader of the Muslim League and instrumental in the creation of Pakistan), all starting with the first legendary icon of Indians: Dadabhai Naoroji, the president of the sister Indian National Association and later the first Indian Member of Parliament in the British House of Commons.

With the rise of Mahatma Gandhi's popularity and his Satyagraha art of revolution came Sardar Vallabhbhai Patel, Pandit Jawaharlal Nehru (the nation's first Prime Minister), Dr. Rajendra Prasad (the nation's first President), Khan Mohammad Abbas Khan, Khan Abdul Ghaffar Khan, Chakravarti Rajgopalachari, Jivatram Kripalani and Maulana Abul Kalam Azad.

With the already existing nationalistic feeling combinded with Gandhi's popularity the Congress became a forceful mass organization in the country, bringing together millions of people by specifically working against caste differences, untouchability, poverty, and religious and ethnic boundaries. Although predominantly Hindu, it had members from virtually every religion, ethnic group, economic class and linguistic group. At the time of the Quit India movement, the Congress was undoubtedly the strongest political and revolutionary organization in India. The Indian National Congress could claim to be the true representative of the Indian people.

The 1929 Lahore session under the presidency of Jawaharlal Nehru holds special significance as in this session "Poorna Swaraj" (complete independence) was declared as the goal of INC. The 26th January 1930 was declared as "Poorna Swaraj Diwas,"

Independence Day although the British remained in India a number of years longer. It was to commemorate this date particularly that The Indian Constitution was formally adopted on 26 January 1950 (even though it was passed on 26 November 1949).

After the First World War the party became associated with Mahatma Gandhi, who remained its unofficial, spiritual leader and mass icon even as younger men and women became party president. The party was in many ways an umbrella organization, sheltering within itself radical socialists, traditionalists and even Hindu and Muslim conservatives.

## The Post-independence Era

The party remained in power for thirty *continuous* years between independence in 1947 and its first taste of electoral defeat (at the national level) in 1977.

## History of the Republic of India

The History of the Republic of India began on August 15, 1947 when India became an independent Dominion within the British Commonwealth. Concurrently the Muslim-majority northwest and east of British India was separated into the Dominion of Pakistan. Lord Louis Mountbatten, and later Chakravarti Rajagopalachari served in the office of the Governor General of India. Jawaharlal Nehru became the first Prime Minister of India and Sardar Vallabhbhai Patel became the Deputy Prime Minister of India and its Minister of Home Affairs.

### *1947–1950*

Independent India's first years were marked with turbulent events – a massive exchange of population with Pakistan, the Indo-Pakistani War of 1947 and the integration of over 500 princely states to form a united nation.

## Aftermath of Partition

An estimated 3.5 million Hindus and Sikhs living in West Punjab, NWFP, Baluchistan, East Bengal and Sind migrated to India in fear of domination and suppression in Muslim Pakistan.

Communal violence killed an estimated 1 million Hindus, Muslims and Sikhs, and gravely destabilized both Dominions along their Punjab and Bengal boundaries, and the cities of Calcutta, Delhi and Lahore. The violence was stopped by early September owing to the cooperative efforts of both Indian and Pakistani leaders, and especially due the efforts of Mohandas Gandhi, the leader of the Indian freedom struggle, who undertook a *fast-unto-death* in Calcutta and later in Delhi to calm people and emphasize peace despite the threat to his life. Both Governments constructed large relief camps for incoming and leaving refugees, and the Indian Army was mobilized to provide humanitarian assistance on a massive scale.

The assassination of Mahatma Gandhi on January 30, 1948 was a major setback to the young nation. Gandhi was murdered by Nathuram Vinayak Godse, allegedly affiliated with the Hindu nationalist movement, who held him responsible for partition and charged that Gandhi was appeasing Muslims. More than one million people flooded the streets of Delhi to follow the procession to cremation grounds and pay their last respects.

In 1949, India recorded close to 1 million Hindu refugees flooded into West Bengal and other states from East Pakistan, owing to communal violence, intimidation and repression from Muslim authorities. The plight of the refugees outraged Hindus and Indian nationalists, and the refugee population drained the resources of Indian states, who were unable to absorb them. While not ruling out war, Prime Minister Nehru and Sardar Patel invited Liaquat Ali Khan for talks in Delhi.

Although many Indians termed this appeasement, Nehru signed a pact with Liaquat Ali Khan that pledged both nations to the protection of minorities and creation of minority commissions. Although opposed to the principle, Patel decided to back this Pact for the sake of peace, and played a critical role in garnering support from West Bengal and across India, and enforcing the provisions of the Pact. Khan and Nehru also signed a trade agreement, and committed to resolving bilateral disputes through peaceful means. Steadily, hundreds of thousands of Hindus returned to East Pakistan, but the thaw in relations did not last long, primarily owing to the Kashmir dispute.

## Union's Integration

British India consisted of 17 provinces and a few hundred princely states. The provinces were given to India or Pakistan, in some cases in particular—Punjab and Bengal—after being partitioned. The princes of the princely states, however, won the right to either remain independent or join either nation. Thus India's leaders faced the prospect of inheriting a nation fragmented between medieval-era kingdoms and provinces organized by colonial powers.

Under the leadership of Sardar Vallabhbhai Patel, the new Government of India employed political negotiations backed with the option (and, on several occasions, the use) of military action to ensure the primacy of the Central government and of the Constitution then being drafted.

There were three States that proved more difficult to integrate than others:

1. Junagadh - a December 1947 plebiscite resulted in a 99% vote to merge with India, annulling the controversial accession to Pakistan, which was made despite the people of the state being overwhelmingly Hindu.
2. Hyderabad - Patel ordered the Indian army to depose the government of the Nizam after the failure of negotiations, which was done between September 13 - September 17, 1948. It was incorporated as a state of India the next year.
3. The area of Kashmir in the far north of the subcontinent quickly became a source of controversy that erupted into the First Indo-Pakistani War which lasted from 1947 to 1949. Eventually a United Nations-overseen ceasefire was agreed that left India in control of two thirds of the contested region.

## Constitution

### *Jawaharlal Nehru Signing the Constitution of India*

The Constituent Assembly adopted the Constitution of India, drafted by a committee headed by B. R. Ambedkar, on November 26, 1949. India became a federal, democratic republic after its

Constitution came into effect on January 26, 1950. Rajendra Prasad became the first President of India.

### *1950s and 1960s*

India held its first national elections under the Constitution in 1952, where a turnout of over 60% was recorded. The Congress Party won an overwhelming majority, and Jawaharlal Nehru began a second term as Prime Minister. President Prasad was also elected to a second term by the electoral college of the first Parliament of India.

## Nehru Administration (1952–1964)

Prime Minister Nehru led the Congress to major election victories in 1957 and 1962. The Parliament passed extensive reforms that increased the legal rights of women in Hindu society, and further legislated against caste discrimination and untouchability. Nehru advocated a strong initiative to enroll India's children to complete primary education, and thousands of schools, colleges and institutions of advanced learning, such as the Indian Institutes of Technology were founded across the nation. Nehru advocated a socialist model for the economy of India – no taxation for Indian farmers, minimum wage and benefits for blue-collar workers, and the nationalization of heavy industries such as steel, aviation, shipping, electricity and mining. An extensive public works and industrialization campaign resulted in the construction of major dams, irrigation canals, roads, thermal and hydroelectric power stations.

## States Reorganization

Potti Sreeramulu's *fast-unto-death,* and consequent death for the demand of an Andhra State in 1953 sparked a major re-shaping of the Indian Union. Nehru appointed the *States Reorganization Commission,* upon whose recommendations, the States Reorganization Act was passed in 1956. Old states were dissolved and new states created on the lines of shared linguistic and ethnic demographics. The separation of Kerala and the Telugu-speaking regions of Madras State enabled the creation of an exclusively Tamil-speaking state of Tamil Nadu. On May 1, 1960, the states of Maharashtra and Gujarat were created out of the Bombay state. The creation of Punjabi Suba on November 1, 1966, an exclusively Punjabi speaking state of Punjab (India), occurred after a long struggle.

## Foreign Policy and Military Conflicts

Nehru's foreign policy was the inspiration of the Non-Aligned Movement, of which India was a co-founder. Nehru maintained friendly relations with both the United States and the Soviet Union, and encouraged the People's Republic of China to join the global community of nations. In 1956, when the Suez Canal Company was seized by the Egyptian government, an international conference voted 18-4 to take action against Egypt. India was one of the 4 backers of Egypt, along with Indonesia, Sri Lanka, and the USSR.

India had controversially opposed the partition of Palestine and the 1956 invasion of the Sinai by Israel, Britain and France, but did not oppose the Chinese occupation of Tibet and the suppression of a pro-democracy movement in Hungary by the Soviet Union.

Although Nehru disavowed nuclear ambitions for India, Canada and France aided India in the development of nuclear power stations for electricity. India also negotiated an agreement in 1960 with Pakistan on the just use of the waters of seven rivers shared by the countries. Nehru had visited Pakistan in 1953, but owing to political turmoil in Pakistan, no headway was made on the Kashmir dispute.

1. India has fought a total of four wars/military conflicts with its rival nation Pakistan, two in this period.In the Indo-Pakistani War of 1947 fought over Kashmir, Pakistan occupied one third of Kashmir (which India claims as its territory), and India occupied three fifths (which Pakistan claims as its territory). In the Indo-Pakistani War of 1965 India attacked Pakistan on all fronts after attempts by Pakistani troops to infiltrate into Indian controlled Kashmir. #In 1961, after continual petitions for a peaceful handover, India invaded and annexed the Portuguese colony of Goa on the west coast of India.

2. In 1962 China and India engaged in the brief Sino-Indian War over the border in the Himalayas. The war was a complete rout for the Indians and led to a refocusing on arms build-up and an improvement in relations with the United States. While China withdrew from occupied lands in the northeast, it continues to occupy Aksai Chin in Kashmir. China disputes India's sovereignty over Arunachal Pradesh and until recently, Sikkim.

## Post-Nehru India

Jawaharlal Nehru died on May 27, 1964. Lal Bahadur Shastri succeeded him as Prime Minister. In 1965 in the Second Kashmir War India and Pakistan again went to war, but without any definitive outcome or alteration of the Kashmir boundary. The Tashkent Agreement was signed under the mediation of the Soviet government, but Shastri died on the night after the signing ceremony. A leadership election resulted in the elevation of Indira Gandhi, Nehru's daughter who had been serving as Minister for Information and Broadcasting, as the third Prime Minister. She defeated right-wing leader Morarji Desai.

The Congress Party won a reduced majority in the 1967 elections owing to widespread disenchantment over rising prices of commodities, unemployment, economic stagnation and a food crisis. Indira Gandhi had started on a rocky note after agreeing to a devaluation of the Indian rupee, which created much hardship for Indian businesses and consumers, and the import of wheat from the U.S. fell through due to political disputes.

Morarji Desai entered Indira's government as Deputy Prime Minister and Finance Minister, and with senior Congress politicians attempted to constrain Indira's authority. But following the counsel of her political advisor P. N. Haksar, Indira resuscitated her popular appeal by a major shift towards socialist policies. She successfully ended the privy purse guarantee for former Indian royalty, and waged a major offensive against party hierarchy over the nationalization of India's banks. Although resisted by Desai and India's business community, the policy was popular with the masses.

When Congress politicians attempted to oust Indira by suspending her Congress membership, Indira was empowered with a large exodus of MPs to her own Congress (R). The bastion of the freedom struggle, the Indian National Congress had split in 1969. Indira continued to govern with a slim majority.

## Nehru and States Reorganisation Act

The States Reorganization Act of 1956 was a major reform of the boundaries and governance of India's states and territories. The act reorganized the boundaries of India's states along linguistic lines, and amended the Indian Constitution to replace the three types of states, known as Parts A, B, and C states, with a single type of state. Although additional changes to India's state boundaries have been made since 1956, the States Reorganisation Act of 1956 remains the single most extensive change in state boundaries since the independence of India in 1947.

## Political Integration after Independence and the Constitution of 1950

South Indian states prior to the *States Reorganisation Act*.

British India, which included most of present-day India as well as Pakistan and Bangladesh, was divided into two types of territories: provinces, which were governed directly by British officials, responsible to the Governor-General of India; and princely states, under the rule of local hereditary rulers who recognised British sovereignty in return for local autonomy, as established by treaty.

As a result of the reforms of the early 20th century, most of the provinces had elected legislatures and governors, although some of the smaller provinces were governed by a chief commissioner appointed by the Governor-General. The 20th century reforms of British India also established the principle of federalism, also known in British India as "dyarchy", which was carried forward into the governance of independent India.

On August 15, 1947, British India was granted independence as the separate dominions of India and Pakistan. The British dissolved their treaty relations with the over 600 princely states, who were encouraged to accede to either India or Pakistan. Most of the states acceded to India, and a few to Pakistan. Bhutan and Hyderabad opted for independence, although the armed intervention of India brought Hyderabad into the Indian Union.

During the 1947-1950 period, the territories of the princely states were politically integrated into the Indian Union. Most were merged into the existing provinces; others were organised into new provinces, like Rajputana, Himachal Pradesh, Madhya Bharat, and Vindhya Pradesh made up of multiple princely states; a few, including Mysore, Hyderabad, Bhopal, and Bilaspur, became separate provinces. The Government of India Act 1935 remained the constitutional law of India pending adoption of a new Constitution. The Constitution of India, which went into effect on January 26, 1950, made India a sovereign, democratic republic, and a union of states (replacing provinces) and territories. The states would have extensive autonomy and complete democracy in the Union, while the Union territories would be administered by the Government of India. The constitution of 1950 distinguished between three types of states.

Part A states, which were the former governors' provinces of British India, were ruled by an elected governor and state legislature. The nine Part A states were Assam, West Bengal, Bihar, Bombay, Madhya Pradesh (formerly Central Provinces and Berar), Madras, Orissa, Punjab, and Uttar Pradesh (formerly United Provinces). The eight Part B states were former princely states or groups of princely states, governed by a rajpramukh, who was often a former prince, along with an elected legislature. The rajpramukh was appointed by the President of India. The Part B states were Hyderabad, Saurashtra, Mysore, Travancore-Cochin, Madhya Bharat, Vindhya Pradesh, Patiala and East Punjab States Union (PEPSU), and Rajasthan.

The ten Part C states included both the former chief commissioners' provinces and princely states, and were governed by a chief commissioner. The chief commissioner was appointed by the President of India. The Part C states included Delhi, Kutch, Himachal Pradesh, Bilaspur, Coorg, Bhopal, Manipur, Ajmer-Merwara, and Tripura. Jammu and Kashmir had special status until 1957. The Andaman and Nicobar Islands was established as a union territory, ruled by a lieutenant governor appointed by the central government.

## The Movement for Linguistic States

Political movements for the creation of new, linguistic-based states developed around India in the years after independence. The movement to create a Telugu-speaking state out of the northern portion of Madras State gathered strength in the years after independence, and in 1953, the 16 northern, Telugu-speaking districts of Madras State became the new State of Andhra. Other small changes were made to state boundaries during the 1950-1956 period.

The small state of Bilaspur was merged with Himachal Pradesh on July 1, 1954, and Chandernagore, a former enclave of French India, was incorporated into West Bengal in 1955.

## The States Reorganisation Commission

In December 1953, Prime Minister Jawaharlal Nehru appointed the States Reorganisation Commission to prepare for the creation of states on linguistic lines. This was headed by Justice Fazal Ali and the commission itself was also known as the *Fazal Ali Commission*. The efforts of this commission was overseen by Govind Ballabh Pant, who served as Home Minister from December 1954. The commission created a report in 1955 recommending the reorganisation of India's states.

## The States Reorganisation Act

The States Reorganisation Act of 1956, which went into effect on November 1, eliminated the distinction between part A, B, and C states. It also reorganised the state boundaries and created or dissolved states and union territories.

## India and the Non-Aligned Movement

India played an important role in the multilateral movements of colonies and newly independent countries that developed into the Non-Aligned Movement.

## Origin of Non Alignment Movement

The founding leaders of the Non-Aligned states meet in New York in October 1960. From left: Nehru of India, Nkrumah of Ghana, Nasser of Egypt, Sukarno of Indonesia and Tito of Yugoslavia.

Nonalignment had its origins in India's colonial experience and the nonviolent Indian independence struggle led by the Congress, which left India determined to be the master of its fate in an international system dominated politically by Cold War alliances and economically by Western capitalism.

The principles of nonalignment, as articulated by Nehru and his successors, were preservation of India's freedom of action internationally through refusal to align India with any bloc or alliance, particularly those led by the United States or the Soviet Union; nonviolence and international cooperation as a means of settling international disputes. Nonalignment was a consistent feature of Indian foreign policy by the late 1940s and enjoyed strong, almost unquestioning support among the Indian elite.

The term "Non-Alignment" itself was coined by Indian Prime Minister Jawaharlal Nehru during his speech in 1954 in Colombo, Sri Lanka. In this speech, Nehru described the five pillars to be used as a guide for Sino-Indian relations, which were first put forth by Chinese Premier Zhou Enlai. Called Panchsheel (five restraints), these principles would later serve as the basis of the Non-Aligned Movement. The five principles were:

1. Mutual respect for each other's territorial integrity and sovereignty
2. Mutual non-aggression
3. Mutual non-interference in domestic affairs
4. Equality and mutual benefit
5. Peaceful co-existence

Jawaharlal Nehru's concept of nonalignment brought India considerable international prestige among newly independent states that shared India's concerns about the military confrontation between the superpowers and the influence of the former colonial powers. New Delhi used nonalignment to establish a significant role for itself as a leader of the Third World in such multilateral organizations as the United Nations (UN) and the Nonaligned Movement.

The signing of the Treaty of Peace, Friendship, and Cooperation between India and the Soviet Union in 1971 and India's involvement in the internal affairs of its smaller neighbors in the 1970s and 1980s tarnished New Delhi's image as a nonaligned nation and led some observers to note that in practice, nonalignment applied only to India's relations with countries outside South Asia.

## Early Developments

The movement had its origins in the 1947 Asian Relations Meeting in New Delhi and the 1955 Asian-African Conference in Bandung, Indonesia. India also participated in the 1961 Belgrade Conference that officially established the Nonaligned Movement, but Jawaharlal Nehru's declining prestige limited his influence. In the 1960s and 1970s, New Delhi concentrated on internal problems and bilateral relations, yet retained membership in an increasingly factionalized and radicalized movement. During the contentious 1979 Havana summit, India worked with moderate nations to reject Cuban president Fidel Castro's proposition that "socialism" (that is, the Soviet Union) was the "natural ally" of nonalignment.

# 3 Charisma of Nehru

The euphoria of independence was short-lived as partition brought disastrous consequences for India in the wake of communal conflict. Partition unleashed untold misery and loss of lives and property as millions of Hindu and Muslim refugees fled either Pakistan or India. Both nations were also caught up in a number of conflicts involving the allocation of assets, demarcation of boundaries, equitable sharing of water resources, and control over Kashmir. At the same time, Indian leaders were faced with the stupendous task of national integration and economic development.

When the British relinquished their claims to paramountcy, the 562 independent princely states were given the option to join either of the two nations. A few princely states readily joined Pakistan, but the rest—except Hyderabad (the largest of the princely states with 132,000 square kilometers and a population of more than 14 million), Jammu and Kashmir (with 3 million inhabitants), and Junagadh (with a population of 545,000)—merged with India. India successfully annexed Hyderabad and Junagadh after "police actions" and promises of privileges to the rulers. The Hindu maharajah of predominantly Muslim Jammu and Kashmir remained uncommitted until armed tribesmen and regular troops from Pakistan infiltrated his domain, inducing him to sign the Instrument of Accession to India on October 27, 1947. Pakistan refused to accept the legality of the accession, and, as a result, war broke out (see The Experience of Wars, ch. 10). Kashmir remains a source of friction between the neighbors (see South Asia, ch. 9).

The assassination of Mahatma Gandhi on January 30, 1948, in New Delhi, by a Hindu extremist opposed to Gandhi's openness to Muslims ended the tenuous celebration of independence and deepened the hatred and mutual suspicion in Hindu-Muslim relations.

Economic backwardness was one of the serious challenges that India faced at independence. Under three successive five-year plans, inaugurated between 1951 and 1964 under Nehru's leadership, India produced increasing amounts of food. Although food production did not allow self-sufficiency until fiscal year (FY—see Glossary) 1984, India has emerged as the nation with the seventh largest gross national product (GNP—see Glossary) in the world (see Industry, ch. 6; Production, ch. 7).

Linguistic regionalism eventually reached a crisis stage and undermined the Congress' attempts at nation building. Whereas in the early 1920s, the Congress had deemed that the use of regional vernaculars in education and administration would facilitate the governance of the country, partition made the leaders, especially Nehru, realize how quickly such provincial or subnational interests would dismantle India's fragile unity (see Diversity, Use, and Policy, ch. 4). However, in the face of widespread agitation for linguistic separation of states, beginning with the Telangana Movement in 1953, in 1956 Nehru reluctantly accepted the recommendations of the States Reorganisation Commission, and the number of states grew by reorganization along linguistic lines. The states became the loci for democratization of political processes at district levels, for expression of regional culture and popular demands against a national culture and unity, for economic development at strategic localities in the rural areas, and for proliferation of opposition parties that ended the possibility of a pan-Indian two-party system

## Jawaharlal Nehru and the Indian National Congress

Jawaharlal Nehru and the Indian National Congress maintained a close relationship that lasted for more than four long and eventful decades of Indian history. Nehru's relationship with the Indian National Congress officially started in 1919, two years after the birth of his daughter, Indira Priyadarshini, and seven years after his return from England. However, his close association with the Indian political scenario started much before his official initiation. Motilal Nehru, Jawaharlal's father, was a veteran Congressman of the moderate school and closely associated with the cause of India's freedom. Soon after his return from England in 1912, Jawaharlal found himself at the very midst of the Indian political scenario.

However, Jawaharlal was not very sure of the ideological position that would be effective for a rapid attainment of Indian Independence. On one side, there was his attachment to the extremist mode of protest, and then there was his loyalty towards his father. His initial dissociation from the ground realities of India also worked as a hindrance for him taking any definitive position. He was overall disturbed at the state of the inane Indian response to the British rule, with Anglophile Indian elite at the helm. The emergence of Gandhi worked as a great impetus to the Indian freedom struggle, and provided Nehru with the much needed direction that he was in search of. Gandhi's success at Champaran and Ahmedabad introduced the power of Satyagraha to the Indian masses. Civic resistance seemed to be a new political weapon that was powerful enough to put even the greatest imperialist power on the back-foot on issues of rightful governance and public rights.

**Apprentice Congressman**: Jawaharlal Nehru as a Congress apprentice started his political career soon after he returned from England. Although he worked in the legal firm of his father, yet it was India's predicament that concerned him more than his legal career. He was highly impressed by the Gandhian philosophy and way of life, and soon found in Gandhi the direction that he long yearned for. The entire Nehru family adopted Gandhian ways, however, but it was Nehru more than others who heartily accepted the Gandhian way of life, much to his father's dismay.

Nehru traveled the country extensively to preach Gandhi's ways and participate in the nationalist movements. The way he was received by the masses filled him with new confidence in his abilities and popular appeal. Gandhi himself was not slow to realize the great popular support that Nehru could harness with his background, charm and liberal education. These sojourns also provided Nehru with an opportunity to see the widespread exploitation that plagued every sphere of Indian civil life. The perils of the Indian populace that he witnessed first hand in these formative years shaped his policies during his tenure as a prime minister later on.

Jawaharlal Nehru participated whole-heartedly in the Non-Cooperation movement. However, he did not join his father to part ways with Gandhi when Motilal Nehru formed the Swaraj Party with CR Das after the movement was called off by Gandhi following the Chauri Chaura incident. Jawaharlal Nehru was caught between divided loyalties between his father and Gandhi. However, his strong faith in Gandhian methodologies made him close ranks with Gandhi in this crucial period of his life. This tension between father and son would be a regular feature in Jawaharlal's life, and it was only after the death of his father that Nehru despite his grief, felt fully free to pursue his own political course. The ascendancy of Nehru in the fullest sense happened only after the death of Motilal Nehru.

**Jawaharlal Nehru as INC President**: Jawaharlal Nehru's rise within the Indian National Congress (INC) was meteoric in the years following the Non-Cooperation movement. He, along with Subhas Chandra Bose, became two dynamic young leaders of the Congress to whom the Indians were glad to look up to for guidance. The Calcutta Congress of 1928 saw the Congress divided on the Nehru report prepared by Motilal Nehru on India's being awarded dominion status by the British government.

Jawaharlal himself took exception to the steps laid down by the Nehru report. Mahatma Gandhi worked towards a compromise, and also single handedly worked for Jawaharlal's election as the Congress President in the historic Lahore Congress in 1929. Despite the universally accepted organizational prowess of Vallabbhai Patel, Jawaharlal Nehru was elected as the Congress president at a young age of forty, prior to the extremely significant Lahore Congress of 1929. Nehru was prompt to use the platform in order to declare his dream of Purna Swaraj or Complete Independence.

**Nehru's Prison Days**: The monumental Lahore Congress introduced the Civil Disobedience Movement. Nehru plunged himself into the movement and courted arrest. It was not the first time Nehru went to prison, and it would not be the last time either. Over the period of the next decade, Nehru would spend most of the time of his life in prison as a political prisoner. However, he was determined to make his solitude count.

During the days of imprisonment, Nehru wrote extensively on a number of topics, particularly history and other social issues. He read a lot and often lectured fellow prisoners. However, with Motilal, Gandhi and Nehru imprisoned, the Indian freedom movement suddenly found itself without a clear direction. A number of factions both within Congress and outside were trying to undermine Satyagraha and offer alternate ways to India's freedom.

**Nehru and the INC in the Years before Indian Freedom**: Nehru spent most of the 1930s in prison, far from the Indian freedom struggle and the Indian National Congress. However, he kept a close watch on the course the movement was taking. On his return from prison to mainstream politics, Nehru had to employ all his reconciliatory skills to bring the warring factions within his party to a common platform. Although his Socialist ideals differed significantly from Gandhi's spiritual bent of civil resistance and the cultural aspects that came along with it. His differences with Gandhian modes came into the open in the Lucknow Conference of 1936.

Throughout the early forties, Nehru visited other Nationalist states as the Congress representative. He returned from China just before the World War II. The World War II brought in new problems for the Indian National Congress. Bose and his followers were willing to cooperate with the Axis forces in order to create pressure on the British officials, a move that Nehru summarily disapproved of. In the mean time, the Second Round Table Conference failed, and the Quit India movement was launched. Nehru was imprisoned once more. He was released in 1945 after the end of the War. Soon he started to work relentlessly towards forming the INA and preparing India for the hour of Independence. The end of the war brought the new Labor government in Britain, and the long held dream of Indian independence did not seem very far from then on.

**The Indian Independence and the INC**: The new government was willing to provide self dominion to India. With Nehru as the Congress president, negotiations were being worked out between the British government and the Congress Party, which was by then elected to be the single most popular party in India. However, the British were willing to play the waiting game and see the outcome of the elections. Moreover, a common ground between the Indian National Congress and the Muslim League was yet to be reached. Nehru tried his best to work out a solution through talks with Jinnah. The talks, expectedly failed. There was an absolute deadlock between the parties, and Partition seemed to be the only way for India to finally attain freedom.

**The Indian Independence finally came in the year 1947**; although the conditions of the much awaited freedom were far from what was expected. For Nehru as the President of the Indian national Congress, it was a bitter-sweet moment of truth. As the President of Congress, Nehru was the automatic choice as the first Prime Minister of Independent India. On 15th August, 1947 Nehru gave his famous 'Tryst with Destiny' speech from the Red Fort. However, it was hardly the end of his troubles. Mahatma Gandhi was murdered soon after and Patel died in 1950. Nehru was vested with the duty of steadying the rocking boat of the tottering economy of a newly emergent nation. This started the second phase of Nehru's work within the folds of the Indian National Congress, the post Independence phase.

**Post-Independence Phase of INC and Nehru**: Indian National Congress was committed to the primary idea of freeing India from British rule. Nehru thought otherwise, and he realized that the widespread popularity of the Congress could be used as a platform to address and solve much of the nation's problems. However, a sudden loss in a sense of direction was imminent in Congress. The Congress party itself had its due share of problems too. The Leftist forces provided a constant threat to the Party, as was the right wing within the Party who opposed Nehru's socialist ideals. At such a time, it was much because of Nehru's personal charisma that the integrity of the Congress could be successfully maintained.

Nehru's imposing internationalism somehow helped to soothe the problems back home. In fact, problems as mounting as the division of the provinces on linguistic lines and the Kashmir debate were also taken care of by Nehru's formidable success in foreign policies. It was with his stature, that Nehru managed to forge together the various warring forces within the Congress. However, Nehru himself was well aware of the decadence that has infested the party ranks and is known to have warned his party members after the Congress victory of 1957.

Nehru's commitment to the Congress party was life-long, and he is still considered to be one of the greatest Congressmen. However, the greatness of Nehru remains in the fact, that he successfully transcended his Congress identity to become a major international political figure.

## Nehru's Nationalism and his role in the Freedom Movement of India

Nehru's Nationalism and his role in the Freedom Movement are closely inter-related, since it was the nature of Nehru's Nationalist ideas that dictated his course of action in the freedom movement of India.

**Nehru's Nationalism**: Nehru's nationalism was not one of mindless jingoism. He was able to reach a common ground between an erudite internationalism and a very keen understanding of the Indian condition. Nehru's nationalism was marked by a fiery pride in the heritage of the country. But he was willing to temper this pride with his readings and his rationalist views that he received from his Western education in the West.

Jawaharlal Nehru's role in the freedom movement of India has probably not received as much historical attention as it deserves. That is, of course no surprise, as Jawaharlal Nehru's astounding success as a statesman who ushered in a new era of international relations through the formation of the NAM, and his stature as the first prime minister of independent India often adumbrate his position as a significant figure in the freedom movement of India. With his charm, highly impressive educational background, and selfless service to the nation, Nehru presented the face of a new and active India to thousands of Indians who looked up to him as a role model and a guide.

**Early Years of Nehru in the Freedom Movement of India:** Jawaharlal Nehru was born into politics. His father Motilal Nehru was a veteran Congressman and committed to the cause of India's freedom for a very long time. Nehru spent much of his educational years in England studying first at Harrow and then at Trinity College, Cambridge. However, the freedom of India was always on his mind. It was therefore no surprise that after his return from the British shores in 1912, the job of a lawyer was the last of Nehru's priorities. As a student he already felt himself closely attached to the cause India's freedom, and had his sympathies with the Extremist leaders of Congress. After his return, he involved himself directly into the political scenario of the country.

However, Nehru was still comparatively without a firm direction in these early years, not sure which path was the right path that would lead towards India's freedom. His father's moderate ideologies and elitist way of life disturbed him, as he thought him, like many other Congressmen of his generation, to be much dissociated from the ground realities of the land and the lives of the common people of India. He also realized that the direct application of Socialist measures would not suit India's socio-economic profile.

It was at that time that he found a direction in the mode of civil resistance as preached by Gandhi. Gandhi's success in Champaran and Ahmedabad renewed and established his belief in Satyagraha. He was not slow to adopt the cultural aspects of Satyagraha as well. He read the Indian scriptures of India, and dressed in home-spun clothes becoming a staunch Gandhian in all senses. Motilal and his entire family adopted the Gandhian way of life. Nehru traveled across India, and was warmly received by the masses. This filled him with a renewed sense of self-confidence. It was time he decided to whole-heartedly commit himself to the cause of Indian freedom.

**Jawaharlal Nehru and the Non-Cooperation Movement**: The first big involvement of Jawaharlal Nehru came at the onset of the non-cooperation movement in 1920. Nehru joined in wholeheartedly in this Satyagraha based movement that stormed India. Nehru was arrested on charges of anti-governmental activities and was released a few months later. In the rift formed within the Congress following the sudden closure of the non-cooperation movement after the Chauri Chaura incident, Nehru remained loyal to Gandhi's camp and denied to join the Swaraj Party formed by Motilal Nehru and CR Das. After his release, Nehru's fame as a dynamic Congress leader was well-established. He soon became the President of the Allahabad Congress Committee in 1923. However, towards the end of the decade, Nehru grew increasingly impatient with the pacifist nature of the senior Congressman. Along with Subhas Chandra Bose, Nehru was intent on complete freedom and believed in giving an ultimatum to the British Government to grant India dominion status. The senior leaders were bent on a slower and more patient approach. The Calcutta Congress of 1928 brought the rift into the open. Jawaharlal openly decried the Nehru Commission framed by Motilal Nehru, and it needed the intervention of Mahatma Gandhi to persuade Nehru to abandon his fiery stance of more direct action.

**Nehru and the Civil Disobedience Movement**: The Lahore Congress of 1929 was monumental in the political career of Nehru as well as the history of India's freedom struggle. Nehru was elected the president of Congress for the first time at a young age of forty. He used the platform of the Lahore conference to declare the goal of complete freedom or Purna Swaraj. The Civil Disobedience movement was formally launched after the Lahore Congress, and Nehru whole heartedly plunged himself in the non-violent protests and picketing that took the nation by storm. Nehru was arrested again in 1930, beginning the second and the longest phase of his prison stays. On his release, he formed the Socialist party within the Congress and insisted on more stern and immediate measures to realize the goal of India's freedom.

**Nehru and the last days of Indian Freedom Struggle**: The Government of India Act of 1935 called for nation-wide elections. Nehru campaigned vigorously for Congress, although he himself did not contest directly in the elections. With Gandhi concentrating on the spiritual development of his followers and gradually dissociating himself from direct political action, the stature of Nehru within the Congress ranks was now more than ever. He became the Congress President in the consecutive years of 1936 and 1937. By 1938, the rift in Congress was clear. With Bose and Gandhi forming the two feuding camps, Nehru was once more faced with a political dilemma. However, he decided to side with Gandhi and his methods. Bose resigned as the Congress president, and Nehru's status in the Congress reached a height previously unattained. This year started a new phase in Nehru's career, especially after his denial to come to a compromise with the Muslim League.

With the clouds of World War II looming large in the horizon, Nehru's skill in international relations would be tested once more. Nehru did not support Bose's policy of siding with the Axis forces, and intended to extend support to the Allies. In the mean time, the Second Round Table conference failed and Gandhi launched the Quit India movement in 1942. Nehru was arrested and was released only in 1945. By the time the World War II was over and the new Labor Government of Britain seemed willing to grant India its long deserved freedom. However, the British Government wanted to adopt a policy of waiting and watching the result of the general elections of 1945.

Nehru was once again at the center of activities. He was arrested. His refusal to comply with Jinnah's claims made partition inevitable, as Jinnah called for direct action. Although his fight for Indian freedom stood on the verge of success, Nehru knew his work was far from over. He had to build a new India and had to guide the nascent economy towards success.

## Jawaharlal Nehru as a Social Reformer

Jawaharlal Nehru was the first Prime Minister of independent India. He was a key figure in the Indian independence movement. Nehru also initiated the process of social reform in the independent Indian Republic. The importance of Jawaharlal Nehru as a social reformer in Indian history cannot be denied.

India gained independence on 15 August, 1947. The India that existed in the 1940's was a cauldron of social unrest. The age-old problem of caste had reared its ugly head and was threatening to tear the social fabric apart. Religious tensions were also a reigning problem in India during those days. The partition of pre-independent India had divided the Indian sub-continent into two countries, India and Pakistan. Pakistan became an Islamic Republic as envisaged by its creator Mohamed Ali Jinnah. India became a secular republic by choice.

Jawaharlal Nehru inherited from the British a country that was bereft of social and economic stability. He inherited a mish-mash of people speaking as many as 16 different languages with different cultural moorings.

The genius of Jawaharlal Nehru as a social reformer shone through in this post-independence period. He took decisive steps to eradicate the evils of the all pervasive caste system. Nehru undertook corrective measures by changing existing Indian legal laws. Legal procedures were enacted to make caste discrimination illegal and punishable by law. The enacted laws were strictly enforced.

Jawaharlal Nehru was one of the few Indian statesmen at that time who understood the need of proper intellectual development of the Indian populace. He had exposure to European educational ideals during his stay at England, where he received education. Nehru also knew that British stress on proper education to run their colonial empire. He understood the importance of proper and healthy intellectual development to run the nascent Indian state. Jawaharlal Nehru wished to combine the best of both worlds, the winning combination of western scientific prowess and Indian civilization wisdom.

Nehru realized that the only way the Indian Republic can reestablish its presence in the world stage is through the intellectual power of its citizens. Jawaharlal stressed on the teaching of science and its practical application fields. He took cognizance of the need of learning vocational science. The teaching of vocational science attracted him. Special focus was put on the development of technology. The famed Indian Institutes of Technology or IIT's were conceived and established during his Prime Minister-ship. The Indian Institutes of Technology are now regarded as one of the premier scientific institutes of higher technological learning throughout the world. IIT graduates are much in demand among the corporate sector. The establishment of such learning centers also indirectly contributed to the emergence of the Indian Republic as a pharmaceutical major in the late 1980's. The cheapest medicines in the world are produced and sold in India. The capabilities of the Indian software industry have also amazed the world.

Jawaharlal Nehru was born in an era when the principal mode of communication was the postal service. Telephones were affordable only by the minuscule economically empowered Indian populace. There were few government hospitals. The rural Indian population lived in pitiable conditions amidst abject poverty.

Nehru was acutely aware of the rural situation of India. He had contested and won democratic elections in Pratapgarh district of Uttar Pradesh. Jawaharlal Nehru knew the many problems faced by the rural populace.

The rural environment was feudal at that time. Literacy was low and social tensions were simmering below the societal surface. Nehru initiated the construction and functioning of a number of schools. The schools provided primary and secondary education to the rural population. The schools are spread throughout India. Primary education was provided free of cost.

The government schools also provided free meals to its students. This scheme was the trump card of Jawaharlal Nehru. The great statesmen understood the importance of food to attract students to schools.

The purchasing power of the rural Indian population at that time was very low. A majority of the rural population subsisted on one meal a day. All members of the family were required to work to keep the home-fires burning. The children were also roped in to earn for the family. Jawaharlal Nehru knew the importance of food in the educational scheme. The food acts as a magnet for the impoverished hungry child. The family of the prospective student was also happy with the subsequent tangible cost savings.

The food given in the primary education programs included milk in addition to pulses for a healthy meal. The specter of malnutrition in the 1950's and 1960's India were fought in this way. Jawaharlal Nehru also established vocational schools for adults. Adult education centers were created both in rural and urban areas. Higher technical schools were also established.

The Indian Republic has a substantial population. Almost half of the population is women. Jawaharlal Nehru enacted laws to guarantee practical universal suffrage to the women population of the country. The laws aimed to secure the social freedoms of Indian women. Female legal rights were also increased under Nehru's able Prime Ministership.

Jawaharlal Nehru was a highly educated man. His western education catalyzed his aspirations for equality of the Indian populace. Nehru actively promoted and brought about the system of reservations in the Indian job sector. A certain percentage of government jobs were reserved for persons born into scheduled castes and scheduled tribes. This was done to ensure the participation of the less privileged Indian population to the mainstream.

Jawaharlal Nehru had many social successes to his credit. He was responsible for promoting the rights of religious minorities. His swift judgment along with his mentor Mahatma Gandhi at the time of independence ensured that the Indian Republic became a secular state. He understood the basic social nature of the Indian population. The Indian population is largely secular, plural and civil and has a number of practicing religions. Nehru fostered the need for tolerance of all religions and respect for people unlike own.

The success of Jawaharlal Nehru's reforms is apparent throughout the modern Indian Republic. The booming economy of contemporary India underscores this fact.

## Economic Policies of Jawaharlal Nehru

The economic policies of Jawaharlal Nehru have been subject to much controversy in the past few decades. However, it is important to place Nehru's economic policies in context for a proper appreciation of his policies. Nehru's commitment to the cause of India's development remains unquestioned, and it is no doubt that much of his plans and speculations were jeopardized by the unexpected partition that came along with the independence of India, which brought about an unprecedented fissure in the economic resources of the Indian mainland.

Nehru himself confessed that the partition brought about a large share of problems, including a great rift in the agricultural and the industrial sectors. A large portion of the most productive agricultural lands fell in Pakistan whereas the corresponding industries remained in Indian dominion. The problem faced by the Jute industry soon after Independence can be stated as a case in the point. The jute producing areas were in Pakistan whereas the Jute processing factories remained in India, thereby affecting jute productions on both sides of the border.

**Early Economic Reforms of Nehru**: Nehru started his career as the Prime Minister of independent India in 1947, and immediately launched a number of economic reforms. Nehru was a firm believer in state control over the economic sectors. His socialist ideals revealed themselves in the way he introduced laws for land redistribution, in order to curtail the economic disparity in India among the landed and the land-less classes. One of Nehru's key economic reforms was the introduction of the Five Years Plan in 1951. It was introduce to determine the mode of government expenditure and grants in important development sectors like agriculture, industries and education.

**The Ideology guiding Nehru's Economic Policies**: Nehru's economic policies have often been considered to be Socialist in nature. It is no doubt that Socialism did play a very important role in Nehru's ideological make-up. But at the same time, it is also important to consider that Nehru himself denied any kind of overt Socialist tendencies in the economic policies adopted by him. Nehru advocated a kind of mixed economy. Any kind of unquestioned ideological adherence to any form of economic tenet, or 'ism', he realized, would be detrimental to India's growth. He wanted a practical approach in framing the Indian economy, which would suit best the country's needs. On the one hand, as a devoted

Gandhian, he had strong belief in the betterment of rural economy. On the other hand, he had a strong belief that heavy industrial development would be the best way to serve India's economic interests.

**Nehru's Industrial Policies**: Nehru wanted to create a balance between the rural and the urban sectors in his economic policies. He stated there was no contradiction between the two and that both could go hand in hand. He denied to carry forward the age old city versus village controversy and hoped that in India, both could go hand in hand. Nehru was intent to harness and fully exploit the natural resources of India for the benefit of his countrymen. The main sector he identified was hydroelectricity, and he constructed a number of dams to achieve that end. The dams would not only harness energy, but would also support irrigation to a great degree. Nehru considered dams to be the very symbol of India's collective growth, as they were the platforms where industrial engineering and agriculture met on a common platform. Nehru also considered the possibility of nuclear growth during his tenure as the prime minister of India.

**The State Control in Nehru's Economic Policies**: The most distinctive, and often debated feature of Nehru's economic policies, was the high level of state and central control that was exercised on the industrial and business sectors of the country. Nehru emphasized that the state would control almost all key areas of the country's economy, either centrally or on a state-wise basis. His Socialist emphasis on state control somehow seemed to undermine his stress on industrial policies. The rigorous state laws and License rules put a great degree of restrain on the free execution of industrial policies. Even the farmers, along with the business personnel, found themselves to be at the receiving end of rigorous state control policies and high taxation. Poverty and unemployment were widespread throughout Nehru's governance.

**Nehru's Views on Rural Economy**: Nehru's policy towards the rural economy of India was also significant. Nehru felt for the rural self-development of India very strongly. He tried to boost India's cottage industries. Much on the lines of Gandhi, Nehru believed that the rural and cottage industries of India played a major role in the economic fabric of the country. But most of his cottage industry development programs were meant as a part of community development. He was also of the belief that small scale industries and cottage industries were effective solutions to the massive employment problems that remained a perpetual issue of concern throughout his tenure.

The economic policies of Nehru are often blamed for the poor economy of India in the subsequent years. However, it cannot be denied that his decisions were necessitated by the needs of the times. India needed to effectively harness its domestic means as well as strengthen its governmental control to lay the base for future privatization. It is often speculated that Nehru would have embraced the economic reforms and economic liberalization of the late twentieth century if he was alive.

## Jawaharlal Nehru as Prime Minister

Jawaharlal Nehru was the first Prime Minister of India. His Prime-Minister-ship was marked by social and economic reforms of the Indian state. A number of foreign policy landmarks like the founding of the Non-Aligned Movement also marked the tenure of Jawaharlal Nehru as Prime Minister.

Jawaharlal Nehru became Prime Minister on the 15th of August 1947. His ascension was plagued by controversy and a bitter power struggle within the Congress Party. The internal struggle of the party was symptomatic of the larger struggle within the Indian Republic itself. The initial period of Jawaharlal Nehru as Prime Minister was marked by communal violence.

Jawaharlal Nehru was forced to concede the creation of Pakistan as per the wishes of the Muslim League leader the leadership of Muhammad Ali Jinnah. Communal violence enveloped the entire country during this period. Maximum bloodshed was witnessed in the national capital Delhi. The Indian states of Punjab and Bengal also witnessed fierce bloodshed.

The first Prime Minister tried to defuse the explosive situation by visiting the violence affected areas. He toured the riot stricken areas with Pakistani leaders to reassure those affected by the violence. Nehru promoted peace in Punjab during that momentous period in Indian history. The secular nature of Jawaharlal Nehru was best exemplified during those times. He took active steps to safeguard the status of Indian Muslims.

The enduring legacy of Nehru rule is the effect of Nehru's economic policies. His economic policies were far reaching and its effects are felt to this day. Jawaharlal Nehru is best known for his enduring brand of 'Nehruvian Socialism' or the Indian version of Socialism. The original socialist policies were watered down by Nehru to gel with the Indian economic context. Jawaharlal Nehru was responsible for the special economic reform policy vehicle, Planning Commission of India.

The Planning Commission of India is Jawaharlal Nehru's brainchild. The Commission is responsible for formulating the 'Five-Year Plans' of the Indian economy. The Planning Commission also conducts a host of other economic functions. The first Five-Year Plan was presented by Prime Minister Jawaharlal Nehru on the 8th of December, 1951.

Prime Minister Jawaharlal Nehru concentrated his economic policies on the rural sector. The Indian rural economy was allotted a lion's share of the first Five-Year Plan fund money. More than 27% of the total funding went to irrigation and energy production. The agricultural sector got more than 17% of the budget resource. About 4% of the fund money was earmarked for land rehabilitation.

The first Five-Year Plan also provided the seed money for setting up the five Indian Institutes of Technology or IIT's. The University Grants Commission or UGC was also set up during this period. The tenth Five-Year Plan is currently in vogue.

Land redistribution plans were undertaken during Jawaharlal Nehru's tenure as a Prime Minister. The redistribution of land ensured a more socially just Indian society. This move helped the Indian economy in many ways. The wealth disparity between sections of the populace lessened. This resulted in a more thriving and healthy societal landscape.

The first Prime Minister Jawaharlal Nehru was one of the first Indian policymakers to understand the importance of cottage industries in the Indian economy. The development of such small scale industries infused much needed production efficiency into the rural Indian economy. The Cottage Industries also helped the agricultural workers to have a better quality of life. This is due to the additional profits generated by the farming community.

A number of educational and social reforms were undertaken when Jawaharlal Nehru was Prime Minister. He was instrumental in starting new Indian institutes of higher learning like the Indian Institutes of Technology, the All India Institute of Medical Sciences or AIIMS and the various branches of the Indian Institutes of Management among others. Primary education was made compulsory. It was also made free of cost. Adult educational units were also established.

Jawaharlal Nehru was also responsible for setting the direction of India's foreign policy. The policy is valid till now. The world in the 1950s was sharply divided into two opposite factions: one side was the west-comprising of the United States and western European countries and the other side was the East- dominated by the erstwhile USSR. India wisely joined neither faction during that period. The Republic of India was one of the founding members of the Non Aligned Movement or NAM.

The negotiating skills of Jawaharlal Nehru came into focus during his dealings with the Pakistani ruling establishment. His consummate skill was on display during the talks with Pakistan on the Kashmir issue. The first Indian Prime Minister cemented India's administrative hold on the northern Indian state. He also arrested the influential politician- Sheikh Abdullah on suspicion of anti-national activities. This led to a smoother administrative transition from the former Kashmiri ruler to civilian Indian rule.

The Indian Prime Minister Jawaharlal Nehru was feted around the world for his efforts to ease global political tensions. The middle of the 1950s saw India criticizing the invasion of the Suez Canal by a combined military force comprising French, British and Israeli troops. Jawaharlal Nehru formally signed the Indus Water Treaty with Pakistan in 1960. This was done with a view to mitigate the long standing dispute between India and Pakistan in sharing the water resources of the major rivers in the shared geographical region of Punjab.

The invasion of India's north-eastern territorial region by China in the 1960s dashed Jawaharlal Nehru's hopes for a peaceful South-East Asia. His decision to grant refuge to the Tibetan Buddhist leader Dalai Lama also came in for severe criticism. The Chinese invasion also forced him to re-examine India's security requirements and act accordingly.

Jawaharlal Nehru's last days as India's Prime Minister were marred by political problems. The Congress Party suffered from corruption within itself. He promoted his daughter Indira Gandhi to the Indian political landscape in that period. Indira Gandhi later became India's first woman Prime Minister. The last period of his Prime Minister-ship also included the Indian invasion of Portugal in 1961. Jawaharlal Nehru died in office on the 27th of May 1964.

## Childhood and Family of Jawaharlal Nehru

Jawaharlal Nehru, the first Prime Minister of India, had a strong and influential lineage. Born on the 14th of November, 1889 at Allahabad, Jawaharlal Nehru was the eldest child of Motilal Nehru and Swarup Rani. His family was from Kashimiri heritage and belonged to a high Hindu caste. They were Saraswat Brahmins, who were revered greatly in Allahabad in those days. Originally part of the Kashmiri Pandit community, the Nehrus had to shift to what was called United Provinces. But the family gelled well with the people there and Motilal Nehru, Jawaharlal's father, started practicing law in Allahabad. He was also a highly influential man, both socially as well as politically. He was a learned scholar too. He excelled in several languages that included Persian, Urdu, Arabic, English and many more.

Jawaharlal Nehru and his entire family lived in a large house called 'Anand Bhawan' in Allahabad. The house is still there. Motilal Nehru was a successful man, who was also well known in the society. He was a barrister by profession and won several accolades for his legal works from different spheres. All these brought him lot of name and fame. As a result, he could give his children the best of everything in life. Jawaharlal Nehru was his only son, while he also had two beautiful daughters named Vijaya Lakshmi Pandit and Krishna Pandit. No discrimination was made between the son and daughters in the family. All of them were provided quality education and privileges. All the children were brought amidst immense luxury and comfort. With a swimming pool and a tennis court in the house premises, Jawaharlal Nehru led a lavish life.

Motilal Nehru never compromised on the education and other facilities that are required to make a happy upbringing for children. He emphasized on English and western education for his children. Jawaharlal Nehru received his initial education at home under an English governess. Hindi and Sanskrit were also taught to the children at the Nehru House. Training was also provided to converse in English fluently. Apart from formal education, various English mannerisms and customs were also taught to Jawaharlal Nehru in his childhood days. The dresses that were adorned by the Nehru family also reflected English style. After some formal education at home, Jawaharlal Nehru also went to a local convent school in Allahabad. At the age of fifteen, he went to England to study at Harrow.

The illustrious family of the Nehrus had a deep impact on the life and childhood of Jawaharlal Nehru. At home, his mother practiced several staunch Hindu customs and even tried to influence young Nehru by them. But she was not much successful in it. Motilal was not a very strong follower of religion, but he was not an absolute atheist too. Motilal Nehru was concerned about very minute details regarding his son. He corresponded with his son, even when he was abroad and enquired about every small detail regarding his stay, studies and all the other curricular activities. Even after coming back from abroad, Jawaharlal Nehru began a firm and solid career with the help of his father. He attained instant fame and glory in his profession and made himself and his family proud.

Motilal Nehru was an active member of the Indian National Congress, which had also influenced and helped in shaping the political life of Jawaharlal Nehru. Motilal Nehru shared extremely good and cordial relation with the British officials. He had a strong belief on British justice and British promises. Several incidents have been sited when Motilal Nehru had been in support of the

British officers. His home was also open to various British officers. British officers also respected him and his family and welcomed them to their homes. As a result of this intermingling, Jawaharlal Nehru and his two sisters also got opportunities to have a glimpse of British lifestyle. Some of the British officers could also fluently speak Urdu and Hindi.

Motilal Nehru was a stylish man and he loved to live life luxuriously. He was a follower of beauty and beautiful things. He had the passion of collecting various beautiful articles from various parts of India as well as from foreign countries. He had made a huge collection of artifacts that were considered as masterpieces and rare articles. One of the most important facts that were seen in the family of Jawaharlal Nehru was that, there were no class restrictions or class distinctions. People of all castes and religions were accepted and welcomed in 'Anand Bhawan'. There were many servants in the Nehru household, who belonged to different castes and religions. The doors of 'Anand Bhawan' remained open for all people irrespective of differences in caste and religion.

Another important part of the family of Jawaharlal Nehru was the active participation of his two sisters, Vijaya Lakshmi Pandit and Krishna Pandit in various matters of the family as well as in politics. They supported him and he had a great influence on their lives. Vijaya Lakshmi Pandit mentioned in one of her lectures about the childhood they had spent together. She also emphasized on the influence that Jawaharlal Nehru had on her political career and personal life.

Jawaharlal Nehru did not have a blissful married life. He was married at a young age in the year 1916. When he was at Harrow, Motilal Nehru and his wife decided to find a perfect match for Jawaharlal Nehru. They started their search and found Kamala Kaul, a girl from a middle-class Kashmiri Brahmin family in 1912. She was a thirteen year old girl, well-educated at home and knew Hindu and Urdu. They waited till 1916, when Kamala attained the age of seventeen years. Kamala was finally married to Jawaharlal Nehru in February, 1916.

The initial years of marriage were not very happy for Kamala as Nehru was then basking in glory and paid little importance to the home front. Kamala Nehru was a strong woman and she endured all this without any protest. She also had to endure several blunt remarks from her husband's relatives regarding her inferior social origins. But she did not retaliate to any of these. She began to involve herself in the Indian freedom struggle and even went to the prison. This event also helped her to come closer to her husband. Jawaharlal Nehru and Kamala Nehru also had a beautiful daughter in 1917, who was called Indira Priyadarshini Gandhi. Kamala Nehru also gave birth to a pre-matured baby boy, who died in 1924. After that she underwent a miscarriage after three years.

Kamala Nehru could not bear this trauma and fell seriously ill. She was diagnosed of tuberculosis and underwent treatment in various hospitals in the country as well as abroad. It was during this time that Jawaharlal Nehru realized his love and passion for her. He used to visit her regularly and even took her abroad for treatment. They also spent few days in Switzerland. Finally she breathed her last in 1936.

To summarize, it has been observed that childhood of Jawaharlal Nehru had a great influence on the later life of this great Indian personality. Though he was brought up amidst immense luxury and glory, it did not restrict him from mingling with general masses and feeling their pulse. His family also had a great influence on his social and political career.

## Nehru and Gandhiji

Mahatma Gandhi and Jawaharlal Nehru were both stalwarts in Indian national struggle for independence. Motilal Nehru, Jawaharlal Nehru's father, was an eminent personality in the Indian National Congress and that fascinated young Jawaharlal Nehru to join politics too. He was greatly influenced by his father's charismatic personality and his elegance and style. Motilal Nehru and Mahatma Gandhi knew each other very well and it became easier for Jawaharlal Nehru to be closely acquainted to 'Bapu'-as the nation called him. Mahatma Gandhi first met Jawaharlal Nehru at the annual meeting of the Indian National Congress in the year 1916 at Lucknow. The first meeting was enough to impress Nehru regarding Gandhi and the charm of this relationship increased and flourished with passing time.

In Mahatma Gandhi, Jawaharlal Nehru had found the absolute leader who was capable of handling the entire nation. This quality he found missing in almost all the Indian political leaders of the time that included his father, Motilal Nehru. Even Motilal Nehru was highly impressed and influenced by Mahatma Gandhi's inner strength and self-confidence.

The greatest quality that went in favor of Mahatma Gandhi was his image. General masses could identify themselves through Gandhiji. In the initial stages of his political career, Jawaharlal Nehru found everything regarding Gandhiji amazing and great.

Gandhiji's plan of action in any field attracted Nehru to a great deal. The Satyagraha movement against the Rowlatt Act fascinated Jawaharlal Nehru greatly and he was keen to join the movement with great deal of enthusiasm. But he was dissuaded by his father to join the movement then and there and asked him to follow the proceedings of the mass-movement. With satyagrahas becoming the common form of revolt against the various forms of British atrocities, Mahatma Gandhi gained an important place in the Indian freedom struggle. There was also immense mass following that helped Gandhiji to attain that grand stature.

The heinous crime that the British committed in Jalianwala Bagh evoked Jawaharlal Nehru into action. He could no longer restrain himself from joining active politics and participate in the Indian independence struggle. Gandhiji also advocated the terms 'ahimsa', meaning non-violence and 'Swaraj', meaning self-rule. These were mainly aimed at improving and changing the economic scenario in the country. Jawaharlal Nehru joined the campaign with full fervor and enthusiasm.

The Congress party was totally reformed and remodeled to reach to the people at the grass root level. This called for involvement of the masses in all the action that was planned for attaining freedom from the shackles of the British rule. Nehru completely supported the idea as he knew that without this support, attaining independence would be a next to impossible job.

In the year 1921, Jawaharlal Nehru was first arrested and sent to prison. After this, he was sent to the prison several times and passed nine years of his life in prison for the freedom struggle. Mahatma Gandhi in the mean time became the supremo of the Indian National Congress. The civil-disobedience movement was also called off by Gandhiji. There was also some political strife that was going on in the Indian National Congress at this time. In 1923, Jawaharlal Nehru was appointed the General Secretary of the Congress just for a period of two years. He again gained back the position in 1927 for two years. Along with this, he was deeply involved in the freedom struggle movement and under Gandhiji's leadership and care he was blooming as an efficient leader.

In 1929, under the patronage of Mahatma Gandhi, Jawaharlal was made the President of the Indian National Congress. This was declared at the annual Congress Session at Lahore. After that Jawaharlal Nehru was made the President of the Indian National Congress six more times. He enjoyed the position and the glory that is attached to the post. But he was frequently arrested and put behind bars during the various movements that were launched to remove the British from India. Even during the Civil Disobedience Movement that was initiated by Mahatma Gandhi against the salt laws that were imposed by the British, Nehru was arrested.

Gandhiji even went to London to attend the Round Table Conference to figure out a peaceful way to attain freedom for the nation. But after coming back from there, he found the situation even worse. In 1932, both Gandhiji and Jawaharlal Nehru were arrested. Once, Motilal Nehru was also arrested and all three of them were behind bars. In 1942, with the beginning of the Quit India Movement, Jawaharlal Nehru was arrested and remained in prison for almost three years, one of the longest periods he had spent in jail. He was finally released in 1945.

In 1946, Jawaharlal Nehru with the influence of Gandhiji was summoned by the British with an idea of forming an interim government. This was done to organize the governmental structure during the transitional pre-independence period. Gandhiji was also against the partition that took place with the independence of the country. He tried his level best to avoid it and even advised the Congressmen to reject the proposals that were put forward by the Cabinet Mission. But the Congress leaders, including Jawaharlal Nehru tried to pacify Gandhiji by explaining that partition was the only way by, which a civil war between the Hindus and Muslims could be avoided. But inspite of this Gandhiji vehemently opposed this approach to freedom. Unfortunately, under great pressure from various sectors of the Congress Party and also from all parts of India, Gandhiji had to give his assent. But from his heart Gandhiji could not accept this and that troubled him till the last day of his life.

After Gandhiji's retirement from active politics, Jawaharlal Nehru became the leader of the Indian National Congress and took charge of the proceedings of the party completely. However, with passage of time and with Nehru's experience in the political field, there were certain difference of opinions and ideologies that cropped up between the two great Indian leaders. There were grave ideological differences between the two leaders. The formation of the Socialist Party within the Congress party by Jawaharlal Nehru was the first point of difference between the leaders. Though Nehru followed several rules of Satyagraha and many other principles of Gandhiji, he also opposed some of them vehemently. Nehru's ideologies matched completely with Subhash Chandra Bose and both of them also came together for the freedom struggle. But their extremist approach was strictly opposed by Gandhiji. The differences between Gandhiji and Jawaharlal Nehru also came to the forefront during the Quit India Movement. Gandhiji insisted that freedom had to be granted in 1942 and he would wait no longer, but Jawaharlal Nehru did not support this.

However, irrespective of the differences, Jawaharlal Nehru respected Mahatma Gandhi. He had influenced Nehru's personal, social as well as political life to a great deal. On his death, Jawaharlal Nehru addressed the nation and expressed his grief on the loss of the great leader. He felt that India had lost the greatest leader. With both good and bad times, the relationship that Jawaharlal Nehru and Mahatma Gandhi shared was a matter of envy for many leaders. It has become an interesting subject of study for many people, even in modern times.

## Education of Jawaharlal Nehru

Jawaharlal Nehru was the first Prime Minister of India. He was also a major persona in the Indian Independence movement. The early education of Jawaharlal Nehru played a major role in his political views and economic policies.

Jawaharlal Nehru was the son of Motilal Nehru. Motilal Nehru was a wealthy barrister by profession. He practiced English law in the colonial Indian courts. The family belonged to the educated genteel class. It was also to a large extent anglicized. Jawaharlal Nehru received primary education under the guidance of an English governess. Young Jawaharlal was taught to converse in English from an early age. He also learnt the appropriate customs of the British Raj.

Motilal Nehru wanted his son to get a proper English education. He wished his son to qualify for and serve the Indian Civil Services or I.C.S. He sent his son Jawaharlal to Harrow, the elite Public school in England. Jawaharlal Nehru was to spend the next six years of his life by studying at the hallowed portals of Harrow and Cambridge.

The young Jawaharlal did not enjoy his schooling at Harrow. He found the school syllabus stifling and the standard of residency conditions unbearable. All students of the school were forced to condition themselves to the daily specter of bathing and washing themselves in cold water. After completing school, Nehru took the University of Cambridge entrance examinations in 1907. The same year, he got admission into the University.

Jawaharlal Nehru studied natural sciences at Cambridge University. His chosen subjects were physics, chemistry and geology. Jawaharlal Nehru was weak in mathematics. For this reason, Physics was later substituted by botany.

The tripos subjects taken up at Cambridge University were not voluntarily chosen by Nehru. He studied the three natural science subjects with only one aim, to pass the Indian Civil Services examination. Nevertheless, Jawaharlal Nehru enjoyed his stay at Cambridge. The liberal atmosphere of the University encouraged him to do a host of non-academic activities. Jawaharlal Nehru passed the final Cambridge degree examinations successfully, where he stood second.

Jawaharlal Nehru joined the Inner Temple for his legal studies in October 1910. This decision, again, was not taken due to Nehru's fascination with the law. The event merely marked a career move as charted by his barrister father Motilal Nehru. Jawaharlal Nehru passed the Bar final examination in 1912. After clearing the examination, he was called to the bar later that year.

Nehru's education years at England fostered in him the Indian nationalist movement. He believed that the colonial English administration willfully discriminated against Indians. This thinking was further fueled by the abrasive attitude of the British Imperial order against Indians. Jawaharlal was attracted by the socialism of the British Fabians. The forte of equality in socialism acted as a magnet for the impressionable Jawaharlal Nehru.

Jawaharlal Nehru was very much influenced by the socialist and liberal political atmosphere prevalent in Europe in those days. The 1900s heralded the culmination of the Western Age of Enlightenment. The atmosphere of liberalism prevalent in that era emphasized the importance of the rights of the individual. It also emphasized on the rights of the equality of opportunity. This liberal viewpoint came to prominence during Nehru's later years. His British sojourn also instilled in him a secular ethos that was far ahead of his time. This moral uprightness would help him to dream of a new India that would accommodate citizens of all religions.

London was a hotbed of political movements in the early part of the 20th century. The student Jawaharlal Nehru liked to visit the cultural attractions of the capital city of the British Empire. He frequented the museums, opera houses and the theaters of London. Nehru was influenced by the deep social cauldron of pre-World War I London. Socialism was one of the prominent influences affecting the English political class at that time.

The early education of Jawaharlal Nehru influenced him in his later life. The influence was clearly visible on the economic policies adopted by the Indian state after its independence in 1947. Nehru clearly favored a more socialist approach when compared to other South Asian economies. The first Prime Minister was clearly thinking about his heady educational period in London when he promulgated the socialist ideology that influenced Indian government of the 1950's. The economy was treated with a mixed control. The Indian government was in control of the primary industries like electricity, mining and heavy engineering workshops.

The socialist leaning of Jawaharlal Nehru was apparent in the land redistribution program announced by the Indian government in the middle of the 20th century. The rural sector was given importance. Nehru correctly thought that since the majority of the Indian population lived in its villages, the rural sector should also get a lion's share of the country's economic resources. Dams were built. Canals were dug. The British education of Nehru is starkly visible in the promotion of fertilizers to increase the crop yield of the land. The British education of Jawaharlal Nehru is also displayed in the Prime Minister's quest for independent energy sufficiency. Nehru actively promoted the acquiring and development of Nuclear Energy. Hydro-electric power projects were also enthusiastically taken. The License Raj was also his creation.

The License Raj was a unique byproduct of Nehru's combined Social-Liberal philosophy. The License Raj was started with the view to help the Indian industrial sector. The intention led to limited success. Indian industries soon became unprofitable and became globally uncompetitive. The failure of the License Raj led to its gradual scrapping by successive Indian governments from the 1980's.

Jawaharlal Nehru was the epitome of a resurgent India in the middle of the 20th century. He had the best of worlds, a privileged British education and an Indian upbringing. His study at the Harrow School helped him to get a firm grounding of the British cultural ethos. This was further cemented by his attendance at the Trinity College in the University of Cambridge. His stint as a Barrister at the Inner Temple in London helped to hone his already sharp negotiation skills at the bar. This legal training would help him to negotiate the treacherous minefield of pre-independence British politics from 1910 to 1947.

## Jawaharlal Nehru and the Indian National Congress

Jawaharlal Nehru and the Indian National Congress maintained a close relationship that lasted for more than four long and eventful decades of Indian history. Nehru's relationship with the Indian National Congress officially started in 1919, two years after the birth of his daughter, Indira Priyadarshini, and seven years after his return from England. However, his close association with the Indian political scenario started much before his official initiation. Motilal Nehru, Jawaharlal's father, was a veteran Congressman of the moderate school and closely associated with the cause of India's freedom. Soon after his return from England in 1912, Jawaharlal found himself at the very midst of the Indian political scenario.

However, Jawaharlal was not very sure of the ideological position that would be effective for a rapid attainment of Indian Independence. On one side, there was his attachment to the extremist mode of protest, and then there was his loyalty towards his father. His initial dissociation from the ground realities of India also worked as a hindrance for him taking any definitive position. He was overall disturbed at the state of the inane Indian response to the British rule, with Anglophile Indian elite at the helm.

The emergence of Gandhi worked as a great impetus to the Indian freedom struggle, and provided Nehru with the much needed direction that he was in search of. Gandhi's success at Champaran and Ahmedabad introduced the power of Satyagraha to the Indian masses. Civic resistance seemed to be a new political weapon that was powerful enough to put even the greatest imperialist power on the back-foot on issues of rightful governance and public rights.

Apprentice Congressman: Jawaharlal Nehru as a Congress apprentice started his political career soon after he returned from England. Although he worked in the legal firm of his father, yet it was India's predicament that concerned him more than his legal career. He was highly impressed by the Gandhian philosophy and way of life, and soon found in Gandhi the direction that he long yearned for. The entire Nehru family adopted Gandhian ways, however, but it was Nehru more than others who heartily accepted the Gandhian way of life, much to his father's dismay.

Nehru traveled the country extensively to preach Gandhi's ways and participate in the nationalist movements. The way he was received by the masses filled him with new confidence in his abilities and popular appeal. Gandhi himself was not slow to realize the great popular support that Nehru could harness with his background, charm and liberal education. These sojourns also provided Nehru with an opportunity to see the widespread exploitation that plagued every sphere of Indian civil life. The perils of the Indian populace that he witnessed first hand in these formative years shaped his policies during his tenure as a prime minister later on.

Jawaharlal Nehru participated whole-heartedly in the Non-Cooperation movement. However, he did not join his father to part ways with Gandhi when Motilal Nehru formed the Swaraj Party with CR Das after the movement was called off by Gandhi following the Chauri Chaura incident. Jawaharlal Nehru was caught between divided loyalties between his father and Gandhi. However, his strong faith in Gandhian methodologies made him close ranks with Gandhi in this crucial period of his life. This tension between father and son would be a regular feature in Jawaharlal's life, and it was only after the death of his father that Nehru despite his grief, felt fully free to pursue his own political course. The ascendancy of Nehru in the fullest sense happened only after the death of Motilal Nehru.

Jawaharlal Nehru as INC President: Jawaharlal Nehru's rise within the Indian National Congress (INC) was meteoric in the years following the Non-Cooperation movement. He, along with Subhas Chandra Bose, became two dynamic young leaders of the Congress to whom the Indians were glad to look up to for guidance. The Calcutta Congress of 1928 saw the Congress divided on the Nehru ıeport prepared by Motilal Nehru on India's being awarded dominion status by the British government. Jawaharlal himself took exception to the steps laid down by the Nehru report. Mahatma Gandhi worked towards a compromise, and also single handedly worked for Jawaharlal's election as the Congress President in the historic Lahore Congress in 1929. Despite the universally accepted organizational prowess of Vallabbhai Patel, Jawaharlal Nehru was elected as the Congress president at a young age of forty, prior to the extremely significant Lahore Congress of 1929. Nehru was prompt to use the platform in order to declare his dream of Purna Swaraj or Complete Independence.

**Nehru's Prison Days:** The monumental Lahore Congress introduced the Civil Disobedience Movement. Nehru plunged himself into the movement and courted arrest. It was not the first time Nehru went to prison, and it would not be the last time either. Over the period of the next decade, Nehru would spend most of the time of his life in prison as a political prisoner. However, he was determined to make his solitude count. During the days of imprisonment, Nehru wrote extensively on a number of topics, particularly history and other social issues. He read a lot and often lectured fellow prisoners. However, with Motilal, Gandhi and Nehru imprisoned, the Indian freedom movement suddenly found itself without a clear direction. A number of factions both within Congress and outside were trying to undermine Satyagraha and offer alternate ways to India's freedom.

Nehru and the INC in the Years before Indian Freedom: Nehru spent most of the 1930s in prison, far from the Indian freedom struggle and the Indian National Congress. However, he kept a close watch on the course the movement was taking. On his return from prison to mainstream politics, Nehru had to employ all his reconciliatory skills to bring the warring factions within his party to a common platform. Although his Socialist ideals differed significantly from Gandhi's spiritual bent of civil resistance and the cultural aspects that came along with it. His differences with Gandhian modes came into the open in the Lucknow Conference of 1936.

Throughout the early forties, Nehru visited other Nationalist states as the Congress representative. He returned from China just before the World War II. The World War II brought in new problems for the Indian National Congress. Bose and his followers were willing to cooperate with the Axis forces in order to create pressure on the British officials, a move that Nehru summarily disapproved of. In the mean time, the Second Round Table Conference failed, and the Quit India movement was launched. Nehru was imprisoned once more. He was released in 1945 after the end of the War. Soon he started to work relentlessly towards forming the INA and preparing India for the hour of Independence. The end of the war brought the new Labor government in Britain, and the long held dream of Indian independence did not seem very far from then on.

The Indian Independence and the INC: The new government was willing to provide self dominion to India. With Nehru as the Congress president, negotiations were being worked out between the British government and the Congress Party, which was by then elected to be the single most popular party in India. However, the British were willing to play the waiting game and see the outcome of the elections. Moreover, a common ground between the Indian National Congress and the Muslim League was yet to be reached. Nehru tried his best to work out a solution through talks with Jinnah. The talks, expectedly failed. There was an absolute deadlock between the parties, and Partition seemed to be the only way for India to finally attain freedom.

The Indian Independence finally came in the year 1947; although the conditions of the much awaited freedom were far from what was expected. For Nehru as the President of the Indian national Congress, it was a bitter-sweet moment of truth. As the President of Congress, Nehru was the automatic choice as the first Prime Minister of Independent India. On 15th August, 1947 Nehru gave his famous 'Tryst with Destiny' speech from the Red Fort. However, it was hardly the end of his troubles. Mahatma Gandhi was murdered soon after and Patel died in 1950. Nehru was vested with the duty of steadying the rocking boat of the tottering economy of a newly emergent nation. This started the second phase of Nehru's work within the folds of the Indian National Congress, the post Independence phase.

Post-Independence Phase of INC and Nehru: Indian National Congress was committed to the primary idea of freeing India from British rule. Nehru thought otherwise, and he realized that the widespread popularity of the Congress could be used as a platform to address and solve much of the nation's problems. However, a sudden loss in a sense of direction was imminent in Congress. The Congress party itself had its due share of problems too. The Leftist forces provided a constant threat to the Party, as was the right wing within the Party who opposed Nehru's socialist ideals. At such a time, it was much because of Nehru's personal charisma that the integrity of the Congress could be successfully maintained.

Nehru's imposing internationalism somehow helped to soothe the problems back home. In fact, problems as mounting as the division of the provinces on linguistic lines and the Kashmir debate were also taken care of by Nehru's formidable success in foreign policies. It was with his stature, that Nehru managed to forge together the various warring forces within the Congress. However, Nehru himself was well aware of the decadence that has infested the party ranks and is known to have warned his party members after the Congress victory of 1957.

Nehru's commitment to the Congress party was life-long, and he is still considered to be one of the greatest Congressmen. However, the greatness of Nehru remains in the fact, that he successfully transcended his Congress identity to become a major international political figure.

## Jawaharlal Nehru's Foreign Policy

Jawaharlal Nehru is considered to be the architect of modern India. Apart from his careful handling of India's tumultuous domestic situation in the years immediately after the Independence, Nehru's major contribution lies in the field of foreign policies. In fact, Nehru determined India's international profile to a great degree in the post-independence years, in his capacity as the foreign minister of India. Jawaharlal Nehru's foreign policy has been made subject to much controversy and debate, like his economic policies. However, taken in the context of India's newly found status as a democratic republic, Nehru's foreign affairs policies seem to be extremely apt.

Socialism can be said to be one of the greatest international influences on Nehru, but Gandhi's ideals of Satyagraha also influenced him to a great degree. But he committed himself to neither point of view in framing his foreign policy. Nehru's foreign policies were characterized by two major ideological aspects. First, he wanted India to have an identity that would be independent of any form of overt commitment to either power bloc, the USA or the Soviet. Secondly, he had an unshaken faith in goodwill and honesty in matters of international affairs.

The first policy led ultimately to the founding of the Non-Alignment Movement (NAM). His second faith was terribly shaken by the Chinese attack of 1962, openly disobeying all the clauses of the Panchsheel or five-point agreement of 1954 between New Delhi and Peking. This breach of faith was a major psychological shock for Nehru, and was partially the reason for his death.

The Founding Principles of Nehru's Foreign Policy: Nehru saw war and violent insurgency from very close quarters as a freedom fighter, and he believed in neither. In his foreign policies, Nehru tried to guide India in such a way, so as to steer clear from any form of violence and militarism. He rightly believed that a newly decolonized nation must invest all its economic and logistic resources towards development and not defense and armament. Just like his economic policies, which were non-committal towards any ideological position, Nehru wanted to bring in a healthy level of pragmatism in his dealings of India's foreign affairs as well. He understood that overt commitment to any of the two major power blocs to emerge in the aftermath of World War II, would not serve India's path. He therefore wanted to tread a third path, which was not necessarily the middle path.

It should be remembered that this dogged non-commitment of Nehru was not seen sympathetically by any of the super powers of either East or West at its initial stage. It was frequently termed as a kind of international opportunism and was accused of 'neutralism' - a stance reckoned to be not only dangerous but also equally immoral in the world of International politics. However, the increasing popularity of NAM among various Asian and African countries and Nehru's growing stature as a statesman situation changed their views. India too benefited from this position, as it managed to secure rebuilding grants from member countries of either bloc. After Nehru's successful mediation in the Korean War and the Congo problem, putting an end to a long and violent struggle, his status as a commendable and efficient statesman reached new heights. Jawaharlal Nehru's theory of ideological non-commitment in a world that was rendered dangerous by the Cold War was appreciated by one and all.

Nehru and the Non-Alignment Movement: The greatest success of Jawaharlal Nehru's non-committal international politics was the formation of the Non-Alignment Movement (NAM). Nehru found allies in Tito, Nasser, Soekarno, U Nu and Nkrumah at a later stage in his formation of this new alliance. An alliance of newly independent and long colonized nations was not taken seriously in the beginning, either by the Eastern or the Western bloc. However, the importance of the alliance was soon felt, and initially led to a great degree of international pressure from both parts of the globe. However, Nehru proceeded with his mission undaunted. It was great test for his courage and it was soon found out that the NAM was not merely a passive platform of neutral and inactive nations.

It had clear objectives that included the gradual decolonization of the world, and a strong statement that the member countries were not party to the ever escalating tension of the Cold War. The favored process of decolonization as adopted by the NAM member countries was one of discussion and peaceful agreement. On many occasions, NAM met with success, often under the leadership of Nehru. Whoever supported its cause was an ally and a friend. Nehru preached a policy of issue based alliance and not one based on political and economic dogmas. He was proud of being an Asian, and wanted Asian nations to be the primary determinants of their political fate, not always guided by Western forces.

Nehru's unshaken belief in the force of international brotherhood was attested with his decision to continue with India's Commonwealth status. He was made subject to much criticism back home because of the support he extended towards the Commonwealth, particularly after the complication of the independence issue by the British government in the post World War II years, leading to the unwanted partition. However Nehru, always the believer in peaceful alliances and solution of international affairs based on discussions, went on with his ideals.

Nehru and the Kashmir Problem: Nehru's Foreign policies did not augur well when it came to deal with the neighbors. Kashmir was a perpetual problem, and he failed to reach any successful negotiation regarding Kashmir with the neighbor Pakistan. Nehru had an innate belief in honest fellow-feeling and political generosity. He tried to force a negotiation with the Pakistani government through the United Nations. But the Pakistani military rulers denied any peaceful agreement. The offer of a possible plebiscite was also taken off in 1950. After India's dogged denial of the two-nation theory, a result in favor of Kashmir in the Muslim dominated Kashmir would be a strategic disaster for India. The Kashmir problem remained unresolved, and not even Nehru's diplomatic expertise could give any positive direction to the problem. It still continues to be the one of the key international problems in South Asia.

Nehru and the China Crisis: Nehru's foreign policies concerning China have been made subject to much criticism. However, even in this case, it was Nehru's faith in transparency in the handling of International relations that is seen to be the root of all problems. Nehru was intent on a very warm and mutually beneficial relationship between India and China. The five-point agreement or the Panchsheel between New Delhi and Peking initiated in 1954 was a result of these negotiations. However, China started patrolling certain parts of the Indian border from 1955 onwards. Delhi started negotiations to solve the problem in a peaceful way. India, under the leadership of Nehru wanted to take one issue at a time and begin the discussions. The Chinese government, under Chou En-lai wanted to treat the border issue in its entirety at one go. It was gross violation of the five-point agreement. The Chinese denial for the arbitration from the International Court of Justice complicated the problem.

Amidst such tensions, the Chinese suddenly started a full-scale invasion in 1962. It was a rude shock, not only to Nehru, but to the entire international society. The Indian military was unprepared and also unequipped. Both USA and the Soviet extended token help. Soviet was quite busy with the Cuban crisis, however soon after the problem subsided, President Kruschev did extend some help. American help was minimum, compared to the massive military help that was extended to Pakistan in 1954. On top of that, the Sandys - Rusk team visited India to hold talks in order to make India concede certain areas of Kashmir to Pakistan, a claim that was squarely denied. Nehru stood firm with this faith in the five-point principle. The international community stood by him, as China withdrew under growing international pressure, fearing isolation and global antagonism. Nehru played his last masterstroke in international policy, as he turned the military defeat in a moral victory for India.

The Chinese invasion had far reaching effects on India's foreign policy. It forced Nehru to change his stance on international affairs. He realized that unmitigated goodwill was not necessary the way the business of foreign affairs was conducted. Nehru's dreams were more or less shattered. It was also a great eye-opener. It made India to see that it is important to strengthen one's military strength and not overtly depend on peaceful negotiations in matters of international affairs. The Chinese invasion was a shock to Nehru, almost shaking his idealistic foundation to the very base. Domestic problems also kept escalating, putting a great degree of mental and physical stress on Nehru.

## Nehru's Message to the Nation on the Independence Day

Jawaharlal Nehru, the first Prime Minister of independent India, was a man, who could influence the masses with his oration. He was an immensely learned man and could feel the pulse of the masses. Nehru's Message to the Nation on the Independence Day was delivered on the brink of midnight of the 14th of August, 1947. The speech focused on various topics related to India and the freedom that she had achieved from the shackles of British colonial rule. The speech also encourages and inspires the countrymen to wake from the long slumber and take steps for the upliftment and development of India.

Jawaharlal Nehru's independence speech aimed at motivating the general masses at building a new India. The speech aimed at boosting the people for working harder and with real zeal and enthusiasm to make India the numero uno nation in the world. There were certain social evils that were dominant in the Indian society in the form of illiteracy, poverty, ignorance, poor health conditions and many more in pre-independent India. The message propagated for the eradication of these social evils and to make India a prospering nation.

The message of the first Prime Minister of independent India, Jawaharlal Nehru, also requested the people of the country to actively participate in the process of nation-building. He also urged the people to have and show confidence in the national leaders of the country, who were bestowed with the duty of carrying the nation forward. The concept of equality was also emphasized in the independence speech made by Jawaharlal Nehru.

The Father of the Nation, Mahatma Gandhi, also finds reference in the speech made by Nehru. He also pays homage to the various freedom fighters, who had sacrificed their lives for the purpose of attaining freedom from the bond of British rule. He also makes a mention of the pains that several people had to endure due to the partition of the country. The speech also motivates the common masses to undergo the initial pains and troubles in the process of making a glorious India.

Last but not the least, Jawaharlal Nehru in the speech pays homage to Mother India and takes vows to defend her in all troubles. He also summons all the countrymen to bind themselves to the services of the Motherland.

The exact speech that was delivered by Pandit Jawaharlal Nehru is as follows:

"Long years ago we made a tryst with destiny, and now the time comes when we shall redeem our pledge, not wholly or in full measure, but very substantially. At the stroke of the midnight hour, when the world sleeps, India will awake to life and freedom. A moment comes, which comes but rarely in history, when we step out from the old to the new, when an age ends, and when the soul of a nation, long suppressed, finds utterance. It is fitting that at this solemn moment we take the pledge of dedication to the service of India and her people and to the still larger cause of humanity.

At the dawn of history India started on her unending quest, and trackless centuries are filled with her striving and the grandeur of her success and her failures. Through good and ill fortune alike she has never lost sight of that quest or forgotten the ideals which gave her strength. We end today a period of ill fortune and India discovers herself again. The achievement we celebrate today is but a step, an opening of opportunity, to the greater triumphs and achievements that await us. Are we brave enough and wise enough to grasp this opportunity and accept the challenge of the future?

Freedom and power bring responsibility. The responsibility rests upon this Assembly, a sovereign body representing the sovereign people of India. Before the birth of freedom we have endured all the pains of labour and our hearts are heavy with the memory of this sorrow. Some of those pains continue even now. Nevertheless, the past is over and it is the future that beckons to us now.

That future is not one of ease or resting but of incessant striving so that we may fulfil the pledges we have so often taken and the one we shall take today. The service of India means the service of the millions who suffer. It means the ending of poverty and ignorance and disease and inequality of opportunity. The ambition of the greatest man of our generation has been to wipe every tear from every eye. That may be beyond us, but as long as there are tears and suffering, so long our work will not be over.

And so we have to labour and to work, and work hard, to give reality to our dreams. Those dreams are for India, but they are also for the world, for all the nations and peoples are too closely knit together today for any one of them to imagine that it can live apart Peace has been said to be indivisible; so is freedom, so is prosperity now, and so also is disaster in this One World that can no longer be split into isolated fragments.

To the people of India, whose representatives we are, we make an appeal to join us with faith and confidence in this great adventure. This is no time for petty and destructive criticism, no time for ill-will or blaming others.

We have to build the noble mansion of free India where all her children may dwell. The appointed day has come-the day appointed by destiny-and India stands forth again, after long slumber and struggle, awake, vital, free and independent. The past clings on to us still in some measure and we have to do much before we redeem the pledges we have so often taken. Yet the turning-point is past, and history begins anew for us, the history which we shall live and act and others will write about.

It is a fateful moment for us in India, for all Asia and for the world. A new star rises, the star of freedom in the East, a new hope comes into being, a vision long cherished materializes. May the star never set and that hope never be betrayed! We rejoice in that freedom, even though clouds surround us, and many of our people are sorrow stricken and difficult problems encompass us. But freedom brings responsibilities and burdens and we have to face them in the spirit of a free and disciplined people.

On this day our first thoughts go to the architect of this freedom, the Father of our Nation [Gandhi], who, embodying the old spirit of India held aloft the torch of freedom and lighted up the darkness that surrounded us. We have often been unworthy followers of his and have strayed from his message, but not only we but succeeding generations will remember this message and bear the imprint in their hearts of this great son of India, magnificent in his faith and strength and courage and humility. We shall never allow that torch of freedom to be blown out, however high the wind or stormy the tempest.

Our next thoughts must be of the unknown volunteers and soldiers of freedom who, without praise or reward, have served India even unto death. We think also of our brothers and sisters who have been cut off from us by political boundaries and who unhappily cannot share at present in the freedom that has come. They are of us and will remain of us whatever may happen, and we shall be sharers in their good [or] ill fortune alike.

The future beckons to us. Whither do we go and what shall be our endeavour? To bring freedom and opportunity to the common man, to the peasants and workers of India; to fight and end poverty and ignorance and disease; to build up a prosperous, democratic and progressive nation, and to create social, economic and political institutions which will ensure justice and fullness of life to every man and woman.

We have hard work ahead. There is no resting for any one of us till we redeem our pledge in full, till we make all the people of India what destiny intended them to be. We are citizens of a great country on the verge of bold advance, and we have to live up to that high standard. All of us, to whatever religion we may belong, are equally the children of India with equal rights, privileges and obligations. We cannot encourage communalism or narrow-mindedness, for no nation can be great whose people are narrow in thought or in action.

*To the nations and peoples of the world we send greetings and pledge ourselves to cooperate with them in furthering peace, freedom and democracy. And to India, our much-loved motherland, the ancient, the eternal and the ever-new, we pay our reverent homage and we bind ourselves afresh to her service. Jai Hind."*

## Nehru-Last Days

Jawaharlal Nehru was one of the pioneering leaders of India, who played an active role in the independence struggle of the country. He was also the first Prime Minister of Independent India. From childhood, Jawaharlal Nehru led a luxurious and glorious life. His father, Motilal Nehru was an eminent personality in the society, both in the social as well as in the political sphere. Jawaharlal Nehru also had a glorious political career and basked in name as well as fame for long time.

Though he had a good career record, his last eight-years as the Prime Minister of the country were not very successful. The country was facing both internal and external crisis during these eight years. Some of the economic policies that were set by Pandit Jawaharlal Nehru were not accepted in the country as well as in the foreign countries. It was also believed that he could not control the ongoing procedures in the country and there was anarchy all around. During the tenure of Nehru as the Prime Minister, Five-Year plans were initiated for the development and progress of the nation. The second Five Year Plan was initiated in the year 1956 and it mainly concentrated on the industrial development of the country. The establishment of several heavy engineering industries was emphasized in this Five Year Plan.

However, there was a problem that hampered the growth of these industries completely. Huge finances were required to set up these establishments, but the Government could fund only about one-third part of the total budget. The rest had to be funded by the several international institutions, World Bank and many more financing companies. This clearly depicted that India was greatly dependent on international financial aids and showed a clear picture of the economic conditions in the country. This pushed Jawaharlal Nehru into back gear. Within a year of the inception of the Second Five Year Plan, the whole plan failed to meet most of the targets that were set. Weather conditions were also unfavorable during this time and this hampered the growth of the nation to a great deal.

Though Jawaharlal Nehru was a great politician, but at some places he was a weak administrator and took some decisions as a Prime Minister, which went against him in various ways. Nehru was himself a devoted and clean man, away from any sort of corruption. But there were some people working in administrative bodies under him, who were corrupt. This was the only failure of Jawaharlal Nehru as a Prime Minister. At this very time, there were problems within the Congress Party. This became evident in the General Elections that were held in 1957. Every year the party framed radical policies that made them more unacceptable with the general masses.

There were also some linguistics problems that were faced by the nation during the period of Jawaharlal Nehru as Prime Minister. Hindi was prescribed as the national language of the country and that was accepted by all. But since, Jawaharlal Nehru had seen the world to a great extent; he knew the importance of the English language. He was a man with great foresight and could sense that English would be the most important and commonly used language in the near future. He stressed on the fact that English should be used as an additional official language. There were also problems with the Urdu language. Jawaharlal Nehru wanted the language to be part of the pluralistic society in India. Urdu was spoken and followed by several people in the country and it was also recognized by the Constitution. These problems affected Nehru to a great deal and he sank deeper and deeper into this.

Jawaharlal Nehru had also established several foreign links that had helped him in enhancing his personal horizon and outlook. He used these experiences for the upliftment and progress of India. However, strains were also seen in the various foreign policies and foreign relations that he had established. During this time, India had managed to include Goa in the Indian Union by making it independent from the Portuguese rule. This was the only positive thing that had happened in the political and social sphere of India in those days. This boosted the morale of Jawaharlal Nehru to a great deal. Congress also won the elections in 1962 that provided some relief to the man, who had dreamt of making a new India.

The Indo-China Relationship was a major issue that had troubled Jawaharlal Nehru in his last days. He was the man, who had tried his best to cultivate harmonious and cordial relations with China. There are also several instances, where India did not react to certain hostilities that were shown by China. Jawaharlal Nehru even went to the extent of visiting the country for improving and enhancing the relation between the two countries. But Sino-Indian relations had reached nadir in the year 1959 with the advent of Dalai Lama in the social and political field.

Jawaharlal Nehru's health was also deteriorating with passing time. He was suffering from a kidney disorder, namely pyelonephritis. It was said that he suffered from this disorder due to excessive workload. He was diagnosed in London and doctors said that if he took rest for a long period of time, he would be absolutely fine. He was a man in his early seventies by then. During the last two years of his life, Jawaharlal Nehru had to endure several harsh conditions, both politically and socially. Several dissatisfactions and disapprovals in the country had made Nehru very upset and that added to the health deterioration.

On 8th January, 1964, he suffered a major stroke that paralyzed him. Many people advised Jawaharlal Nehru to resign at this time, but he refused to do so. He still went to the Parliament on 10th February, but it clearly showed that he was not completely fit, though he denied that he was unwell. In the few months after this, he had recovered a bit and Congressmen were happy that they would get their leader back in power. But on 27th May, he fell severely ill and was in great pain. He was in great discomfort and doctors were called at once. Doctors confirmed that his aorta had ruptured and death was inevitable. He also asked for sedatives and was provided with it, but that did not bring him much relief. Doctors informed all his relatives that nothing more could be done to save him. On the same day at about 1.44p.m Jawaharlal Nehru breathed his last. This marked the end to a grand and glorious personality, who had excelled in political, social as well as in professional life. India lost a great leader on this day and his presence is still felt in times of crisis.

# 4 Nehru and Political Integration of India

### *Immediate Situation Post-1947 Independence*

At the time of Indian independence, India was divided into two sets of territories, the first being the territories under the control of the British Empire, and the second being the territories over which the Crown had suzerainty, but which were under the control of their hereditary rulers. In addition, there were several colonial enclaves controlled by France and Portugal.

The political integration of these territories into India was a declared objective of the Indian National Congress, which the Government of India pursued over the next decade. Through a combination of factors, Vallabhbhai Patel and V.P. Menon convinced the rulers of the various princely states to accede to India.

Having secured their accession, they then proceeded to, in a step-by-step process, secure and extend the central government's authority over these states and transform their administration until, by 1956, there was little difference between the territories that had formerly been part of British India and those that had been part of princely states. Simultaneously, the Government of India through a combination of diplomatic and military means acquired de facto and de jure control over the remaining colonial enclaves, which too were integrated into India.

Although this process successfully integrated the vast majority of princely states into India, it was not as successful in relation to a few states, notably the former princely states of Kashmir, Tripura and Manipur, where active secessionist movements exist.

## Princely States in British India

The early history of British expansion in India was characterised by the co-existence of two approaches towards the existing princely states. The first was a policy of annexation, where the British sought to forcibly absorb the Indian princely states into the provinces which constituted their Empire in India. The second was a policy of indirect rule, where the British assumed suzerainty and paramountcy over princely states, but conceded some degree of sovereignty to them.

During the early part of the nineteenth century, the policy of the British tended towards annexation, but the Indian Rebellion of 1857 forced a change in this approach, by demonstrating both the difficulty of absorbing and subduing annexed states, and the usefulness of princely states as a source of support. In 1858, the policy of annexation was formally renounced, and British relations with the princely states thereafter were based on indirect rule, whereby the British exercised paramountcy over all princely states with the British crown as ultimate suzerain, but at the same time respected and protected them as allies.

The exact relations between the British and each princely state were regulated by individual treaties, and varied widely, with some states having significant autonomy, some being subject to significant control in internal affairs, and some being in effect the owners of a few acres of land with little autonomy.

During the 20th century, the British made several attempts to integrate the princely states more closely with British India, creating the Chamber of Princes in 1921 as a consultative and advisory body, transferring the responsibility for supervision of smaller states from the provinces to the centre in 1936, and creating direct relations between the Government of India and the larger princely states superseding political agents. The most ambitious was a scheme of federation in the Government of India Act, 1935, which envisaged the princely states and British India being united under a federal government.

This scheme came close to success, but was abandoned in 1939 as a result of the outbreak of the Second World War. As a result, in the 1940s, the relationship between the princely states and the crown remained regulated by the principle of paramountcy and the various treaties between the British crown and the states.

Neither paramountcy nor these arrangements could continue after Indian independence. The British took the view that because they had been established directly between the British crown and the princely states, they could not be transferred to independent India. At the same time, they imposed obligations on Britain that it was not prepared to continue to carry out, such as the obligation to maintain troops in India for the defence of the princely states. The British government therefore decided that paramountcy, together with all treaties between them and the princely states, would come to an end upon the transfer of power.

## Reasons for Integration

The Saurashtra and Kathiawar regions of Gujarat were home to over two hundred princely states, many with non-contiguous territories, as this map of Baroda shows.

The termination of paramountcy would have in principle have meant that all rights that flowed from the states' relationship with the British crown would return to them, leaving them free to negotiate relationships with the new states of India and Pakistan "on a basis of complete freedom." Early British plans for the transfer of power, such as the offer produced by the Cripps Mission, recognised the possibility that some princely states might choose to stand out of independent India.

This was unacceptable to the Congress, which regarded the independence of princely states as a denial of the course of Indian history, and consequently regarded this scheme as a "Balkanisation" of India. The Congress had traditionally been less active in the princely states because of their limited resources which restricted their ability to organise there and their focus on the goal of independence from the British, and because Congress leaders, in particular Gandhi, were sympathetic to the more progressive princes as examples of the capacity of Indians to rule themselves. This changed in the 1930s as a result of the federation scheme contained in the Government of India Act, 1935 and the rise of socialist Congress leaders such as Jayaprakash Narayan, and the Congress began to actively engage with popular political and labour activity in the princely states. By 1939, the Congress' official stance was that the states must enter independent India, on the same terms and with the same autonomy as the provinces of British India, and with their people granted responsible government. As a result, it insisted on the incorporation of the princely states into India in its negotiations with Mountbatten.

A few British leaders, particularly Lord Mountbatten, the last British viceroy in India, were also uncomfortable with breaking links between independent India and the princely states. The development of trade, commerce and communications during the 19th and 20th centuries had bound the princely states to British India through a complex network of interests. Agreements relating to railways, customs, irrigation, the use of ports, and other similar agreements would disappear, posing a serious threat to the economic life of the subcontinent.

Mountbatten was also persuaded by the argument of Indian leaders such as V.P. Menon that the integration of the princely states into independent India would to some extent assuage the wounds of partition. The result was that Mountbatten personally favoured and worked towards the accession of princely states to India following the transfer of power, as proposed by the Congress.

## Accepting Integration

### *The Princes' Position*

The rulers of the princely states were not uniformly enthusiastic about integrating their domains into independent India. Some, such as the kings of Bikaner and Jawhar, were motivated to join India out of ideological and patriotic considerations, but others insisted that they had the right to join either India or Pakistan, to remain independent, or form a union of their own.

Bhopal, Travancore and Hyderabad announced that they did not intend to join either dominion. Hyderabad went as far as to appoint trade representatives in European countries and commencing negotiations with the Portuguese to lease or buy Goa to give it access to the sea, and Travancore pointed to the strategic importance to western countries of its thorium reserves while asking for recognition. Some states proposed a subcontinent-wide confederation of princely states, as a third entity in addition to India and Pakistan. Bhopal attempted to build an alliance between the princely states and the Muslim League to counter the pressure being put on rulers by the Congress.

A number of factors contributed to the collapse of this initial resistance and to nearly all princely states agreeing to accede to India. An important factor was the lack of unity amongst the princes. The smaller states did not trust the larger states to protect their interests, and many Hindu rulers did not trust Muslim princes, in particular Hamidullah Khan, the Nawab of Bhopal and a leading proponent of independence, who they viewed as an agent for Pakistan.

Others, believing integration inevitable, sought to build bridges with the Congress, hoping thereby to gain a say in shaping the final settlement. The resultant inability to present a united front or agree on a common position significantly reduced their bargaining power in negotiations with the Congress. The decision by the Muslim League to stay out of the Constituent Assembly was also fatal to the princes' plan to build an alliance with it to counter the Congress, and attempts to boycott the Constituent Assembly altogether failed on 28 April 1947, when the states of Baroda, Bikaner, Cochin, Gwalior, Jaipur, Jodhpur, Patiala and Rewa took their seats in the Assembly.

Many princes were also pressured by popular sentiment favouring integration with India, which meant their plans for independence had little support from their subjects. The king of Travancore, for example, definitively abandoned his plans for independence after the attempted assassination of his dewan, Sir C.P. Ramaswamy Aiyar. In a few states, the chief ministers or dewans played a significant role in convincing the princes to accede to India. The key factors that led the states to accept integration into India were, however, the efforts of Lord

Mountbatten, the last Viceroy of British India, and Vallabhbhai Patel and V.P. Menon, who were respectively the political and administrative heads of the Indian Government's States Department, which was in charge of relations with the princely states.

## Mountbatten's Role

Lord Louis Mountbatten played an important role in convincing reluctant monarchs to accede to the Indian Union.

Mountbatten believed that securing the states' accession to India was crucial to reaching a negotiated settlement with the Congress for the transfer of power. As a relative of the British Emperor, he was trusted by most of the princes and was a personal friend of many, especially the Nawab of Bhopal, Hamidullah Khan. The princes also believed that he would be in a position to ensure the independent India adhered to any terms that might be agreed upon, because Jawaharlal Nehru and Patel had asked him to become the first Governor General of the Dominion of India.

Mountbatten used his influence with the princes to push them towards accession. He declared that the British Government would not grant dominion status to any of the princely states, nor would it accept them into the British Commonwealth, which meant that the states would sever all connections with the British crown unless they joined either India or Pakistan. He pointed out that the Indian subcontinent was one economic entity, and that the states would suffer most if the link were broken. He also pointed to the difficulties that princes would face maintaining order in the face of threats such as the rise of communal violence and communist movements.

Mountbatten stressed that he would act as the trustee of the princes' commitment, as he would be serving as India's head of state well into 1948. He engaged in a personal dialogue with reluctant princes, such as the Nawab of Bhopal, who he asked through a confidential letter to sign the Instrument of Accession making Bhopal part of India, which Mountbatten would keep locked up in his safe. It would be handed to the States Department on 15 August only if the Nawab did not change his mind before then, which he was free to do. The Nawab agreed, and did not renege over the deal.

At the time, several princes complained that they were being betrayed by Britain, who they regarded as an ally, and Sir Conrad Corfield resigned his position as head of the Political Department in protest at Mountbatten's policies. Mountbatten's policies were also criticised by the opposition Conservative Party. Winston Churchill compared the language used by the Indian government with that used by Adolf Hitler before the invasion of Austria. Modern historians such as Lumby and Moore, however, take the view that Mountbatten played a crucial role in ensuring that the princely states agreed to accede to India.

## Pressure and Diplomacy

Vallabhbhai Patel as Minister for Home and States Affairs had the responsibility of welding the British Indian provinces and the princely states into a united India

By far the most significant factor that led to the princes' decision to accede to India was the policy of the Congress and, in particular, of the two key figures in the States Department, Sardar Vallabhbhai Patel and V.P. Menon. The Congress' stated position was that the princely states were not sovereign entities, and as such could not opt to be independent notwithstanding the end of paramountcy. The princely states, it declared, must therefore accede to either India or Pakistan.

In July 1946, Nehru pointedly observed that no princely state could prevail militarily against the army of independent India. In January 1947, he said that independent India would not accept the Divine Right of Kings, and in May 1947, he declared that any princely state which refused to join the Constituent Assembly would be treated as an enemy state. Other Congress leaders, such as C. Rajagopalachari, argued that as paramountcy "came into being as a fact and not by agreement", it would necessarily pass to the government of independent India, as the successors of the British.

Patel and Menon, who were charged with the actual job of negotiating with the princes, took a more conciliatory approach than Nehru. The official policy statement of the Government of India made by Patel on 5 July 1947 made no threats. Instead, it emphasised the unity of India and the common interests of the princes and independent India, reassured them about the Congress' intentions, and invited them to join independent India "to make laws sitting together as friends than to make treaties as aliens." He reiterated that the States Department would not attempt to establish a relationship of domination over the princely states. Unlike the Political Department of the British Government, it would not be an instrument of paramountcy, but a medium whereby business could be conducted between the states and India as equals.

## Instruments of Accession

Patel and Menon backed up their diplomatic efforts by producing treaties that were designed to be attractive to rulers of princely states. Two key documents were produced. The first was the Standstill Agreement, which confirmed that the agreements and administrative practices that existed as between the princely state in question and the British would be continued by India. The second was the Instrument of Accession, by which the ruler of the princely state in question agreed to the accession of his kingdom to independent India, and to granting India control over specified subject matters. The nature of the subject matters varied depending on the acceding state.

The states which had internal autonomy under the British signed an Instrument of Accession which only ceded three subjects to the government of India – defence, external affairs, and communications, each defined in accordance with List 1 to Schedule VII of the Government of India Act, 1935. Rulers of states which were in effect estates or talukas, where substantial administrative powers were exercised by the Crown, signed a different Instrument of Accession, which vested all residuary powers and jurisdiction in the government of India. Rulers of states which had an intermediate status signed a third type of Instrument, which preserved the degree of power they had under the British.

The Instruments of Accession implemented a number of other safeguards. Clause 7 provided that the princes would not be bound to the Indian constitution as and when it was drafted. Clause 8 guaranteed their autonomy in all areas in which authority was not expressly ceded to the Government of India. This was supplemented by a number of promises.

Rulers who agreed to accede would receive guarantees that their extra-territorial rights, such as immunity from prosecution in Indian courts and exemption from customs duty, would be protected, that they would be allowed to democratise slowly, that none of the eighteen major states would be forced to merge, and that they would remain eligible for British honours and decorations.

In discussions, Lord Mountbatten reinforced the statements of Patel and Menon by emphasising that the documents gave the princes all the "practical independence" they needed. Mountbatten, Patel and Menon also sought to give princes the impression that if they did not accept the terms put to them then, they would subsequently have to accede on substantially less favourable terms. The Standstill Agreement was also used as a negotiating tool, as the States Department categorically ruled out signing a Standstill Agreement with princely states that did not sign an Instrument of Accession.

## The Accession Process

The limited scope of the Instruments of Accession and the promise of a wide-ranging autonomy and the other guarantees they offered, gave sufficient comfort to many rulers, who saw this as the best deal they could strike given the lack of support from the British, and popular internal pressures. Between May 1947 and the transfer of power on 15 August 1947, the vast majority of states signed Instruments of Accession. A few, however, held out.

Some simply delayed signing the Instrument of Accession. Piploda, a small state in central India, did not accede until March 1948. The biggest problems, however, arose with a few border states, such as Jodhpur, which tried to negotiate better deals with Pakistan, with Junagadh, which actually did accede to Pakistan, and with Hyderabad and Kashmir, which declared that they intended to remain independent.

## Border States

The ruler of Jodhpur, Hanwant Singh, was antipathetic to the Congress, and did not see much future in India for him or the lifestyle he wished to lead, and entered into negotiations with Jinnah, who was the designated head of state for Pakistan, along with the ruler of Jaisalmer. Jinnah was keen to attract some of the larger border states, hoping thereby to attract other Rajput states to Pakistan and compensate for the loss of half of Bengal and Punjab. He offered to permit Jodhpur and Jaisalmer to accede to Pakistan on any terms they chose, giving their rulers blank sheets of paper and asking them to write down their terms, which he would sign.

Jaisalmer refused, arguing that it would be difficult for him to side with Muslims against Hindus in the event of communal problems. Hanwant Singh came close to signing. However, the atmosphere in Jodhpur was in general hostile to accession to Pakistan. Mountbatten also pointed out that the accession of a predominantly Hindu state to Pakistan would violate the principle of the two-nation theory on which Partition was based, and was likely to cause communal violence in the State. Hanwant Singh was persuaded by these arguments, and somewhat reluctantly agreed to accede to India.

## Junagadh

Although the states were in theory free to choose whether they wished to accede to India or Pakistan, Mountbatten had pointed out that "geographic compulsions" meant that most of them must choose India. In effect, he took the position that only the states that shared a border with Pakistan could choose to accede to it.

The nawab of Junagadh, a princely state located on the south-western end of Gujarat and having no common border with Pakistan, chose to accede to Pakistan ignoring Mountbatten's views, arguing that it could be reached from Pakistan by sea. The rulers of two states that were subject to the suzerainty of Junagadh—Mangrol and Babariawad—reacted to this by declaring their independence from Junagadh and acceding to India. In response, the nawab of Junagadh militarily occupied the states. The rulers of neighbouring states reacted angrily, sending their troops to the Junagadh frontier and appealed to the Government of India for assistance. A group of Junagadhi people, led by Samaldas Gandhi, formed a government-in-exile, the *Aarzi Hukumat* ("temporary government").

India believed that if Junagadh was permitted to go to Pakistan, the communal tension already simmering in Gujarat would worsen, and refused to accept the accession. The government pointed out that the state was 80% Hindu, and called for a plebiscite to decide the question of accession. Simultaneously, they cut off supplies of fuel and coal to Junagadh, severed air and postal links, sent troops to the frontier, and reoccupied the principalities of Mangrol and Babariawad that had acceded to India. Pakistan agreed to discuss a plebiscite, subject to the withdrawal of Indian troops, a condition India rejected. On 26 October, the Nawab and his family fled to Pakistan following clashes with Indian troops. On 7 November, Junagadh's court, facing collapse, invited the Government of India to take over the State's administration. The Government of India agreed. A plebiscite was conducted in February 1948, which went almost unanimously in favour of accession to India.

## Kashmir

Shown in green is the Kashmiri region under Pakistani control. The dark-brown region represents Indian-administration Jammu and Kashmir while the Aksai Chin is under Chinese administration

At the time of the transfer of power, Kashmir was ruled by Maharaja Hari Singh, a Hindu, although the state itself had a Muslim majority. Hari Singh was equally hesitant about acceding to either India or Pakistan, as either would have provoked adverse reactions in parts of his kingdom. He signed a Standstill Agreement with Pakistan and proposed one with India as well, but announced that Kashmir intended to remain independent. However, his rule was opposed by Sheikh Abdullah, the popular leader of Kashmir's largest political party, the National Conference, who demanded his abdication.

Pakistan, attempting to force the issue of Kashmir's accession, cut off supplies and transport links. The chaos in Punjab resulting from Partition had also severed transport links with India, meaning that Kashmir's only links with the two dominions was by air. Rumours about atrocities against the Muslim population of Poonch by the Maharajah's forces caused the outbreak of civil unrest. Shortly thereafter, Pathan tribesmen from the North-West Frontier Province of Pakistan crossed the border and entered Kashmir.

The invaders made rapid progress towards Srinagar. The Maharaja of Kashmir wrote to India, asking for military assistance, offering an Instrument of Accession, and setting up an interim government headed by Sheikh Abdullah. The accession was accepted, but Nehru declared that it would have to be confirmed by a plebiscite although there was no legal requirement to seek such confirmation.

Indian troops secured Jammu, Srinagar and the valley itself during the First Kashmir War, but the intense fighting flagged with the onset of winter, which made much of the state impassable. Prime Minister Nehru, recognising the degree of international attention brought to bear on the dispute, declared a ceasefire and sought U.N. arbitration, arguing that India would otherwise have to invade Pakistan itself, in view of its failure to stop the tribal incursions.

The plebiscite was never held, and on 26 January 1957, the Constitution of India came into force in Kashmir, but with special provisions made for it in the Constitution's Article 370. India did not, however, secure administrative control over all of Kashmir. The northern and western portions of Kashmir came under Pakistan's control in 1947, and are today Pakistan-administered Kashmir. In 1962, China occupied Aksai Chin, the north-eastern region bordering Ladakh, which it continues to control and administer.

## Hyderabad

Hyderabad state in 1909. Its former territories are today incorporated in the Indian states of Andhra Pradesh, Karnataka and Maharashtra.

Hyderabad was a landlocked state that stretched over 82,000 square miles (over 212,000 square kilometres) in south-eastern

India. Whilst 87% of its 17 million people were Hindus, its ruler Nizam Osman Ali Khan was a Muslim, and its politics were dominated by a Muslim elite. The Muslim nobility and the Ittehad-ul-Muslimeen, a powerful pro-Nizam Muslim party, insisted that Hyderabad must remain an independent state and stand on an equal footing to India and Pakistan. Accordingly, the Nizam in June 1947 issued a *firman* announcing that on the transfer of power, his state would be resuming independence. The Government of India rejected the firman, terming it a "legalistic claim of doubtful validity." It argued that the strategic location of Hyderabad, which lay astride the main lines of communication between northern and southern India, meant it could easily be used by "foreign interests" to threaten India, and that in consequence, the issue involved India's peace and security. It also pointed out that the state's people, history and location made it unquestionably Indian, and that its own "common interests" therefore mandated its integration into India.

The Nizam was prepared to enter into a limited treaty with India, which gave Hyderabad safeguards not provided for in the standard Instrument of Accession, such as a provision guaranteeing Hyderabad's neutrality in the event of a conflict between India and Pakistan. India rejected this proposal, arguing that other states would demand similar concessions. A temporary Standstill Agreement was signed as a stopgap measure, even though Hyderabad had not yet agreed to accede to India. By December 1947, however, India was accusing Hyderabad of repeatedly violating the Agreement, while the Nizam alleged that India was blockading his state, a charge India denied.

The situation deteriorated further in 1948. The Razakars ("volunteers"), a militia affiliated to the Ittehad-ul-Muslimeen and set up under the influence of Muslim radical Qasim Razvi, assumed the role of supporting the Muslim ruling class against upsurges by the Hindu populace, and began intensifying its activities and was accused of attempting to intimidate villages. The Hyderabad State Congress Party, affiliated to the Indian National Congress, launched a political agitation. Matters were made worse by Communist groups, which had originally supported the Congress but now switched sides and began attacking Congress groups. Attempts by Mountbatten to find a negotiated solution failed and, in August, the Nizam, claiming that he feared an imminent invasion, attempted to approach the UN Security Council and the International Court of Justice. Patel now insisted that if Hyderabad was allowed to continue its independence, the prestige of the Government would be tarnished and then neither Hindus nor Muslims would feel secure in its realm. On 13 September, the Indian Army was sent into Hyderabad in Operation Polo on the ground that the law and order situation there threatened the peace of South India.

The troops met little resistance and between 13 and 18 September took complete control of the state. The Nizam was retained as the head of state in the same manner as the other princes who acceded to India. He thereupon disavowed the complaints that had been made to the UN and, despite vehement protests from Pakistan and strong criticism from other countries, the Security Council did not deal further with the question, and Hyderabad was absorbed into India.

## Completing Integration

Central Provinces and Berar, which form part of modern Madhya Pradesh and Maharashtra.

The Madras Presidency was divided and merged with neighbouring princely states to produce Kerala, Tamil Nadu, Karnataka and Andhra Pradesh.

The Instruments of Accession were limited, transferring control of only three matters to India, and would by themselves have produced a rather loose federation, with significant differences in administration and governance across the various states. Full political integration, in contrast, would require a process whereby the political actors in the various states were "persuaded to shift their loyalties, expectations, and political activities towards a new center," namely, the Republic of India. This was not an easy task.

Whilst some princely states such as Mysore had legislative systems of governance that were based on a broad franchise and not significantly different from those of British India, in others, political decision-making took place in small, limited aristocratic circles and governance was, as a result, at best paternalistic and at worst the result of courtly intrigue. Having secured the accession of the princely states, the Government of India between 1948 and 1950 turned to the task of welding the states and the former British provinces into one polity under a single republican constitution.

## Fast-track Integration

The first step in this process, carried out between 1947 and 1949, was to merge the smaller states that were not seen by the Government of India to be viable administrative units either into neighbouring provinces, or with other princely states to create a "princely union." This policy was contentious, since it involved the dissolution of the very states whose existence India had only recently guaranteed in the Instruments of Accession.

Patel and Menon emphasised that without integration, the economies of states would collapse, and anarchy would arise if the princes were unable to provide democracy and govern properly. They pointed out that many of the smaller states were very small and lacked resources to sustain their economies and support their growing populations. Many also imposed tax rules and other restrictions that impeded free trade, and which had to be dismantled in a united India. Given that merger involved the breach of guarantees personally given by Mountbatten, Patel and Nehru initially intended to wait until after his term as Governor-General. An adivasi uprising in Orissa in late 1947, however, forced their hand.

In December 1947, princes from the Eastern and Chhatisgarh Agencies were summoned to an all-night meeting with Menon, in the course of which they were persuaded to sign Merger Agreements integrating their states into Orissa, the Central Provinces and Bihar with effect from 1 January 1948. Later that year, sixty-six states in Gujarat and the Deccan were merged into Bombay, including the large states of Kolhapur and Baroda. Other small states were merged into Madras, East Punjab, West Bengal, the United Provinces and Assam. Not all states that signed Merger Agreements were integrated into provinces, however. Thirty states of the former Punjab Hill States Agency which lay near the international border and had signed Merger Agreements were integrated into Himachal Pradesh, a distinct entity which was administered directly by the centre as a Chief Commissioner's Province, for reasons of security.

The Merger Agreements required rulers to cede "full and exclusive jurisdiction and powers for and in relation to governance" of their state to the Dominion of India. In return for their agreement to entirely cede their states, it gave princes a large number of guarantees. Princes would receive an annual payment from the Indian government in the form of a privy purse as compensation for the surrender of their powers and the dissolution of their states. Whilst state property would be taken over, their private property would be protected, as would all personal privileges, dignities and titles. Succession was also guaranteed according to custom. In addition, the provincial administration was obliged to take on the staff of the princely states with guarantees of equal pay and treatment.

Although the Merger Agreements were principally intended for smaller, non-viable states, they were also applied to a few larger states. Kutch in western India, and Tripura and Manipur in North-East India, all of which lay along international borders, were also asked to sign Merger Agreements, despite being larger states, following which they became Chief Commissioners' Provinces. Bhopal, whose ruler was proud of the efficiency of his administration and feared that it would lose its identity if merged with the Maratha states that were its neighbours, also became a directly-administered Chief Commissioner's Province, as did Bilaspur, much of which was likely to be flooded on completion of the Bhakra dam.

## Four-step Integration

### *Merger*

The bulk of the larger states, and some groups of small states, were integrated through a different, four-step, process. The first step in this process was to convince groups of large states to combine to form a "princely union" through the execution by their rulers of Covenants of Merger. Under the Covenants of Merger, all rulers lost their ruling powers, save one who became the Rajpramukh of the new union. The other rulers were associated with two bodies, the council of rulers whose members were the rulers of salute states, and a presidium, one or more of whose members were elected by the rulers of non-salute states, with the rest elected by the council.

The Rajpramukh and a deputy Rajpramukh, or *Uprajpramukh*, were chosen by the council from amongst the members of the presidium. The Covenants made provision for the creation of a constituent assembly for the new union which would be charged with framing its constitution. In return for agreeing to the extinction of their states as discrete entities, the rulers were given a privy purse and guarantees similar to those provided under the Merger Agreements.

Through this process, Patel obtained the unification of 222 states in the Kathiawar peninsula of his native Gujarat into the princely union of Saurashtra in January 1948, with six more states joining the union the following year. Madhya Bharat emerged on 28 May 1948 from a union of Gwalior, Indore and eighteen smaller states. In Punjab, the Patiala and East Punjab States Union was formed on 15 July 1948 from Patiala, Kapurthala, Jind, Nabha, Faridkot, Malerkotla, Nalargarh, and Kalsia. The United State of Rajasthan was formed as the result of a series of mergers, the last of which was completed on 15 May 1949. Travancore and Cochin were merged in the middle of 1949 to form the princely union of Travancore-Cochin. The only princely states which signed neither Covenants of Merger nor Merger Agreements were Kashmir, Mysore and Hyderabad.

## Democratisation

Merging the administrative machineries of each state and integrating them into one political and administrative entity was not easy, particularly as many of the merged states had a history of rivalry. In the former Central India Agency, whose princely states had initially been merged into a princely union called Vindhya Pradesh, the rivalry between two groups of states became so bad that the Government of India persuaded the rulers to sign a Merger Agreement abrogating the old Covenants of Merger, and took direct control of the state as a Chief Commissioner's State. As such, the mergers did not meet the expectations of the Government of India or the States Department.

In December 1947, Menon suggested requiring the rulers of states to take "practical steps towards the estabiishment of popular government." The States Department accepted his suggestion, and implemented it through a special covenant signed by the rajpramukhs of the merged princely unions, binding them to act as constitutional monarchs. This meant that their powers were de facto no different from those of the Governors of the former British provinces, thus giving the people of their territories the same measure of responsible government as the people of the rest of India.

The result of this process has been described as being, in effect, an assertion of paramountcy by the Government of India over the states in a more pervasive form. Whilst this contradicted the British statement that paramountcy would lapse on the transfer of power, the Congress position had always been that independent India would inherit the position of being the paramount power.

## Centralisation and Constitutionalisation

Democratisation still left open one important distinction between the former princely states and the former British provinces, namely, that since the princely states had signed limited Instruments of Accession covering only three subjects, they were insulated from government policies in other areas. The Congress viewed this as hampering its ability to frame policies that brought about social justice and national development.

Consequently, they sought to secure to the central government the same degree of powers over the former princely states as it had over the former British provinces. In May 1948, at the initiative of V.P. Menon, a meeting was held in Delhi between the Rajpramukhs of the princely unions and the States Department, at the end of which the Rajpramukhs signed new Instruments of Accession which gave the Government of India the power to pass laws in respect of all matters that fell within the seventh schedule of the Government of India Act, 1935. Subsequently, each of the princely unions, as well as Mysore and Hyderabad, agreed to adopt the Constitution of India drafted by the constituent assembly as the constitution of that state, thus ensuring that they were placed in exactly the same legal position vis-à-vis the central government as the former British provinces.

The only exception was Kashmir, whose relationship with India continued to be governed by the original Instrument of Accession, and the constitution produced by the state's Constituent Assembly.

The Constitution of India classified the constituent units of India into three classes, which it termed Part A, B, and C states. The former British provinces, together with the princely states that had been merged into them, were the Part A states. The princely unions, plus Mysore and Hyderabad, were the Part B states. The former Chief Commissioners' Provinces and other centrally administered areas, except the Andaman and Nicobar Islands, were the Part C states.

The only practical difference between the Part A states and the Part B states was that the constitutional heads of the Part B states were the Rajpramukhs appointed under the terms of the Covenants of Merger, rather than Governors appointed by the central government.

In addition, Constitution gave the central government a significant range of powers over the former princely states, providing amongst other things that their governance shall be under the general control of, and comply with such particular directions, if any, as may from time to time be given by, the President." Apart from that, the form of government in both was identical.

## Reorganisation

The distinction between Part A and Part B states was only intended to last for a brief, transitional period. In 1956, the States Reorganization Act reorganised the former British provinces and princely states on the basis of language. Simultaneously, the Seventh Amendment to the Constitution removed the distinction between Part A and Part B states, both of which were now treated only as "states", with Part C states being renamed "union territories." The Rajpramukhs lost their authority, and were replaced as the constitutional heads of state by Governors, who were appointed by the central government. These changes finally ended the princely order to an end. In both legal and practical terms, the territories that formerly were part of the princely states were now fully integrated into India and did not differ in any way from those that were formerly part of British India. The personal privileges of the princes-the privy purse, the exemption from customs duty, and customary dignities-survived slightly longer, but were abolished in 1971.

## Post-integration Issues

### *The Princes*

Whilst the progressive integration of the princely states into India was largely peaceful, not all princes were happy with the outcome. Many had expected the Instruments of Accession to be permanent, and were unhappy about losing the autonomy and the guaranteed continued existence of their states they had expected to gain. Some felt uneasy about the disappearance of states that generations of their family had controlled, whilst others were unhappy about the disappearance of administrative structures they had worked hard to build up and which they believed to be efficient.

The majority, however, despite the "strain and tension" of adapting to life as private citizens, content to retire on the generous pension provided by the privy purse. Several took advantage of their eligibility to hold public offices under the central government. The Maharaja of Bhavnagar, for example, became the Governor of Madras State, while several others were appointed to diplomatic posts overseas.

## Colonial Enclaves

Yanaon was one of five French colonial enclaves in India

The integration of the princely states raised the question of the future of the remaining colonial enclaves in India. At independence, the regions of Pondicherry, Karikal, Yanaon, Mahe and Chandernagore were still colonies of France, and Daman and Diu, Dadra and Nagar Haveli and Goa remained colonies of Portugal. An agreement between France and India in 1948 provided for an election in France's remaining Indian possessions to choose their political future. A plebiscite held in Chandernagore on 19 June 1949 resulted in a vote of 7,463 to 114 in favour of being integrated with India. It was ceded to India on a de facto basis on 14 August 1949 and de jure on 2 May 1950.

In the other enclaves, however, the pro-French camp, led by Edouard Goubert, used the administrative machinery to suppress the pro-merger groups. Popular discontent rose, and in 1954 demonstrations in Yanam and Mahe resulted in pro-merger groups assuming power. A referendum in Pondicherry and Karaikal in October 1954 resulted in a vote in favour of merger, and on 1 November 1954, de facto control over all four enclaves was transferred to the Republic of India. A treaty of cession was signed in May 1956, and following ratification by the French National Assembly in May 1962, de jure control of the enclaves was also transferred.

Demonstrators demanding the integration of Goa into India march against the Portuguese on 15 August 1955

Portugal, in contrast, resisted diplomatic solutions. It viewed its continued possession of its Indian enclaves as a matter of national pride and, in 1951, it amended its constitution to convert its possessions in India into Portuguese provinces. In July 1954, an uprising in Dadra and Nagar Haveli threw off Portuguese rule. The Portuguese attempted to send forces from Daman to reoccupy the enclaves, but were prevented from doing so by Indian troops. Portugal initiated proceedings before the International Court of Justice to compel India to allow its troops access to the enclave, but the Court rejected its complaint in 1960, holding that India was within its rights in denying Portugal military access.

In 1961, the Constitution of India was amended to incorporate Dadra and Nagar Haveli into India as a Union Territory.

Goa, Daman and Diu remained an outstanding issue. On 15 August 1955, five thousand non-violent demonstrators marched against the Portuguese at the border, and were met with gunfire, killing 22. In December 1960, the United Nations General Assembly rejected Portugal's contention that its overseas possessions were provinces, and formally listed them as "non-self-governing territories." Although Nehru continued to favour a negotiated solution, the Portuguese suppression of a revolt in Angola in 1961 radicalised Indian public opinion, and increased the pressure on the Government of India to take military action. African leaders, too, put pressure on Nehru to take action in Goa, which they argued would save Africa from further horrors.

On 18 December 1961, following the collapse of an American attempt to find a negotiated solution, the Indian Army entered Goa, Daman and Diu. The Portuguese took the matter to the Security Council but a resolution calling on India to withdraw its troops immediately was defeated by the USSR's veto. Portugal surrendered on 19 December. This take-over ended the last of the European colonies in India. Goa was incorporated into India as a centrally-administered union territory and, in 1987, became a state.

## Secessionism and Sub-nationalism

Whilst the majority of princely states absorbed into India have been fully integrated, a few outstanding issues remain. The most prominent of these is in relation to Kashmir, where a violent secessionist insurgency has been raging since the late 1980s.

Some academics suggest that the insurgency in Kashmir is at least partly a result of the manner in which it was integrated into India. Kashmir, uniquely amongst princely states, was not required to sign either a Merger Agreement or a revised Instrument of Accession giving India control over a larger number of issues than the three originally provided for.

Instead, the power to make laws relating to Kashmir was granted to the Government of India by Article 5 of the Constitution of Jammu and Kashmir and was, under Article 370 of the Constitution of India, somewhat more restricted than in relation to other states. Widmalm argues that during the 1980s, a number of Kashmiri youth began to feel that the Indian government was increasingly interfering in the politics of Jammu and Kashmir. The elections of 1987 caused them to lose faith in the political process and begin the violent insurgency which is still ongoing. Similarly, Ganguly suggests that the policies of the Indian government towards Kashmir meant that the state, unlike other parts of India, never developed the solid political institutions associated with a modern multi-ethnic democracy. As a result, the growing dissatisfaction with the status quo felt by an increasingly politically aware youth was expressed through non-political channels which Pakistan, seeking to weaken India's hold over Kashmir, transformed into an active insurgency.

Separatist movements also exist in two other former princely states located in North-East India, Tripura and Manipur. These separatist movements are generally treated by scholars as being part of the broader problem of insurgencies in North-east India, rather being a result of specific problems in integrating the princely states into India, as the Kashmir problem is and, in particular, to reflect the failure of the Government of India to adequately address the aspirations of tribal groups in the Northeast, or to tackle the tensions arising from the immigration of people from other parts of India to the north-eastern areas.

The integration of former princely states with other provinces to form new states has also given rise to some issues. The Telengana region, comprising the Telugu-speaking districts of the former Hyderabad State, were in many ways different from the Telugu-speaking areas of British India with which they were merged. In recognition of these differences, the States Reorganisation Commission originally recommended that Telengana be created as a separate state, rather than as part of a broader Telugu-speaking entity.

This recommendation was rejected by the Government of India, and Telengana was merged into Andhra Pradesh. The result was the emergence in the 1960s of a movement demanding a separate Telengana state, which continues to be strong in the region. A similar movement, although less strong, exists in the Vidarbha region of Maharashtra, which consists of the former Nagpur state and the Berar region of the former Hyderabad state.

## Critical Perspectives on the Process of Integration

Jinnah supported the right of princely states to remain independent, a position rejected by Nehru and the Congress

As this article has discussed, the integration process repeatedly brought Indian and Pakistani leaders into conflict. During negotiations, Jinnah, representing the Muslim League, strongly supported the right of the princely states to remain independent, joining neither India nor Pakistan, an attitude which was diametrically opposed to the stance taken by Nehru and the Congress and which was reflected in Pakistan's support of Hyderabad's bit to stay independent.

Post-partition, the Government of Pakistan accused India of hypocrisy on the ground that there was little difference between the accession of the ruler of Junagadh to Pakistan – which India refused to recognise – and the accession of the Maharajah of Kashmir to India, and for several years refused to recognise the legality of India's incorporation of Junagadh, treating it as de jure Pakistani territory.

Different theories have been proposed to explain the designs of Indian and Pakistani leaders in this period. Rajmohan Gandhi postulates that an ideal deal working in the mind of Patel was that if Muhammad Ali Jinnah let India have Junagadh and Hyderabad, Patel would not object to Kashmir acceding to Pakistan. In his book *Patel: A Life*, Gandhi asserts that Jinnah sought to engage the questions of Junagadh and Hyderabad in the same battle.

It is suggested that he wanted India to ask for a plebiscite in Junagadh and Hyderabad, knowing thus that the principle then would have to be applied to Kashmir, where the Muslim-majority would, he believed, vote for Pakistan. A speech by Patel at the Bahauddin College in Junagadh following the latter's take-over, where he said that "we would agree to Kashmir if they agreed to Hyderabad" suggests that he may have been amenable to this idea. Whilst Patel's opinions were not India's policy, nor were they shared by Nehru, both leaders were angered at Jinnah's courting the princes of Jodhpur, Bhopal and Indore, leading them to take a harder stance on a possible deal with Pakistan.

Modern historians have also re-examined the role of the States Department and Lord Mountbatten during the accession process. Ian Copland argues that the Congress leaders did not intend the settlement contained in the Instruments of Accession to be permanent even when they were signed, and at all times privately contemplated a complete integration of the sort that ensued between 1948 and 1950.

He points out that the mergers and cession of powers to the Government of India between 1948 and 1950 contravened the terms of the instruments of accession, and were incompatible with the express assurances of internal autonomy and preservation of the princely states which Mountbatten had given the princes. Menon in his memoirs stated that the changes to the initial terms of accession were in every instance freely consented to by the princes with no element of coercion. Copland disagrees, on the basis that foreign diplomats at the time believed that the princes had been given no choice but to sign, and that a few princes expressed their unhappiness with the arrangements. He also criticises Mountbatten's role, saying that whilst he stayed within the letter of the law, he was at least under a moral obligation to do something for the princes when it became apparent that the Government of India was going to alter the terms on which accession took place, and that he should never have lent his support to the bargain given that it could not be guaranteed after independence.

Both Copland and Ramusack argue that, in the ultimate analysis, one of the reasons why the princes consented to the demise of their states was that they felt abandoned by the British, and saw themselves as having little other option. Older historians such as Lumby, in contrast, take the view that the princely states could not have survived as independent entities after the transfer of power, and that their demise was inevitable. They therefore view successful integration of all princely states into India was a triumph for the Government of India and Lord Mountbatten, and as a tribute to the sagacity of the majority of princes, who jointly achieved in a few months what the Empire had attempted, unsuccessfully, to do for over a century -- unite all of India under one rule.

## Freedom at Midnight

Freedom at Midnight by Larry Collins and Dominique Lapierre was recommended to me by zackq and KO (who has his own thoughts here). It is a highly readable book with a great writing style.

The major fault of the book lies with the authors' reliance on Mountbatten. One of their major sources is a personal interview with Mountbatten. In addition, they got some of Mountbattens personal papers about the events of his viceroyalty in India. In my opinion, the authors seem to be smitten with Mountbatten. Every mention of him has something really nice to say. His charm, persuasiveness, greatness, administrative and military genius are praised over and over again. No skepticism is applied to Mountbatten's account. Since I am not a Mountbatten fan, this turned me off quite a bit.

Freedom at Midnight starts when Mountbatten was appointed Viceroy of India in March 1947 and ends with Gandhi's assassination in January 1948. Thus it is an account of the last year of British India. If you don't know anything about the Indian independence movement, you might be better off reading a more comprehensive account. There is, however, a lot that happened in 1947 and "Freedom at Midnight" covers it in good detail, taking almost 500 pages to do so.

One of the side-effects of the authors' Mountbatten-worship is that most of the major figures, like Gandhi, Nehru, and Jinnah, are seen mostly through Mountbatten's eyes. One result of this is the extremely negative portrayal of Jinnah. I don't usually have much of a problem with his negative portrayal since that is quite common in history books not written by Pakistanis. But "Freedom at Midnight" tries a negative adjective for Jinnah every time he's mentioned. I know Jinnah was a determined fellow who was arrogant and vain as well, but still the authors lost me there. I do agree with this statement though:

> *Jinnah himself celebrated the day [of independence] by assuming full powers for his supposedly ceremonial office. In the year of life remaining to him, the London-trained lawyer who for years*

> *had not ceased to proclaim his faith in the constitutional process would govern his new nation as a dictator.*

This, in my view, was one of the problems with Pakistani democracy since its founding. Contrast Jinnah's behavior with Nehru. Nehru became Prime Minister of India and set up a parliamentary government. In the end, Nehru probably had as much dictatorial power as Jinnah but the foundation of parliamentary democracy had been set up in India while Pakistan became a land of dictators.

The authors also do not seem well-versed in Indian history before the British. For example, they mention that Islam came to India "after the cohorts of Genghis Khan and Tamerlane had battered their way down the Khyber Pass to weaken the Hindus' hold on the Gangetic plain." I guess they are confusing Muslims and Mughals. It was during the slave dynasty and then the Khaljis that the battles with the Mongols took place. Oh and Tamerlane himself was Muslim (not that it matters) and defeated Mahmud Tughluq in 1398.

The imperialist attitude of the British is captured well by the authors.

> Their rule was paternalistic, that of the old public-school master disciplining an unruly band of boys, forcing on them the education that he was sure was good for them. With an occasional exception they were able and incorruptible, determined to administer India in its own best interests – but it was always they who decided what those interests were.

This description of the Viceroy's travel reminded me of Pakistan's President-General.

> Whenever the viceroy's white-and-gold train moved across the vast spaces of India, guards were posted every one hundred yards along its route twenty-four hours in advance of its arrival.

Mountbatten impulsively decided the date of partition (Aug 15, 1947) at a press conference. No prior thought or discussions on this. And this is a guy who, according to the authors, had provided the Congress and Muslim League leaders with a 34-page document titled "The Administrative Consequences of Partition when partition had been agreed on because He [Mountbatten] had forced these seven men to come to grips with a problem so imposing that it would leave them neither the time nor the energy for recrimination in the few weeks of coexistence left to them.

He had chosen the date because it was the anniversary of Japanese surrender. To top that impulsive decision, he decided not to reveal the Boundary Commission awards until a couple of days after independence. This created a lot of confusion in the provinces of Punjab and Bengal which were being partitioned.

I talked about dual loyalties in a previous post. Two instances in this book provide some food for thought.

- When the tribal irregular forces from Pakistan invaded the state of Kashmir (which was sort of independent at the time) on Ocober 24, 1947, this news was relayed to the British commander-in-chief of the Indian army, Lt. Gen. Sir Rob Lockhart, by the British general commanding the Pakistani army, Maj. Gen. Douglas Gracey. Do you think Gracey was being disloyal to the country hc served, Pakistan? Why? Or why not?
- Sahibzada Yaqub Khan, then a major in the army (later foreign minister of Pakistan), opted to leave for Pakistan from his home in Rampur. He led a battalion of the Pakistani army in the war in Kashmir in 1947-8. His younger brother, Younis Khan, had decided to remain in his ancestral Rampur. He too was an army officer. And he too fought in Kashmir. But on the Indian side. What did these two guys think of loyalty? What do you think?

Any thoughts on the matter?

***Why did Nehru find difficulty in fitting Jinnah and the idea of Pakistan into his own conception of a 'Modern India'?***

The former British colony, India, became independent in August 1947. Indeed two new states emerged from it-India and Pakistan. Jawaharlal Nehru was the first prime minister of India, while Muhammad Ali Jinnah held office as Pakistan's first governor general. Nehru had, as one of the most important leaders, fought many years for India's independence. During this fight, he developed his own views about what modernity meant to him and how a future free Indian modernity would look like. In his opinion, it would be connected with democratic, secular, and socialistic principles, and also with equal rights for every Indian independent of his or her religion, language, caste, sex and so on.

This essay is concerned with Nehru's perceptions about modernity, its features and the role religion should play in it and in politics. The question, which shall be answered, is why did Nehru find difficulty in fitting Jinnah and the idea of Pakistan into his own conception of a modern India. The first of the two main arguments to be discussed is that, in his opinion, all Indians belonged to one nation. The second argument, which Nehru discussed in his writings, is that for him a modern India should be a secular state.

In this state, politics and economics should not be mixed with religious matters, and political parties and organisations not be formed along religious lines. Before the author goes into detail with these arguments, it has to be pointed out what modernity meant to Nehru.

Democracy was one basic principle, which Nehru favoured in connection with modernity and with a modern India. As early as the first half of the 1920s, he interpreted *Swaraj*, the objective of the Non-Cooperation-Movement, as "political independence,..., and a democratic form of government". Later in his *Discovery of India,* he stated again that the establishment of a democratic state was one of the important demands made in India.A second basic principle of modernity was, in Nehru's opinion, socialism. During the 1930s, his interest in socialist and communist ideas started. The social issue could, for him, no longer be separated from political freedom and in 1938 he stated:

I am convinced that the only key to the solution ... of India's problems lies in socialism .... I see no way of ending poverty, the vast unemployment, the degradation and the subjection of the Indian people except through socialism. That involves vast and revolutionary changes in our political and social structure, ... Socialism is thus for me not merely an economic doctrine which I favour, it is a vital creed which I hold with all my head and heart.

Socialism was thus, in Nehru's opinion, one of the forces which could lead to a better life for all Indians. It presented for him the only opportunity to bring modernity to India in a fair way. The opposite world order, the capitalist system, he disliked. One last aspect should be shortly mentioned in connection with the question what modernity and, especially Indian modernity, meant to Nehru. This aspect is secularism. The author will go into further detail with it in the following paragraphs when the two formulated arguments will be discussed.

With its manifold cultures, traditions, histories and peoples, India was not easy to grasp for Nehru, but in the course of time he developed his own ideas and concepts about these topics. In his *Discovery of India*, he tried to show that there is continuity in his homeland; that India remains India. He stated that, of course there are distinctive features amongst the Indian people, but he was also convinced that they had a common ground due to the same virtues, national heritage and moral as well as mental qualities. Starting from this point of view, Nehru disagreed with Jinnah's theory that India consisted of two nations.

Jinnah, who led a political party, the Muslim League, argued that a Hindu and a Muslim nation existed in India. As a consequence, he adopted the already existing conception of Pakistan for political claims and as the political objective of the Muslim League respectively. The idea of Pakistan contained the perception that Muslims as a nation should have their own homeland and state where they could live regarding spiritual, cultural, economic, social, and political aspects in accordance with their ideals.

Nehru rejected both ideas, the theory of two nations within India and the concept of Pakistan. In his opinion, the Indian people belonged to one nation, independently of their religion. He argued that if nationality would be based on religion, there would be more nations within the Indian territory than only the Hindu one and the Muslim one. The distinctive feature that separated one nation from another was, in this view, not religion, but rather "a sense of belonging together and of together facing the rest of mankind". He declared that there was no other difference between a Hindu and a Muslim who, for example, both lived as peasants in the same village than a religious one. Their language, customs and traditions were, in his views, the same.

Because of this perception, Nehru believed that a Muslim nation therefore: means that there is no nation at all but a religious bond; it means that no nation in the modern sense must be allowed to grow; it means that modern civilisation should be discarded and we should go back to the medieval ways; it means either autocratic government or a foreign government; it means, finally, just nothing at all except an emotional state of mind and a conscious or unconscious desire not to face realities, especially economic realities.

This statement is, in the author's opinion, a clear piece of evidence for Nehru's view that such a religious based nation would not be a part of the modern world.

In addition, this quotation shows one other facet which is important in order to answer the posed question. In regard to economic realities, Nehru argued that the Indian people have the same concerns and problems independent of their religion. He asked: "In what way are the interests of the Muslim peasant different from those of the Hindu peasant? Or those of a Muslim labourer or artisan or merchant or landlord or manufacturer different from those of his Hindu protype?" He added that the "ties that bind people are common interest, and, in the case of a subject country especially, a common national interest." Nehru believed that in a modern state political participation and claims would develop because of common economic interests and problems, not because of belonging to the same religious group.

In connection with the economic and also with the social issue, one more facet should be mentioned. In Nehru's perception, both could only be solved with the help of socialist methods and the participation of the masses. He believed that the formation of a modern Indian state would only be possible when the masses were involved in the freedom struggle, and in the politics of a future free India. Nehru stressed therefore that "the Congress had further developed agrarian, economic, and social programmes. Neither the Muslim League nor the Hindu Mahasabha had ever considered any such question or attempted to frame a programme." In addition, he added that the Congress, the party which led the Indian struggle for independence from the British colonial masters, "represented not only the nationalist urge of India ..., but also, to a large extent, proletarian urges for social changes." In connection with the Muslim League and Jinnah, he believed that "the communal organizations, ..., were closely associated with feudal and conservative elements and were opposed to any revolutionary social change."

This opinion of his-that the Muslim League was, as a result of their conservative and feudal elements, not connected with the masses and their claims-clearly shows his difficulties in fitting Jinnah and the idea of Pakistan in his own views of modernity. Thoughts about economic and social changes, which would be, in Nehru's perception, inevitable for the constitution of a modern society, were not shared by Jinnah and the Muslim League. Nehru gave, regarding this aspect, the following judgement about Jinnah: "He belonged to an older generation which was hardly aware of modern political thought or development. Of economics, ..., he appeared to be entirely ignorant." This perceived absence of modern ideas in regard to economic and social issues was problematic for Nehru and his views of modernity.

Besides these difficulties, there were also some concerning politics and secularism. Nehru did not believe in the mixture of religion and politics. He rejected communalism, which normally can be described as the policy of a group, or community that is formed along religious lines. Communalism meant, for him, "a narrow group mentality basing itself on a religious community but in reality concerned with political power and patronage for the interested group." This quotation again makes clear that, in his opinion, the religious appeal to win political power for a certain group was an example for a policy which was out of fashion.

It also shows that he had the opinion that a communal party like the Muslim League could not appeal to the masses; neither to all Indians nor only to all Muslims. In this context, Nehru defined the Muslim League as follows: "It represents a group of

Muslims, not doubt highly estimable persons, but functioning in the higher regions of the upper class and having no contact with the Muslim masses and few even with the Muslim lower middle classes." The confinement to the interests of special, mostly backward looking groups within the religious community prevented, in Nehru's view, the existence of modern ideas.

Communalism was outdated for him in this aspect. He stated, "... to think in terms of communal groups functioning politically is to think in terms of medievalism." As a result of this opinion, he had difficulties with Jinnah's views and the concepts of the Muslim League. He acknowledged that in fact, the Muslim League was a political organisation, but at the same time he held the view that, because of its confinement to a religious group, it was primarily a religious or communal organisation. Nehru rejected the idea that the religion of a person should also define his/her political view and his/her automatically belonging to a certain party, as obsolete. He believed that among Muslims, Hindus, Sikhs, Christians, Parsees, etc., "one may find Congressmen, socialists, anti-socialists, communists, liberals, direct-actionists, revolutionaries, moderates, extremists, believers in different kinds of economy theory ... ". He stated in this connection that "to appeal to Mussalmans or Hindus as religious groups on politcal matters is obviously the wrong thing. It is the medieval attitude, when politics and economics were in the background, and it cannot possibly fit in with the modern world. It is because of this that I say I find it difficult to think on communal lines."

In conclusion, it can be declared that Nehru had difficulties in fitting Jinnah and the idea of Pakistan into his own conception of a modern India because of his belief that modernity should contain inter alia a secular and socialist order. Jinnah had, in Nehru's perception, a wrong, backward looking political view. Nehru rejected the idea that there were two different nations in India because of religious differences and that the adoptive Muslim nation would need its own homeland, its own state, as being medieval. He had the modern opinion that all Indians belong to one nation. Only with the help of this unified nation could India be liberated and a free state in which every person would have the same rights.

But not only in regard to this aspect did Nehru disagree with Jinnah's ideas. A modern India should be, in his perception, a secular state in which politics and economy should not be mixed with religious matters. Nehru believed that in a really modern society parties and organisations should be formed on the basis of the same economic and political interests, not on the basis of the same religion.

Retrospective it must be stated in connection with the impact of Nehru's views on the further development of the Indian independence struggle that recent historians admire his ideas, but at the same time show that his ideas were not fit to solve all problems and did not respect some of the political, social and religious conditions. B. Zachariah states in this context that Nehru, who was unconcerned with caste, religion and religious nationalism, did not take the communal problem seriously enough, it was a minor problem for him. Michael Mann points out that Nehru, because of his unaccomodating attitude, is blamed to have hindered the unity of India. In conclusion, it can be stated that Nehru's views about a 'modern India' and his denial of concepts like religious nationalism had a strong influence on the events which led to the partition and on the development of an democratic Indian state after 1947 in which emerged a typical Indian type of secularism

***Idols of Division***

BJP and Congress recently had a war of words about Jinnah and Nehru. The war was about who did it? That is, who was responsible for the partition of India, Jinnah or Nehru? Gandhi although not a principle character in this debate remains firmly placed on the pedestal. It was a historical drama. The time setting was the British Raj.

All three of them were role models of the time. They came from well-to-do families of varying degrees. Jawarharlal's father Motilal Nehru was the wealthiest and the most illustrious. While all three of them went to become barristers, their fathers came from different professions. Mohandas Gandhi's father was prime minister to the tiny western state of Porbandar in Gujrat. Although, grocers by caste the Gandhis rose by dint of merit and service.

Jinnah's father Jinnah Poonja, originally from Kathiawar, Gujrat, was a prosperous merchant of Karachi. They belonged to the Khoja community and the Ismaili sect of Islam. Jawarharlal's father Motilal was a highly placed barrister of Allahabad High Court. He came from a cultured and enlightened family background.

Gandhi's family was the most devout in their faith. He was to become far more religious and developed into Mahatma. Cleanliness of soul and penitence was his way of attaining godliness. Gandhi applied himself to the fullest to attain the attributes of the Hindu god Rama. The path he travelled was 'Satyagrah' or firmness in truth. There was a spiritual content in his struggle. Ahimsa or non-violence, precisely passive resistance or what American writer David Thoreau calls Civil Disobedience was a method of protest, that earned lasting recognition.

Jinnah was a strictly private person modelled on the British. Not much is known about his religious beliefs and practices. For that matter the Ismailias are known to be more businessmen than Muslims. While Jinnah was not a businessman, he preferred doing things the way business is done. Like, 'tell me your business, do your business, and let me do my business'. The Jinnah who fought for Pakistan was for everybody to see, but Jinnah the person was off-limits. The Muslims of British India was his political agenda but he did not fight to establish Islam. Pakistan was to be a country for the Muslims but never did he speak of a land of Islam. He was not irreligious neither was he pious. Jinnah looked on the Islamic identity as a way of empowering the backward Muslims of India. He was much too a 'pucca sahib' to indulge in the obscurantism of religious bigotry and communalism. The most revealing of his statement on the issue was when he spoke in his inaugural address as the governor general of Pakistan. He said, 'You will find that in the course of time, Hindus would cease to be Hindus and Muslims would cease to be Muslims, not in the religious sense because that is the personal faith of each individual but in the political sense as the citizens of the state'.

Nehru on the other hand came from a Hindu Brahmin family. But he was a professed agnostic. Both Nehru and Jinnah shared western thought. He however imbibed himself with Hindu cultural heritage. Both Nehru and Jinnah responded almost in similar fashion regarding the marriage of their daughters Indira and Dina. Gandhi had to lend his family name to Feroz, a Parsi, while Jinnah was even harsh in never accepting Dina's marriage to a Parsi. Indira's marriage ended in separation and Dina as reported was not allowed by Jinnah to see him on his deathbed.

Among the three, Nehru was the politician. He had the gifts for it and was influenced by Hindu tradition of politics. Besides, he was the brightest of intellectuals. His was the sharpest mind of the time. A Fabian (named after Fabian Maximus Verrcusos) Socialist one who believed in gradualist approach, Nehru applied cautious and dilatory tactics and proceeded by meandering ways. He believed in his destiny and worked accordingly. That he was destined to be the Prime Minister of India. If it meant adopting the populist approach, so be it, he gave up western Attire for Khadi. India got two national icons in loincloth-clad sanyasi Gandhi and the impeccably dressed Nehru in Gandhi cap.

The stand of the three against the British Raj was also different. The background and the social context of their participation in India's independence movement varied too. Gandhi was the populist of the three. His contact with the general people was more direct and personal. In fact, the years he spent in South Africa baptized him. Apartheid was not the best of social circumstances. The discrimination in it treated self-respect brutally. Gandhi was appalled by the denial of civil liberties. His soul was not however encumbered by the frailty of his physique. It ruled his spirit. His form of protest did not have a rebel in it but disgraced the wrongdoer by the loftiness of his spirit and the orderly method of his resistance. The world found an apostle of dignity in protest and the mighty were in distress in containing this peaceable form of passive resistance. Even the racist government of South Africa acceded to his demand for the recognition of Indian marriages and the abolition of poll tax imposed on them.

Gandhi then returned to India. Among the three, he was the first to engage the British directly and he kept on doing so to the end of British Raj. His first encounter with the Raj was when the British Parliament passed the Rowlatt Acts in 1919 giving Indian colonial authorities the emergency powers to deal with the so-called Revolutionaries. Gandhi launched a non-cooperation movement, in his words Satyagraha and it spread through out India. Thousands were arrested and Gandhi was jailed. Swaraj (self-rule) or Swadeshi movement further emboldened Indian Freedom movement by spreading the call of boycotting imported goods and thef using homespun fabrics. He kept the freedom movement steaming with his populist form of passive protest.

For the British he was not the ideal man to confer with. Gandhi's undying zeal and lofty spirit in spreading the gospel of self-rule made the British concede with every move. They however looked to it that they retreat with grace. For that, they had Pandit Nehru and Mr. Jinnah to talk to.

Jinnah was more a barrister than a politician. On return from England, he started legal practice at the Bombay High Court and befriended the Parsi community. He made his formal political appearance by acting as the private secretary to the then Congress President Dababhoy Naurozi at the Calcutta session of All India Congress held in 1906. There was very little Indian or for that matter Muslim in him. Leaving aside his origin, he developed his mind and lifestyle in the mould of an Englishman. Physically he was lean and upright with sharp features. Like his features, he was upright, precise, unbending, determined, quick and sharp. His wit and intelligence endowed him with the skill and showmanship of a swordsman. When he believed, he believed with all his faith and determination, leaving no room for doubt, indecision or delay. Those who came across him or had to engage him, it was a matter of black and white. Either to love or to leave him, or even to hate him. To Mountbatten he was a villain and a hero to those who wanted Pakistan.

At the beginning, he worked for Hindu-Muslim unity and is credited for the success of Lucknow Pact in 1916 accepting the principle of separate electorate for the Muslims. He was a strict disciplinarian and rejected brinkmanship. All through he differed with agitation and expressed disapproval of precipitous methods that are destined to fail. By that account, he was never a populist and would not allow his followers to wake him up from sleep at the railway station to accept their adulation. When he came back from retirement in England in 1935, the Muslim League was in dire straits. He galvanized the Muslims of India uniting them in the faith of their separateness as a nation.

It is the unbending nature of his resolve and straightforwardness of his method that established the separateness of the Muslims as a nation. The concept of Pakistan, which was in limbo, even few years before madeir into the agenda of Freedom for British India. It prospered with the niggardliness and hesitant approach of Congress. And there was Pakistan, even though moth-eaten as Jinnah called.

Nehru came from the best of circumstances and from a politician's family. Born into an illustrious and wealthy family, he had a privileged upbringing. He received his schooling from Harrow and obtained his law degree from Trinity College Cambridge. Afterward he spent seven years in England to widen his horizons of knowledge. As told earlier, Nehru was influenced by the sceptical and rationalist outlook of Fabian Socialism and drew his patriotic inspiration from Irish Nationalism. His western upbringing was complete. On returning from England, he got into politics as Gandhi's disciple and took part in the Non-cooperation Movement. He also held public office as the President of Allahabad Municipal Corporation and served for two years. Pandit Nehru was outstanding as a politician and remained so. His next move was everybody's guess. The vehicle that carried him forward was Gandhi's sequential engagement with the British. The voice that talked to the British was Nehru who possessed a charming personality. He had the advantage of remarkable enlightenment and a natural rapport with the British, particularly with Lord Mountbatten.

The Congress had everything to gain through Nehru. He added all round balance to Gandhi's populist effervescence and spiritual naiveté. As a devoted disciple of 'Bapuji' Nehru protected Gandhi from the perils and pains of an errant protégé. He was a perfect foil for Jinnah's quick thrust, sharp, and unencumbered judgement. His privileged background and western education enabled him to walk the corridors of power with great ease and grace. He had all the elements in his favour, enlightenment, dignity, poise, confidence and a natural knack for office. He walked the corridors of power as if he had been there for a long time. And then eased into the office of the Prime Minister of India.

There is little doubt that these are the three most interesting personalities of British India-Gandhi, Jinnah and Nehru. These three outstanding leaders dominated a greater and in fact the most important part of the proceedings of the British India with their beliefs, thoughts, actions and utterances. The freedom movement of India was as diverse and complex in its ways as the land itself and the leaders who led it.

It is natural that the three men cannot be to everybody's liking. They were patriotic men who judged and acted in accordance with what they believed to be right for the people they led. Those of us who live in a different time cannot, by our judgements of varying nature, take away from them what history has given them. All three of them became what history wanted them to be. A Mahatma, a founder of a new nation and the builder of the largest democracy of the world. They belong to the rank of all time great leaders of Asia along with Mao Ze Dong and Ho Chi Minh.

# 5 Nehru Relations with Jinnah

People who had devoted major part of their adult lives in prison felt themselves getting closer to power and the prospects of an independent India seemed much brighter than ever before and they did not want to postpone what they have been seeking for years.

Looking back to 1942, when the Congress rejected the "Cripps Plan", Rajaji came up with his "CR-Plan". He advised the Congress to accept the formation of Pakistan but was violently opposed by the party. Some historians think that if only the Congress had only accepted the CR-Plan, the trauma of Partition in 1947 could well have been avoided. Do you agree?

The CR-Plan anticipated in acute detail what actually happened later in 1947. In a way he paved the way for talks if not a solution. Rajagopalachari largely engineered the Gandhi-Jinnah Talks of 1944. It gave Jinnah much publicity, much propaganda of his cause, much force and increased the chances of formation of Pakistan.

CR was the most brilliant, serious, rational and clever-thinking man India ever produced. Here was a man who could see far ahead but he could not grasp the human frailties in the situation. We now know that Cripps did not have the support of the Home Government in London! Winston Churchill was not for any proposals. And he did not want the Cripps Plan to work. FDR was pressing Churchill that he should do something for India and her demand for freedom. So Churchill knew he had to make some of gesture to the Americans to get them off his back.

So he was trying to please Roosevelt more than anything else!

I think that, as far as Churchill was concerned, it was his perceptual objective that there should be no offer to India for freedom especially in the war situation. Cripps was entirely in a false position. He thought it would work. He did not know that Amery (the Secretary of Sate for India) was hand in glove with Churchill!

There is an interesting incident not known to many. Sir C. P. Ramaswamy Aiyer, then the Dewan of Travancore State, met Sardar Patel in Bombay. Both were on their way to meet Sir Stafford Cripps. Patel told Sir C. P that nothing would come out of the Cripps Plan. The whole thing was a front engineered by Nehru to become the Prime Minister of India and it would not happen for he (Patel) was putting it down and going to kill it! He had already told Gandhi and he had agreed that it should be done! Sir C. P. was taken aback at this revelation. So he wrote a secret communication to Lord Linlithgow who was equally surprised! He narrated it all in a secret letter to Amery in London, which I read in the " Transfer of Power" Documents.

In 1942 Nehru was genuinely anxious that the Cripps proposals should work, though on Congress terms. He was a genuine democrat – anti-fascist. He was anxious to get the Congress to agree to some arrangement with the Raj, He felt that it would help to avert in the future the partition of India.

Talking of Jinnah, do you think that his role on Indian politics was much bigger than Gandhi's?

In terms of their moral presence Gandhi was by far a greater man. Jinnah had two moments of dominance in the Indian story. One was during the First World War (1914-1918), which the Congress just frittered away. Here was a man who could be a very powerful and useful ally but they alienated him and allowed him to drift into negative relationship with the Congress. And he comes back in 1935 with a new proposition, he has to work extremely hard to build up his position as the all India Muslim leader, and by 1945 he is a key player. But Jinnah was an impossible man to negotiate with.

Was it part of his psyche or a mere put-on?

He was naturally reserved, he had so many human setbacks, his marriage, the importance that Gandhi got from the "Khilafat Movement", he never really recovered from the serious hurt of the series of injuries he had in life. He was a very secretive man, kept his ideas well in control, a loner. I recognise him as master tactician of real politique. You may not like him but you have to recognise his political talents and manoeuvring skills. In the beginning he didn't want Pakistan but some all-India settlement for Muslims. He allowed the Pakistan Movement to become the vehicle to manoeuvre the politics of the Indian sub-continent.

It was a case of the means becoming the end. Perhaps the means was Pakistan and the end was the Prime Ministership of India. He very much hoped in 1946 and was shattered when Lord Wavell (then Viceroy of India) didn't allow him and Nehru became the Prime Minister of the Interim Government. Gandhi did invite him to take over but it did not happen. We do not know when the tuberculosis he suffered from became rampant — he kept it a closely guarded secret but he knew he had not long to live. That's why he chose to become the President of Pakistan, and not Prime Minister.

### *Jinnah and Nehru*

I Seek the reader's indulgence for inviting attention to my letter 'Jinnah before and after' (Dawn, June 29). The letter had challenged Mr M. J. Akbar's contention in his article "Jinnah before and after the 1920 Congress session" (Dawn, June 14) that the Cabinet Mission plan of 1946, that would have kept India united and which had been accepted by both the Congress and the Muslim League 'collapsed inexplicably'.

In my letter I argued that the Congress had accepted the plan with disabling reservations and by putting a disingenuous interpretation of its own, in line with Mr Gandhi's thinking. So, it was Gandhi and the Congress leadership who were squarely responsible for the collapse of the plan and that there could not be any two opinions on the subject.

My argument was based on documentary evidence produced by eminent Bombay jurist A. G.Noorani in one of his articles from which I quoted fairly extensively. I was hoping that Mr M. J. Akbar or some other Indian from amongst Dawn's vast Internet readership would respond to what I had stated. But there has been no response at all. As I had referred to in my letter, Nehru told the Cabinet Mission categorically, on June 10, 1946 that the "Congress was going to work for a strong centre and break the grouping system and that they did not think Mr Jinnah had any real place in the country".

In this context, even more revealing information about Nehru's attitude to Jinnah has come to my notice recently. Mr A. G. Noorani, in his article, 'Punjab and Pakistan', in Frontline of March 12-25, 2005 has quoted what Nehru wrote in his prison Diary on Dec 28, 1943: "Instinctively I think it is better to have Pakistan or almost anything if only to keep Jinnah far away". On this, Noorani has commented: "His aversion to Jinnah was as visceral as was the Congress's to power-sharing. When it wrecked the Cabinet Mission scheme finally in December 1946 (after the London conference convened by the British government), Jinnah had no option but to acquire a 'truncated' Pakistan established in rancour. No alternative was in sight nor was one even offered."

### *The Third Side of the Partition Coin*

There's a third side to the coin that the Partition debate seems to ignore: the British.

The British did 'divide-and rule', and did it quite successfully for two centuries over the Indo-Pak subcontinent. And, we not only had the kind of homegrown 'diversity' such a policy needs but also provided it generously.

The seeds of communalism were already in the fertile Indian soil, long before partition. The British couldn't have ignored them. Besides, you don't build an empire, a far- flung one at that covering nearly a quarter of the world's population and area, without a well-trained eye for such pathology and an ability to exploit it.

**We already had slogans**: "Quit India" (Congress, 1942) and "Divide and Quit" (Muslim League, 1943), both of which caused, directly or indirectly, sectarian violence and bloodshed. Both sides had extremists. We had satyagrahas and "Direct Action" riots. We had a vocal minority that felt increasingly alienated, and found the majority's promises unacceptable.

No matter who initiated or precipitated it or how, such complex situations often have shared responsibility. To consider them otherwise is just politically naïve. We can keep pointing fingers at each other, calling names, throwing around poorly-understood, inflammatory labels, and we seem to have an inexhaustible reservoir of all this, even after some 58 years. We can continue to wallow in the same, or bury the hatchet, learn from our mistakes and start a bold new page as neighbors with a shared heritage.

When Clement Attlee (Labor) was elected Prime Minister of Britain in 1945 (soon after the WWII), he decided that India was strategically indefensible, and Britain could no longer afford to govern it. He also did not believe that Britain had the right to govern it. He sent a Cabinet Mission to India to work out a plan for a Hindu-Muslim working together in undivided India. All parties accepted it initially because the plan provided for protection of Muslim minority rights, but after the elections for the new Assembly, Nehru decided not to have anything to do with the new government. Jinnah also refused and called for Direct Action on August 16, 1946 (a year to the day before Partition).

Amid all this, Attlee appointed Louis Mountbatten as Viceroy to India in March 1947 (just five months before the Partition). He had instructions to keep India united if at all possible. Attlee had even set a deadline for the freedom of India: "No later than June 1948." Mountbatten did one-up, and suggested an earlier date and swifter transfer of power. He also thought the confederal proposals were essentially unworkable and acceded in principle the partition of the subcontinent. He presented a Partition plan to all parties on June 3, 1947, which they accepted. To Mountbatten's annoyance, it seems Jinnah told him (according to Alan Campbell-Johnson, viceroy's press secretary), "I do not agree, but I accept." Basically, no one liked Partition. It wasn't just one of the most desirable options, it was "the only solution," as Campbell-Johnson puts it, and thus they "accepted what they got."

Then, to devise a partition plan, Attlee appointed a distinguished barrister, Cyril Radcliffe, who had never been to the subcontinent, and had no first hand knowledge of the situation, the problems or the people. He was chosen because he was 'unbiased', and was expected to remain so. He was provided with the services of four judges, two Hindu, two Muslim, who almost constantly fought along the partisan lines and weren't much help to him at all. Radcliffe had the 1943 census (the figures were probably old, and never confirmed) and the maps of the region (perhaps out-dated). Radcliffe's former press secretary, Christopher Beaumont, thinks Radcliffe had an "impossible assignment." When Radcliffe met Mountbatten for the first time, he learned that he actually had 36 days. Still, Radcliffe managed to complete the task on 13 August, 1947, two days ahead of schedule.

Karl Meyer, a veteran journalist, scholar and a long-time editorial board member of the New York Times, is quite critical of the British in his book "The Dust of Empires: The Race for Mastery in the Asian Heartland" (May 2003). He concludes that the 'shabby' and 'hasty' departure of the British, together with Mountbatten-Nehru friendship (particularly between Mountbatten's wife, Edwina and Nehru), turned a bad outcome into worse. Meyer rejects the view (promoted by the movie Gandhi) that Jinnah and the Muslim League were "the only culprits." In Meyer's view the "real villain" was Mountbatten, "in collusion" with Nehru, and Jinnah was "nearly blameless by comparison." He thinks Mountbatten's method of drawing borders between these countries was "at best arbitrary, at worst reckless. His timetable for partition left the Indian army on the sideline when communal slaughter began.

Some people in Britain were very critical of Mountbatten, right from the beginning, suggesting that his friendship with Nehru interfered with fairness. Mountbatten supporters obviously disagree. There is no way that the issue can now be independently reviewed, because Radcliffe destroyed all the records when he completed the assignment, refused any discussion of his Commission's work, and never went back to the subcontinent again. His aide, Christopher Beaumont, did however make some things clear in 1992.

He gave the British conservative newspaper, The Daily Telegraph, a copy of the memo he had prepared on the deliberations of the Radcliffe Commission, which he had already donated to All Souls College at Oxford. Beaumont confirms that borders were secretly redrawn, to Pakistan's disadvantage, particularly in case of Ferozepore, a 400 sq. mile area, where the canal head-water controlled irrigation in Bikaner. Nehru somehow got the wind of the still-confidential work, and he and Maharajah of Bikaner appealed to the Viceroy. The Viceroy then asked Radcliffe for a private lunch (his second and last meeting with him), and after that, Radcliffe promptly altered the border he had originally drawn. According to this Beaumont memo, "This episode reflects great discredit on Mountbatten and Nehru."

Two other major cases in which Mountbatten intervened were: Chittagong Hill Tracts (CHT) and Gurdaspur District. Despite a higher non-Muslim population, Radcliffe had CHT going to Pakistan and Gurdaspur (with a Muslim majority) to India. In Radcliffe's initial proposal, Gurdaspur District was in Pakistan, but it was changed later because of Mountbatten's intevention.

It's not that the British are suddenly forthcoming with their criticism now. One of the Indian supporters of the British also had some tough words. In the second volume of his autobiography "Thy Hand, Great Anarch !" Nirad Chaudhuri says: (i) " ... then an apologia emerged ex post facto which is the most shameless sophistry I have read anywhere. It was argued, and is still being argued, that if the British had not left – the manner of their leaving being conveniently glossed over – there would have been uprisings and therefore loss of life far exceeding what was seen. Now, the conjuring of the hypothetical bogeys which no one can prove or deny is the best defense of every coward who yields at the first sign of trouble." (ii) [and this is on Jinnah], "I must set down at this point that Jinnah is the only man who came out with success and honor from the ignoble end of the British Empire in India. He never made a secret of what he wanted, never prevaricated, never compromised, and yet succeeded in inflicting unmitigated defeat on the British Government and the Indian National Congress. He achieved something which not even he could have believed to be within reach in 1946."

India received most of the 562 scattered princely states, among other things. Karl Meyer is quite astute when he says there's some "provincial unfinished quality" about Pakistan: 7 different Constitutions, not a single Chief of the State completing his/her term, or managing to have a peaceful transfer of power. Meyer thinks Pakistan got the "loser's share of the Raj spoils." India did receive most of everything (even most of 562 princely states).

Out of the thousands of Indian Civil servants and other elite, Meyers notes Pakistan got just a tiny fraction: about 100 Civil Service and national police, supported by 50 British civil servants, 11 Indian army officers that "overnight had to create Pakistan's administration, judicial and diplomatic realms.

Jinnah was a complex character, much different from Nehru and Gandhi. He was autocratic, aloof, much anglicized and distrustful of the British attitude toward Muslims. His relationship with Mountbatten was stiff, frosty, and decidedly unfriendly (Mountbatten had some choice words, including "awfully cold," to describe an arrogant Jinnah). It's hard to say whether this worked against his cause, but it didn't quite earn him the brownie-points that Nehru seems to have gotten plenty of. He, according to some, was Pakistan's Charles de Gaulle: haughty, impervious, nationalistic and the country, personified.

The question, again, is not whether the British withdrawal was hasty: In the eyes of the Indian group, it was long over-due. As to the British, they saw the light and had their own deadline, announced well in advance. The important questions are: (i) Whether, in haste to withdraw, did the British thoroughly explore ALL options ? (ii) Were adequate security precautions taken to protect the public at large from the inevitable violence and massacre? The answer to both questions is probably NO! Among facile rationalizations offered are: Since independence was announced before Partition, it was up to the new governments of India and Pakistan to keep public order; no large population movements were suspected; the plan did call for the protection of minorities in both countries, but both of them failed; and some Mountbatten supporters hypothesize that by rushing, Mountbatten actually saved more lives than those who died on the eve of

Partition, and had he delayed the partion/independence any longer, there would have been a huge civil war, with much greater loss of life. As a rationale, this is unbecoming and bizarre.

For another, non-political perspective from one of my favorite British poets, W. H. Auden ('Partition', May 1966):

*Unbiased at least he* was when he arrived on his mission, Having never set eyes on this land he was to partition Between two peoples fanatically at odds, With their different diets and incompatible gods. "Time," they had briefed him in London, "is short***. It's too late for mutual reconciliation or rational debate: the only solution now lies in separation. The Viceroy** thinks, as you will see from his letter, That the less you are seen in his company the better, So we've arranged to provide you other accommodations. We can give you four judges, two Muslim, two Hindu, To consult with, but the final solution must rest with you." Shut up in a lovely mansion, with police night and day Patrolling the gardens to keep assassins away, He got down to work, to the task of settling the fate Of millions. The maps at his disposal were out of date And the Census# returns almost certainly incorrect, But there was no time to inspect Contested areas. The weather was frightfully hot And a bout of dysentery kept him constantly on the trot, But in seven weeks it was done, the frontiers decided, A continent for better or worse divided. The next day he sailed for England where he quickly forgot The case as a good lawyer must. Return he would not Afraid, as he told his Club, that he might get shot."*

## Flashback to Indian Partition

Astrologers could not decide on an auspicious day for the independence of India so it fell at midnight between 14 and 15 August 1947.

The British colony was divided along religious lines and two nations were born-the secular but Hindu-dominated India and the Islamic Republic of Pakistan.

But even as the celebrations were getting under way it was questioned whether partition could lead to peace among the subcontinent's different groups.

Some observers say it has fuelled regional animosities and argue that it established a sinister precedent.

Since partition, India and Pakistan have waged three wars against each other-two of them over the unresolved issue of Kashmir.

### *Peace Declaration*

The first ceremonies to symbolise the transfer of power from Britain to one of the new dominions took place in Karachi on the morning of 14 of August.

*"At the stroke of midnight hour, when the world sleeps, India will wake up to life and freedom."*

### *Free India*

After the ceremony in Pakistan, Lord and Lady Mountbatten flew to Delhi, where special events to mark the transfer of power took place. He was to stay on as Governor General of India, while Pandit Jawaharlal Nehru became the country's first prime minister.

*"That night people were very expectant, very hopeful of things to come"*

### *Saeed Suhrawardy*

The special ceremony began at 11pm in the State Council building.

"At the stroke of midnight hour, when the world sleeps, India will wake up to life and freedom," Nehru said.

As the last chimes of midnight died, an assembly member blew a conch shell and a great cheer rose in the hall.

Tens of thousands of people celebrated outside the building-many more did so in cities around India.

Mahatma Gandhi, regarded as the father of Indian independence, did not attend the celebrations. Instead, Gandhi-who strived for a united India-spent the day with Indian Muslims in Calcutta.

### *Exodus*

Journalist Saeed Suhrawardy, an Indian Muslim from the town of Mirzapur, was 17 at the time and remembers the night clearly.

"I think the whole town was awake," he said. "There was no television at that time and few radios. So radio shops were very crowded with people waiting for the speech of Pandit Jawaharlal Nehru. It was like a festival, at least in my place there was no tension.

"That night people were very expectant, very hopeful of things to come."

But Saeed Suhrawardy recalls that there were also fears that night.

"Reports coming from other places made the minorities fearful for events to come.

"In our town we did not have any record of communal violence. But there were stories of violence, riots, attacks on trains and bloodstained trains arriving with dead bodies."

Saeed Suhrawardy did not think of migrating after partition. Many others did.

As soon as the new borders were known some 10 million Hindus, Muslims and Sikhs fled from their homes on one side of the newly demarcated borders to the other side.

About one million people were killed during the exodus, and to this day many families are separated by the border.

### *Religious Rivalry*

The origin of partition is still a matter of debate.

The name Pakistan-or "Land of the Pure"-did not come into existence until 1933, when it was coined by Rahmatullah Chowdhry, a Cambridge student.

### *Partition Timeline*

- 1930: Alama Iqbal advocates the two-nation theory
- 1933: The name Pakistan is coined

- 1940: Jinnah calls for a separate Muslim state
- May/June 1946: Both parties accept Cabinet Mission Plan
- July: Plan collapses
- Aug: Hindu-Muslim violence kills thousands
- June 1947: Mountbatten plan for partition approved
- July: India Independence Act passed in Britain
- Aug: Separate states of Pakistan and India are born

Three years earlier, the poet Alama Iqbal had advocated the establishment of a separate Muslim state at a Muslim League conference. But it was not until 1940 that his two-nation theory was adopted by the League.

The 1930s saw a growing mistrust between the Muslim League and the All India Congress.

The League's leader, Mohammed Ali Jinnah-until 1940 reluctant to advocate the creation of two nations-is said to have feared that the country's Muslim minority would be subjugated by the Hindu majority.

***Deadline***

During World War II Britain's mobilisation of the Indian economy and military forces was opposed by Congress.

Fearing the movement's ability to sabotage the war effort, Britain is said to have exploited the Hindu-Muslim rivalry in an effort to curtail the Congress.

After the war, Labour Prime Minister Clement Attlee came to power in Britain.

In 1946, he sent a Cabinet Mission to India that put forward a plan for Hindus and Muslims to work together.

This was initially accepted by both sides, but within week the plan had collapsed. Some say it was Nehru who changed his mind, others say it was Jinnah.

Jinnah called for Direct Action on 16 August 1946 to protest against Congress and the British.

In Calcutta this led to three days of Hindu-Muslim violence-the bloodiest in nearly a century-and thousands of deaths.

A year later, Lord Mountbatten was sent to India to replace Lord Wavell as viceroy, with plans to transfer power no later than June 1948.

### *Demarcation*

The new viceroy is said to have found the situation too dangerous to wait even that brief period, and to have become convinced that partition was unavoidable.

On 3 June 1947, he presented his plan to Nehru and Jinnah. They both accepted it.

A month later, the British Parliament passed the Indian Independence Act, ordering the demarcation of the dominions of India and Pakistan by midnight 14-15 August.

Two boundary commissions worked against the clock to partition the states of Bengal and Punjab in such a way as to leave a majority of Muslims to the west of the new Punjab border (what is currently Pakistan) and to the east of the new Bengal border (East Pakistan, which in 1971 would become Bangladesh).

Under the partition plan, Kashmir was free to accede to India or Pakistan.

### *Sharp Reminder*

Three days before partition, the Hindu ruler of Muslim-majority Kashmir, Maharajah Hari Singh, said that he wanted to remain independent.

However, in a series of events which are still the subject of controversy to this day, a Pathan tribal force entered Kashmir with Pakistani backing. The Maharajah decided to accede to India, allowing Indian troops to be airlifted to the state.

Pakistani and Indian forces ended up at the point now known as the Line of Control, splitting the territory unevenly.

Nearly 55 years and two wars later, the status of Kashmir remains unresolved-one of the many reminders of a partition that has left thousands of families separated by the line which divides India and Pakistan.

When Edwina met Nehru

The first is a brisk account of Britain's involvement with India and of the backgrounds of those people who were principally responsible for unscrambling that relationship.

It contains most of the facts that matter, if rather too much social trivia that does not, and is generally fair. Where it is unfair is in its dismissal of Mountbatten as a trivial playboy. It is permissible to make fun of some of the wilder schemes which he championed during his time at Combined Operations—notably the iceberg-aircraft carrier Habbakuk—but unreasonable to dismiss the ingenuity, energy and formidable organising powers which created the machine that made possible the invasion of Europe in 1944.

Mountbatten was, indeed, often preoccupied with trifles, or with his status as a member of the royal family, but to claim that he 'engaged himself almost full time' in arranging the marriage between his nephew Philip and the future Queen is absurdly to underestimate the range of his activities and to exaggerate his role as matchmaker.

By the time that the second part of this book begins—dealing with the coming of independence and the partition of India—the reader (or, at any rate this reader) is therefore expecting a hatchet job on the last Viceroy, a reprise of the gospel according to Saint Andrew Roberts.

The contrary proves to be true. Harold Nicolson in his diary remarked how curious it was that 'we should regard as a hero the man who liquidates the empire which other heroes such as Clive, Warren Hastings and Napier won for us'.

But, von Tunzelmann goes on:

Mountbatten was serving his country with as much loyalty, courage and determination as had those other heroes. Mountbatten turned a stagnating mess into perhaps the most successful retreat from empire in history—from the point of view of the imperialist nation, at least.

She examines the three main charges against him—that he mishandled the problem of the Sikhs, failed to make proper use of the British army, and transferred power with disastrously reckless speed—and acquits him on all of them.

Certainly she criticises certain aspects of his operations but she is equally ready to show that all the main protagonists—Gandhi, Nehru and Jinnah in particular—were at times guilty of obstinacy, pride, ill-temper and rank bad judgment.

She conveys vividly the terrifying pressures under which they were all working: the massacres that besmirched partition were bad enough, but von Tunzelmann leaves one in no doubt as to how much worse they might have been.

The heroes are all shown to have had their frailties; the heroine, Edwina Mountbatten, is alone almost immaculate. Her achievements were, indeed, prodigious, but the author exaggerates her importance—sometimes it seems as if Mountbatten would have been incapable of performing his task without her constant guidance, if not control.

The remarkable relationship between Nehru and the two Mountbattens is described with sympathetic understanding.

Von Tunzelmann suggests that the 'affair' between Nehru and Edwina began far earlier than May 1948—'the line later perfected by official biographers'. It depends what you mean by 'affair'. No one doubts that a close friendship existed while Mountbatten was still Viceroy but Nehru himself dates to a weekend in Simla in midMay the discovery that 'there was a deeper attachment between us, that some uncontrollable force, of which I was only dimly aware, drew us to one another'.The point is of importance, since Pakistani historians in particular insist that Mountbatten as Viceroy was prejudiced in favour of the Indians because of Nehru's baleful influence, exercised through the Viceroy's wife.

The subtitle of this book, 'The Secret History.. .' suggests that the author has had access to hitherto unknown sources and is offering the reader sensational revelations. If such sources exist they are singularly well concealed.

Von Tunzelmann has, however, worked conscientiously through a mass of published and unpublished material.

From it she has created a compelling narrative, sometimes controversial, occasionally perverse, never boring or unintelligent. It will be interesting to see what she tackles next; there is every reason to hope that it will be well worth reading.

### *Mountbatten Redrafted Plan for Nehru: Viceroy's Daughter*

New Delhi, Jul 19 (PTI) India's last Viceroy Lord Mountbatten had to redraft the plan to give dominion status to both India and Pakistan after Jawaharlal Nehru, who shared a "special relationship" with the Viceroy's wife, Edwina, rejected many points of the plan saying it was tantamount to the "Balkanisation" of the country.

Nehru, who was prone to mood swings, was invited by Lord Mountbatten to Simla to get a feedback on the plan. But Nehru turned down the plan and wrote a "bombshell" letter to the Viceroy, writes Pamela Mountbatten, the Viceroy's younger daughter in her book "India Remembered: A Personal Account of the Mountbattens During the Transfer of Power".

"... My father began soul-searching and decided to show Nehru the Mountbatten Plan to get his feedback. Nehru was incandescent and kept Krishna Menon up till dawn the night that he arrived, dictating the bombshell letter dated the 11th May (1947) to my father which rejected many points of the plan which he saw as the Balkanisation of his country. My father rethought and with the incredible and brilliant V P Menon, redrafted the whole plan...," writes Pamela, who travelled with her parents to India in 1947.

Following Nehru's rejection of the plan, Lord Mountbatten "rethought and...Resubmitted it (the plan) to London—much to the India Office and Attlee's confusion and perturbation", points out Pamela, who was 17 at the time.

Mountbatten then travelled to London and got the amendments to the plan—already agreed to by Nehru—"approved".

Mountbatten returned "...To India victorious and able to press ahead urgently with the moves that would lead to Dominion

Status for both India and Pakistan. The first thing that was needed was to meet and get the Indian leaders' agreement (of course he already had that from Nehru), and secondly, it needed announcing to the country and the wider world," she writes. The Viceroy also saved Nehru—"a Kashmiri Brahmin—"who was emotional about the (Kashmir) problem" humiliation by convincing the Maharaja of Kashmir to accept the Mountbatten plan.

"Nehru being a Kashmiri was intent on travelling to Kashmir himself to see the Maharaja, but my father realised the dangers inherent in that plan and luckily we could take up a long-standing invitation to visit the Prince ourselves. There was therefore a political expedient to our trip to Kashmir—to convince the Maharaja to accept the plan—and save Nehru the humiliation," writes Pamela, who was coaxed by her daughter India to record her 15-month stay in India.

Edwina's "special relationship" with Pandit Nehru was very useful for the Viceroy too. "Pandit Nehru was a Kashmiri himself, so he was emotional about the problem. If things were particularly tricky my father would say to my mother, 'Do try to get Jawaharlal to see that this is terribly important...'" However, Lord Mountbatten's charm offensive—a tool he used before launching his pragmatic strategies—fell flat on Mohammed Ali Jinnah, who was intent on creating Pakistan.

The Mountbattens, who were very optimistic about the chance to mediate between Jawaharlal Nehru and Congress and Jinnah and the Muslim League, found it difficult to "crack" Jinnah. "My father could talk of nothing else because he could not crack Jinnah and this had never happened to him before. He later admitted that he didn't realise how impossible his task was going to be till he met Jinnah," writes Pamela.

In a letter to his elder daughter the last Viceroy signalled just how depressed he was with the situation. "'I have boobed', he wrote mournfully. It was the only time he admitted it," writes Pamela.

In a section titled "Operation Seduction" Pamela points out that Jinnah was intent on creating Pakistan ever since he had been introduced to the concept at the history-shaping meeting in Waldorf in London in 1933. However, Mountbatten thought that Partition was an absurd idea but inevitable as the Indians wanted independence and couldn't agree.

Edwina also recorded her impressions of the Nehru-Jinnah meet: "Two very clever and queer people. I rather liked them but found them fanatical on this Pakistan and quite impractical." In another diary entry she calls Jinnah a "meglo-maniac (sic)" and says "god help Pakistan". Jinnah even put paid to Lord Mountbatten's plan who wanted to become Governor-General (G-G) of both India and Pakistan—by announcing that he (Jinnah) would become G-G of Pakistan.

"This left my father to decide whether to accept the offer to become G-G of India and therefore to go against every non-partisan plan he had stood for in his tenure. Indeed his later acceptance of the governor-generalship of India did tarnish his impartial reputation and kindled persistent rumours that he was anti-Muslim League," she writes.

The only time "Mr Jinnah" —as Lord Mountbatten called him—showed "emotion" was when he was seeing the Mountbattens off after the Independence Day function in Karachi.

"Jinnah was an icy man, but on this occasion he showed emotion. He leant over to my father, put his hand on his knee and said with evident feeling...'Your Excellency, I'm so glad to get you back safely.'"

## Nehru on Others Perspective

The story of the end of the Raj is one of the greatest tales of 20th Century history and since the day the last Union Jack was pulled down in Delhi there has been a stream of books on one or other aspects of the subject. ALEX VON TUNZELMANN has now added to these a very racy account of the whole saga in her debut work, *INDIAN SUMMER: THE SECRET HISTORY OF THE END OF AN EMPIRE*. This is a book which has already earned her a place amongst the growing band of popular historians now re-writing, and thankfully enlivening, history for the modern reader. Her account of the unraveling of the Raj and of the chief characters who unraveled it provides a very welcome and rivetingly lively summary of the lengthy and tortuous process that started in the late 19th Century and was concluded, at least formally, on two days in August 1947 (a day each for the two successor states, first Pakistan then India).

Von Tunzelmann handles this massive story, and the huge amount of information that she has absorbed from the books and files that lie behind it, adeptly and without over-burdening the reader with her erudition. Her writing is so fluid that it reads deceptively like a novel, though there is no make believe in it. She has the panache Edith Simon displayed in her *Luther Alive*. This is indeed a history that is alive. Her account of the horrors that engulfed India after partition is particularly vivid; I have not read a better account of the deaths, maimings, abductions, rapes and arson that accompanied the mass emigration of the fleeing millions seeking a home on the other side of the artificial line between the Muslim state of Pakistan and the secular state of India that was drawn by the departing British administration.

She is a terrific biographer; her characterisations are succinct and, for the most part, sympathetic. Her characters play their roles in this tragedy as realistic human beings, their failings balanced judiciously by their achievements, the weighty affairs of state they handle enlivened by the human touch, Gandhi's arm on the Vicereine, Edwina Mountbatten's, shoulder, Edwina's walks in the forest with Jawaharlal Nehru.

The book is not really a 'secret history' for there is not much of it that has not been penned elsewhere, as her excellent bibliography demonstrates, but it is what could be described as almost a multi-personality biography, for von Tunzelmann uses the life histories of the principal players (Gandhi, Nehru, the two Mounbattens and, to a much lesser, extent Jinnah and Churchill) to weave the story of the Indian national struggle from the late years of the 19th century to its denouement in the second half of the 20th.

Minor characters, if they can be called so, get similar treatment with lesser star billing; Edward VIII in his earlier, happier days as David, Prince of Wales; the many members of Gandhi's family; Jinnah's sister, Fatima; Nehru's daughter, Indira. This approach has the advantage of telling what is in reality a very winding story, with its countless sub-plots, dead ends, unexplained causes and confused outcomes, intelligibly. It allows von Tunzelmann to show how that story made sense to each of these participants, and so gives it a form that we can grapple with. If you are to cover all of this, as she does, in only 318 pages, and not produce a dry-as-dust summary, this is a better way than most to do it.

This approach does, inevitably, have its drawbacks, for over such a huge period of time (the book ranges over more than one hundred years) much occurs that cannot be explained by, or attached to, a small number of lives, no matter how key they were. The Indian (by which I mean what became both the Indian and Pakistani) national struggles are therefore on occasion reduced rather to the activities of Gandhi, Nehru and Jinnah.

The complicated chicaneries that have for ever obfuscated a true understanding of the Kashmir problem are not easily dealt with in this fashion. This is less damaging than the concentration upon the Mountbattens for the British side of the story. Theirs is no doubt by far the most attractive part of the British participation; they were young, they were glamorous and, amazingly for who they were (Mountbatten was a minor Royal in his own right and his wife, Edwina, one of the richest women in the world in hers), they were politically radical. Amongst the rather moth eaten assemblage of British dignitaries who handled British Indian affairs at the end of the Raj, they sparkled as if they themselves were the jewels in the Imperial Crown that they were busily giving away.

And they genuinely liked and loved, the latter particularly in Edwina's case, Indians. But the dreary succession of British policy, of scheme after scheme, commission after council, that trudged on from the early years of the 20th Century as the British tried to deal with, then finally rid themselves of, their Indian problem was something in which the Mountbattens had no part, and to which they provided, only on very rare occasions, the odd scintillating noise off in the wings. To some extent, then, history here takes second place to biography.

There is another problem with the balance in this book, which is its denigration of Gandhi. This is deliberate, though it is not a new phenomenon. Others before von Tunzelmann have focused on Gandhi's horrible treatment of his family; his inflexibility, particularly when faced with an attack on anything he took to be a matter of principle (which was, in reality, most things); his, at the times when he wasn't being inflexible, impossible vacillation; his naive unrealism when suggesting courses affecting the life or death of millions; his incredibly selfish, immoral really, use of the naked bodies of his own teenage relatives to test his purity.

Von Tunzelmann clearly doesn't like him at all, and though she tries hard to give Gandhi credit, giving full space to a few of his major deeds, such as the salt march, the picture she paints of him is lacking and leaves one wondering why there was so much of an outpouring of grief across India when he died and why her hero, Nehru, was so totally devoted for all of his life to the Mahatma.

Her treatment of Churchill is, to a lesser degree, similar. Here are all Churchill's anti-Indian-isms paraded again, and none of them are deniable, most are reprehensible. But it is really not possible to maintain that the diehards would have died less hard without them or that they had much effect on the overall course of events. They were, no doubt, a disagreeable part of his character, but he was, as was Gandhi, a bigger figure than the one we see here in the margins of this story. Both men were symbols of many facets of their times and nationalities. Big men can have mud on their boots.

Big men and women can also fall in love, and von Tunzelmann's account ends as the story of a love affair, the unlikely and touching relationship between Edwina Mountbatten and Jawaharlal Nehru. She is right to give this such pride of place in her final pages. It was an affair directly touching on the survival and future of India and on the relations between India and Britain. The affair also proves, albeit circumstantially, her assessment of these two principal characters. For one of the real virtues of this book is that von Tunzelmann will have none of the post-Strachian cynicism that leaves us with no one to admire. She recognises, nay trumpets, these facts: that individual human beings can rise above prejudice and background and find common ground; and that some human beings can, for at least part of their lives, be heroes and heroines.

It is difficult to think of a man and a woman better fitted for those accolades than Nehru and Edwina, or whose relationship could more authoritatively have overturned the pessimistic final parting of Briton and Indian of Forster's *Passage to India*. For then the very stars were against Fielding and Aziz. Thirty years later, Britain and India parted in Edwina and Nehru's farewell kiss.

It is not sentiment to recognize greatness of character and bravery of conduct nor the effect of love on human affairs. Alex von Tunzelmann has this, as she has the major things in her book, absolutely right.

### *Gandhi Sent Word to Jinnah that he would not Object to Jinnah being the Leader of Free India Instead of Nehru*

Nehru gets a lot of blame for going with Mountbatten's desire for not just partitioning the country hastily but also for agreeing to divide Punjab and Bengal.

Gandhi had refused for seven years, since Jinnah proposed a separate Muslim nation, to support a 'vivisection of the Mother,' arguing 'Muslims can never cut themselves away from their Hindu or Christian brethren. We are all children of the same Mother.'

He was so serious about saving India that he sent word, a few months before Partition, to Jinnah through Mountbatten that he would not object to Jinnah being the leader of free and united India instead of Nehru. But Jinnah—who always mistrusted the Mahatma, calling him 'wily Gandhi'—had no use for such overtures.

Nehru is also faulted for not listening to Gandhi in getting Jinnah to mediate in the escalating violence in undivided Kashmir. Gandhi even wondered if holding a plebiscite in Kashmir could end the looming violence there.

Why did Nehru listen so much to Mountbatten?

Those who forget history...

Nehru had talked about Mountbatten's fatal charm," Wolpert says. "Of course, he was flattering Mountbatten when he said that. But Nehru unfortunately came too much under the influence of Mountbatten, exacerbated by Nehru's education in England. Nehru was charmed by the English upper world, he thought he could trust and work with Mountbatten.

"Mountbatten's royal blood appealed as much to the rulers of princely states in India ," Wolpert continues, "as his radical views and social charms did to Nehru. His charm was so much Nehru was blinded by it."

Asked if Nehru's relationship with Mountbatten's wife Edwina played a role, the historian says, "It helped him cloud the danger of what Mountbatten was doing."

Wolpert doesn't fight the idea that Partition looked inevitable by 1947, and he understands why Nehru, seeing the way Hindus had been killed in Bengal and Punjab, agreed to the partition of the two provinces.

"But the real solution to any massacre is not to make more violence by drawing a line blindly through a province," the historian points out.

Years later, Mountbatten would whisper now and then how he had botched up the Independence process.

Years after Partition, Mountbatten would whisper now and then how he had botched up the Independence process.

Nehru 'finally awakened,' and admitted in a letter to the Nawab of Bhopal, a friend, 'Partition came and we accepted it because we thought that perhaps that way, however painful it was, we might have some peace.

'And yet, the consequences of that Partition have been so terrible that one is inclined to think that anything else would have been preferable,' Nehru added.

At the end of his six-year research and writing, Wolpert was looking for a picture for the book's dust jacket. He had gone through hundreds of pictures of Partition. And he had also seen pictures offering glimpses of thousands of people who perished in the tragedy – some estimates believe over a million were killed.

"Suddenly, I came across an image that encapsulated the tragedy," he says. It is a picture by the well-known photographer

Margaret Bourke-White, showing mostly bare-footed refugees going to places they felt would be safe from the communal carnage.

The image of a Sikh man in the same photograph carrying a woman on his shoulders also spoke volumes, Wolpert says. "The picture brought to our attention the fact that these poor, barefoot people with no possessions had to make the perilous journey because of the idiocy and arrogance of those who had a duty to protect them."

Partition - an event that even after so many years arouses multi-faceted responses, where long silences give way to sudden outbursts, where as much is buried as is revealed.

The recent years particularly have seen a rich body of literature on Partition, which is as vast as it is diverse. More intriguing than the fictional recalling of the traumatic times has been the new excitement in portals of academe to combine a study of the whys and hows of Partition with an analysis of pain and the limits of violence epitomised by it.

One is often troubled by this new-found interest in Partition. Memory, after all, is not just about remembering, it is also about forgetting. At the same time, to look at Partition through memory has also to do with the general dissatisfaction with the way conventional history about it has been written. And in spite of the vast, extremely rich writings now available on Partition, particularly the works of Urvashi Butalia, Ritu Menon and Gyanendra Pandey, one is still not sure if we have managed to grasp it in its totality, and more important, to come to terms with it.

The present book under review, put together in two volumes by the editors of the Indian Council of Historical Research, adds another chapter to the narratives on Partition. What is important here is that it covers a vast arena, in a total of 40 essays. However, I am not quite sure if it anywhere breaks new ground. Many of its writers have written more eloquently and extensively on the subjects covered elsewhere. While many of the essays are immensely readable, I think the main purpose that the volumes serve is to provide a peep into some of the work on the subject at one place.

Let me at the outset comment on the weakness of the two volumes. I think what they lack is a comprehensive introduction. It is the same for both the volumes, revealing that not much has gone into its writing.

There is no attempt by the editors to weave together a narrative thread and build certain key theoretical arguments, broad themes and insights on the basis of the rich array and variety of essays. They fail to address crucial questions of politics of identity.

At one place in the introduction the editors remark, "In any case, the fear of the Muslims has proved unfounded in the end as a substantial section of this community found a secure home in India and are thriving as freely as any other community in independent India" (emphasis mine) (p 8). I think the statement is too sweeping, especially when the memories of recent pogrom in Gujarat are fresh, and fails to even acknowledge the increasing communalisation of politics in recent times, the mounting insecurity, and attacks on Muslims and other minorities, and a greater than ever need to acknowledge and combat communalism.

The introduction also resorts to a simplified binary dualism between popular view and scholarly view, between historian's history and people's history, while actually the two deeply intersect, with no neat divisions between the two, as the essays themselves prove. In fact, there is a greater need for a space where the two commentaries are intermeshed.

Having said this, I must say that some of the essays in the volumes are a pleasure, especially in the second volume. Let me however begin with the first volume, which is more concerned with 'high' politics, of Congress and Gandhi, individuals like Mountbatten and the formation of the Constituent Assembly.

The first chapter by V N Dutta attempts to figure out the role of Lord Mountbatten in the Radcliffe Award, and if he unduly influenced him to change the boundary award in favour of Indian Pakistan – a question which does not have a definite answer. Gandhi was the saddest and at his heroic best during the days of Partition, a well known fact, different facets of which are covered in two articles by B R Nanda and Chittabrata Palit.

The imperialist stand is reviewed and questioned by Bishwa Mohan Pandey. Lal Bahadur Verma writes on a subject, which I think is much more eloquently covered from a different angle by Krishna Kumar in the second volume and more so in his recent book, on the impact of different approaches to Partition in the writing of history books in India and Pakistan. The late Partha Sarathi Gupta highlights the importance of documents as a corrective to stereotyped accounts. Sucheta Mahajan analyses the role of Congress in failing to keep the country united, an issue covered in a much more detailed fashion by her elsewhere. Salil Mishra, in chronicling the coalition politics in UP during 1937, lucidly reveals a turning point in the history of Partition.

The papers by Jayanta Sengupta, K S Singh and Bir Good Gill respectively show the happenings in the Oriya princely states, the role of some prominent tribal leaders and tribal politics in central India and the north-east and the role of the Akalis in Punjab. Dwijendra Tripathi and Sri Prakash essentially explore the politics of economics, in relation to the event. While most essays are competent, I found them often dry reading, perhaps because they are often 'official', 'statist' narratives, dissatisfaction with which has been often expressed by those working on Partition, and avidly by Gyanendra Pandey in his latest book *Remembering Partition.* Incidentally, I am surprised that there is no essay by him in the volumes, since he has written in depth on the subject.

### *The Human Dimension*

What has interested me more in the present work under review has been the second volume, which highlights the literary representations of Partition and the human dimension of the event. The essays here roughly cover personal reminiscences, recollections by contemporaries, impressions mirrored in creative literature and events and incidents which inspired the visual media, narratives and popular culture. Krishna Kumar's essay on the way Partition is written about in school textbooks across the divide provides us with a starting point to examine mentalities and attitudes.

However, since his book is recently out, it is much better to read that. The linguistic divide in northern India, particularly from the early twentieth century and the final triumph of sanskritised Khari Boli Hindi over Hindustani and Urdu has been covered widely in the writings of Christopher King, Suniti Chatterjee, and many others in a detailed fashion. R K Agnihotri writes on this well trodden field, but I am surprised that there is no reference to King's *One Language Two Script's* in it.

Literature dominates in this volume, and naturally so, since nowhere else has Partition been expressed more poignantly. A number of leading lights of literature have lent their pen to the volume, including Mrinal Pandey, Alok Bhalla and K S Duggal. Mrinal Pandey's short essay is actually almost a review of Urvashi Butalia's book *The Other Side of Silence*. Some essays are very short and almost read like literary notes, for example that of Duggal. Alok Bhalla has two essays and in the one where he undertakes a long and detailed interview with Bhisham Sahni, whose Tamas will rank among some of the best literature on Partition, is of great interest and relevance to us.

It is a delight to read Sahni, where there is almost a nostalgia for the syncretic culture of the past. His second essay talks of the problems in Khalid Hasan's English translation of Manto's Partition stories, simultaneously raising critical questions on the ethics of a translator. Alok Bhalla features yet again, this time through the essay of M Asaduddin, who finds in the stories on Partition collected by Alok Bhalla in three volumes multiple perspectives and visions of the event. Nandi Bhatia, Anindita Mukhopadhyay, Ameena K Ansari, Jayanti Chattopadhyay, M Asaduddin, Kamlesh Mohan, Shikoh Mohsin Mirza - all cover various literary writers and diverse dimensions of literary representations of the Partition. The paradoxical question of why partition found only fleeting presence in Bengali literature is taken up by Tapati Chakravarty.

Perhaps the most readable paper in the two volumes is one by Satish Gujral, where he reveals that he is not only a sensitive painter but can also narrate his reminiscences of Partition in a moving personal manner, revealing fragments and moments of brutality and indignity. Combined with the essay by Kehsav Malik, on the paintings of Satish Gujral on Partition, we get an insight into a sensitive and creative mind and heart. The short but well written essay by Partha Chatterjee reveals how in Ritwik Ghatak's films, Partition never figures directly; rather it is a riveting memory image of a cataclysmic event. Some essays are very short, like that of Badri Narain Tiwari on the way Partition is perceived in the popular mind in the Bhojpuri region.

Urvashi Butalia can be regarded as one of those who has shown deep sensitivity on Partition and particularly what it meant for women. In an essay, interspersed with thought provoking anecdotes, she reveals how silences speak and how oral histories deeply enrich conventional historical sources in understanding Partition. Combined with the essay by Monmayee Basu on the suffering of the Hindu women in Bengal directly affected by Partition, they make an effective case for oral evidence, especially to get women's side of the story.

Minus footnotes, many of the essays in this volume make for easy and touching reading. This volume is much more involving, since it touches a core, and brings forward the pain and tragedy in a sensitive manner. The two volumes together have so many essays that it is impossible for a reviewer to cover all of them, and thus I have just been able to provide a bird's-eye view on them.

Finally, I think that any work on Partition is incomplete if it is not plural. Suvir Kaul, in his recent edited book on the subject, *Partition of Memories,* has lucidly remarked that each time we teach the story of Partition in order to demonstrate Jinnah's guilt or the culpability of the Muslim League, and ignore the role played by religious chauvinists within the Congress or other political and social organisations, we tell a tale that deepens the divides signified by Partition.

Only a history which makes an attempt to underline the different and plural truths of what happened at the time, can help us to be more tolerant and better human beings. Literary narratives, oral accounts, constructs and interpretations as much as actual events, local happenings – all these acquire a critical importance for this very reason. The two volumes, in spite of their limitations and the fact that they break no new ground, are partially successful in bringing together these plural and multifaceted dimensions of Partition.

## Nehru, Jinnah Over Junagadh Issue

In New Delhi the only issue was when and how to move in. The Governor-General, Mountbatten, reported to the King: "A Cabinet meeting to consider the Junagadh situation summoned for 5 p.m. on 17th September. I was informed that the members of the Cabinet had, prior to this meeting, decided among themselves that military action was the only answer." He sent for Nehru and Patel and persuaded them "to take no decision which the world could interpret as putting India in the wrong and Pakistan in the right, and that all the resources of negotiation should first be exhausted".

A second track was set afoot, however, with Patel's blessings. V.P. Menon, Secretary to the Ministry of States, and N.M. Buch, Government's Regional Commissioner at Rajkot, along with military officers, discussed the situation with local politicians. U.N. Dhebar, later Congress president, reported to Patel on September 21, setting out the agreed strategy-a proclamation denouncing the Nawab of Junagadh and appointing a provisional government. "The Manifesto or Proclamation will be drawn upon American lines." The headquarters of the government "will be on Indian soil. As we acquire Junagadh territories, Government will shift there. We shall receive moral and material support. We will hold the meeting in course of the next week in Bombay. We shall send draft proclamation tomorrow .

Jinnah complained to Mountbatten about Indian troop movements in the region (September 18). Mountbatten's reply (September 22) reiterated India's position denying "information about large troop concentrations around Junagadh." He said: "Pakistan Government unilaterally proceeded to action which, it was made plain, Government of India could never and do not acquiesce in. Acceptance of accession to Pakistan cannot but be regarded by the Government of India as an encroachment on Indian sovereignty and inconsistent with friendly relations that should exist between the two Dominions.

This action of Pakistan is considered by the Government of India to be a clear attempt to cause disruption by extending the influence and boundaries of the Dominion of Pakistan in utter violation of the Principles on which partition was agreed upon and effected". None could doubt "the Principles" he was hinting at. He asked Pakistan to reconsider (that is, nullify) the accession or face "responsibility of consequences". He repeated Nehru's offer-"accept the verdict of the people of Junagadh in the matter of accession, the plebiscite being carried out under joint supervision of Indian and Junagadh governments"; effectively, under India's since the decrepit regime of Junagadh could hardly perform (page 608). It was a demand for surrender. Pakistan had no cards to play. India held them securely in its hands and decided to play them to a decisive conclusion.

September 25 was a fateful day. The Ministry of States issued a detailed press note complaining that Pakistan had accepted the accession "without any warning" (Sardar's Letters, page 80). In Bombay on that day, a Provisional Government of Free Junagadh was set up with Samaldas Gandhi as its president. Narendra P. Nathwani, later a High Court Judge, was one of its members. K.M. Munshi, who was close to Patel, drafted the "Declaration by the Subjects of Junadagh State" (vide K.M. Munshi; Somanatha: The Shrine Eternal; pages 68-9 for the text).

Pakistan had accepted the accession "in disregard of such declared wishes and in defiance of all natural ties which bind the people of Junagadh (82 per cent of whom are non-Muslims) to the people of Kathiawar and to the Dominion of India and in breach of the understanding on the basis of which certain parts of India were allowed to secede and form into a separate State of Pakistan; namely that only contiguous areas predominantly inhabited by Muslims were to be included into the Dominion of Pakistan with the free and willing consent of the people inhabiting those areas."

Munshi recorded: "The Provisional Government of Junagadh moved to Saurashtra and took possession of the Junagadh House at Rajkot. Young men from all over Saurashtra flocked to its banner of freedom. Large sums of money flowed in, volunteers were armed and trained. On the Dessehra Day, the "Day of Victory"-October 24, 1947-the volunteers of the Provisional Government began their operations. People rose against the Nawab's rule in several parts of Junagadh."

Did Jinnah and Liaquat follow contradictory policies? For Liaquat asked Mountbatten's Chief of Staff Ismay in Karachi: "Why, if it was suggested that a referendum should be held in Junagadh one should not be held in Kashmir?" This was discussed by the Indian Cabinet on September 22. Ismay was of the opinion that "one of the main objects of the Pakistan Government was to use Junagadh as a bargaining counter for Kashmir".

Liaquat and Nehru met in New Delhi on October 1 under Mountbatten's auspices. He reiterated the commitment to the democratic principle: "Nehru nodded his head sadly. Liaquat Ali Khan's eyes sparkled. There is no doubt that both of them were thinking of Kashmir." Nehru took Patel into confidence on September 25: "We are already considering the possibility of military action".

V.P. Menon records that on October 4, the Government of India considered the Junagadh situation: "It was decided to inform the Prime Minister of Pakistan that the only basis on which friendly negotiations could start and be fruitful was the reversion of Junagadh to the status quo preceding the accession of Junagadh to Pakistan and that the alternative to negotiations was a plebiscite." So much for the sanctity of the Instrument of Accession.

In a statement on October 5, 1947, the Government of India said: "Any decision involving the fate of large numbers of people must necessarily depend on the wishes of these people. This is the policy which the Government of India accept in its entirety and they are of the opinion that a dispute involving the fate of the people of any territory should be decided by a referendum or plebiscite of the people concerned. This is a method at once democratic, peaceful and just. They suggest, therefore, that the issues regarding Junagadh should be decided by a referendum or plebiscite of the people of the State. Such a referendum or plebiscite should be held under impartial auspices to be determined by the parties concerned."

Two days later, the Government of Pakistan issued a statement setting out its views on the accession of Junagadh. The statement suggested the withdrawal of troops by the Government of India from Sardargarh and Batva and by Junagadh from Babariawad:

"The Pakistan Government have also informed the Government of India of their willingness to discuss the conditions and circumstances in which a plebiscite should be taken by any State or States." Why did Jinnah not affirm this on November 1?

Unable to bear the pressures, Shah Nawaz Bhutto pleaded with Jinnah, on October 27, urging that "you immediately arrange for a conference of the representatives of the two Dominions to decide the Junagadh issue." On November 5, the Junagadh State Council decided on "a complete reorientation of the State policy... even if it involves a reversal of the earlier decision to accede to Pakistan". The Dewan was authorised to negotiate.

Bhutto cashed the blank cheque by opening negotiations with Samaldas Gandhi on November 7 through Capt. Harvey Jones, Senior Member of the Junagadh State Council, asking him to take over the State's administration. It was decided, however, to hand over the State to the Government of India instead. On November 8, Bhutto wrote to Buch on these lines (V.P. Menon, Integration of Indian States; page 137).

On November 9, the Indian Army moved into Junagadh. Nehru formally informed Liaquat about the move. Admiral Satyindra Singh has recorded the Navy's plans "to land the Indian Army for the Junagadh operations-Exercise Peace as it was called" (The Statesman; September 21, 1997). On December 8, at a meeting with Liaquat in New Delhi, as Mountbatten recorded: "Pandit Nehru, while openly admitting that India had been in some ways in the wrong about Junagadh, claimed that the parallel with Kashmir was not tenable because of the vast differences in scale between the two".

Both Nehru and Mountbatten realised now what India was up against. "The fact is that Kashmir is of the utmost vital significance to India as well as to Pakistan. There lies the rub," Nehru wrote to Sri Prakasa, High Commissioner to Pakistan. Earlier he had dismissed Pakistan's interest in Kashmir and began doing just that later. New Delhi sticks to this stand even in 2001, rendering compromise impossible. Nehru admitted: "Kashmir is going to be a drain on our resources, but it is going to be a greater drain on Pakistan.

In a military sense we are stronger." India could not quit. "Kashmir gives us an example of communal unity and cooperation. This has had a healthy effect in India and any weakening in Kashmir by us would create a far more difficult communal situation in India" (SWJN; Vol. 4; pages 346-7). Nehru lived to see the situation in Kashmir deteriorate to a point where Jan Sangh leader S.P. Mookerjee could exploit it in 1952-53 to whip up communalism. Things have worsened since. The "drain" on resources continues.

Mountbatten told both Nehru and Liaquat on December 8 that "the whole future welfare of India depended on an agreement over Kashmir between the two Dominions. The effect that such an agreement would have on world opinion would also be very great" (ibid; p. 361). But, Sir Chimanlal Setalvad had foreseen it all even as the events had begun to unfold. In a letter to The Times of India (October 3, 1947) he wrote: "Many of those who are enthusing over the activities of the so-called 'Provisional Government' of Junagadh do not seem to realise the dangerous consequences that are likely to follow from what is happening.

The Junagadh Government has acted unwisely in acceding to Pakistan, ignoring geographical considerations and the wishes of its subjects, but that affords no justification for what is being done. The 'Provisional Government' was formed and functioned for some days in Bombay with the avowed object of overthrowing by force the established Government in Junagadh."

He renewed his plea after the Kashmir crisis erupted. "Pandit Nehru in his broadcast has rightly asked the Pakistan Government how and why the invaders of Kashmir came across the Frontier Province or West Punjab, and how they came to be fully armed. He charges the Pakistan Government with violation of international law and an unfriendly act towards India. He alleges that the Pakistan Government was either too weak to prevent the invaders of Kashmir from marching across its territory or that it was willing that this should happen. Exactly the same poser can be put to the Indian Dominion with regard to Junagadh".

The Government of India held a plebiscite in Junagadh as well as five of its erstwhile feudatories on February 20, 1948. It was conducted by an ICS officer C.B. Nagarkar. Out of an electorate of 2,01,457, 1,90,870 cast their votes. Only 91 voted for Pakistan. Of the 31,434 votes cast in the five princeling areas, only 39 voted for accession to Pakistan (Menon; page 142). The result would not have been different even if the U.N. had conducted this plebiscite.

But it puts paid to the debating ploys about "no self-determination for a part of the nation" and "the core of nationalism". Junagadh was quintessentially Indian. Negotiations on plebiscite in Kashmir came to a naught because for five years (1949-53) Nehru would not yield on the powers of the Abdullah government or on the strength of Indian forces in the State. Their presence was not in issue. He then proceeded to argue that efflux of time had rendered the accord on plebiscite obsolete.

Pakistan's aggression in 1965 extinguished the option of plebiscite. But its grievances of old persist. Thanks to India's policies, the alienation of Kashmiris has deepened. Time has not extinguished the "Kashmir dispute". None in the wide world believes it has.

Today, in 2001, India needs seriously to grapple with the problem of forging a sound and realistic foreign policy in a democracy so that it can craft a Kashmir solution which does not entail the State's secession-yet goes beyond the Line of Control. India cannot countenance the former; Pakistan cannot, the latter. Therein lies a challenge to diplomatic creativity.

The Volume gives glimpses of Jinnah's remarkable personality. A man of sterling integrity, courage and sharp and cold intelligence, he stumbled badly in the hour of triumph and left the State he had created a heritage it could have well done without. Nehru did likewise.

While respecting their memory, we need to learn from their mistakes in order to chart a new course. Recall the murky record, we must. For, as George F. Kennan wrote: "When the ambivalence of one's virtue is recognised, the total inequity of one's opponent is also irreparably impaired". This applies to both sides-and Junagadh remains a dark chapter which neither wishes to recall.

# 6 Nehru Relations with Patel

Sardar Vallabhbhai Patel's letter to Jawaharlal Nehru on 7 November 1950 not only deploring Indian Ambassador KM Panikkar's action but also warning about dangers from China

My dear Jawaharlal,

Ever since my return from Ahmedabad and after the cabinet meeting the same day which I had to attend at practically fifteen minutes' notice and for which I regret I was not able to read all the papers, I have been anxiously thinking over the problem of Tibet and I thought I should share with you what is passing through my mind.

I have carefully gone through the correspondence between the External Affairs Ministry and our Ambassador in Peking and through him the Chinese Government. I have tried to peruse this correspondence as favourably to our Ambassador and the Chinese Government as possible, but I regret to say that neither of them comes out well as a result of this study. The Chinese Government has tried to delude us by professions of peaceful intention. My own feeling is that at a crucial period they managed to instill into our Ambassador a false sense of confidence in their so-called desire to settle the Tibetan problem by peaceful means.

There can be no doubt that during the period covered by this correspondence the Chinese must have been concentrating for an onslaught on Tibet. The final action of the Chinese, in my judgement, is little short of perfidy. The tragedy of it is that the Tibetans put faith in us; they chose to be guided by us; and we have been unable to get them out of the meshes of Chinese diplomacy or Chinese malevolence. From the latest position, it appears that we shall not be able to rescue the Dalai Lama. Our Ambassador has been at great pains to find an explanation or justification for Chinese policy and actions.

As the External Affairs Ministry remarked in one of their telegrams, there was a lack of firmness and unnecessary apology in one or two representations that he made to the Chinese Government on our behalf. It is impossible to imagine any sensible person believing in the so-called threat to China from Anglo-American machinations in Tibet. Therefore, if the Chinese put faith in this, they must have distrusted us so completely as to have taken us as tools or stooges of Anglo-American diplomacy or strategy. This feeling, if genuinely entertained by the Chinese in spite of your direct approaches to them, indicates that even though we regard ourselves as the friends of China, the Chinese do not regard us as their friends. With the Communist mentality of "whoever is not with them being against them", this is a significant pointer, of which we have to take due note.

During the last several months, outside the Russian camp, we have practically been alone in championing the cause of Chinese entry into UN and in securing from the Americans assurances on the question of Formosa. We have done everything we could to assuage Chinese feelings, to allay its apprehensions and to defend its legitimate claims in our discussions and correspondence with America and Britain and in the UN. Inspite of this, China is not convinced about our disinterestedness; it continues to regard us with suspicion and the whole psychology is one, at least outwardly, of scepticism perhaps mixed with a little hostility. I doubt if we can go any further than we have done already to convince China of our good intentions, friendliness and goodwill.

In Peking we have an Ambassador who is eminently suitable for putting across the friendly point of view. Even he seems to have failed to convert the Chinese. Their last telegram to us is an act of gross discourtesy not only in the summary way it disposes of our protest against the entry of Chinese forces into Tibet but also in the wild insinuation that our attitude is determined by foreign influences. It looks as though it is not a friend speaking in that language but a potential enemy.

In the background of this, we have to consider what new situation now faces us as a result of the disappearance of Tibet, as we knew it, and the expansion of China almost up to our gates. Throughout history we have seldom been worried about our north-east frontier. The Himalayas have been regarded as an impenetrable barrier against any threat from the north. We had a friendly Tibet which gave us no trouble. The Chinese were divided. They had their own domestic problems and never bothered us about frontiers.

In 1914, we entered into a convention with Tibet which was not endorsed by the Chinese. We seem to have regarded Tibetan autonomy as extending to independent treaty relationship. Presumably, all that we required was Chinese counter-signature. The Chinese interpretation of suzerainty seems to be different. We can, therefore, safely assume that very soon they will disown all the stipulations which Tibet has entered into with us in the past. That throws into the melting pot all frontier and commercial settlements with Tibet on which we have been functioning and acting during the last half a century. China is no longer divided.

It is united and strong. All along the Himalayas in the north and north-east, we have on our side of the frontier a population ethnologically and culturally not different from Tibetans and Mongoloids. The undefined state of the frontier and the existence on our side of a population with its affinities to the Tibetans or Chinese have all the elements of the potential trouble between China and ourselves. Recent and bitter history also tells us that Communism is no shield against imperialism and that the communists are as good or as bad imperialists as any other. Chinese ambitions in this respect not only cover the Himalayan slopes on our side but also include the important part of Assam.

They have their ambitions in Burma also. Burma has the added difficulty that it has no McMahon Line round which to build up even the semblance of an agreement. Chinese irredentism and communist imperialism are different from the expansionism or imperialism of the western powers. The former has a cloak of ideology which makes it ten times more dangerous. In the guise of ideological expansion lie concealed racial, national or historical claims.

The danger from the north and north-east, therefore, becomes both communist and imperialist. While our western and north-western threat to security is still as prominent as before, a new threat has developed from the north and north-east. Thus, for the first time, after centuries, India's defence has to concentrate itself on two fronts simultaneously. Our defence measures have so far been based on the calculations of superiority over Pakistan. In our calculations we shall now have to reckon with communist China in the north and in the north-east, a communist China which has definite ambitions and aims and which does not, in any way, seem friendly disposed towards us.

Let us also consider the political conditions on this potentially troublesome frontier. Our northern and north-eastern approaches consist of Nepal, Bhutan, Sikkim, Darjeeling and the tribal areas in Assam. From the point of view of communication, there are weak spots. Continuous defensive lines do not exist. There is almost an unlimited scope for infiltration. Police protection is limited to a very small number of passes. There, too, our outposts do not seem to be fully manned. The contact of these areas with us is by no means close and intimate.

The people inhabiting these portions have no established loyalty or devotion to India. Even Darjeeling and Kalimpong areas are not free from pro-Mongoloid prejudices. During the last three years, we have not been able to make any appreciable approaches to the Nagas and other hill tribes in Assam. European missionaries and other visitors had been in touch with them, but their influence was in no way friendly to India or Indians. In Sikkim, there was political ferment some time ago.

It is quite possible that discontent is smouldering there. Bhutan is comparatively quiet, but its affinity with Tibetans would be a handicap. Nepal has a weak oligarchic regime based almost entirely on force: it is in conflict with a turbulent element of the population as well as with enlightened ideas of the modern age.

In these circumstances, to make people alive to the new danger or to make them defensively strong is a very difficult task indeed and that difficulty can be got over only by enlightened firmness, strength and a clear line of policy. I am sure the Chinese and their source of inspiration, Soviet Union, would not miss any oppoıtunity of exploiting these weak spots, partly in support of their ideology and partly in support of their ambitions.

In my judgement the situation is one which we cannot afford either to be complacent or to be vacillating. We must have a clear idea of what we wish to achieve and also of the methods by which we should achieve it. Any faltering or lack of decisiveness in formulating our objectives or in pursuing our policies to attain those objectives is bound to weaken us and increase the threats which are so evident.

Side by side with these external dangers, we shall now have to face serious internal problems as well. I have already asked Iengar to send to the External Affairs Ministry a copy of the Intelligence Bureau's appreciation of these matters Hitherto, the Communist Party of India has found some difficulty in contacting communists abroad, or in getting supplies of arms, literature, etc., from them. They had to contend with the difficult Burmese and Pakistan frontiers on the east or with the long seaboard. They shall now have a comparatively easy means of access to Chinese communists and through them to other foreign communists.

Infiltration of spies, fifth columnists and communists would now be easier. Instead of having to deal with isolated communist pockets in Telengana and Warrangal we may have to deal with communist threats to our security along our northern and north-eastern frontiers, where, for supplies of arms and ammunition, they can safely depend on communist arsenals in China. The whole situation thus raises a number of problems on which we must come to an early decision so that we can, as I said earlier, formulate the objectives of our policy and decide the method by which those objectives are to be attained. It is also clear that the action will have to be fairly comprehensive, involving not only our defence strategy and state of preparations but also problem of internal security to deal with which we have not a moment to lose. We shall also have to deal with administrative and political problems in the weak spots along the frontier to which I have already referred.

It is of course, impossible to be exhaustive in setting out all these problems. I am, however, giving below some of the problems which, in my opinion, require early solution and round which we have to build our administrative or military policies and measures to implement them.

a) A military and intelligence appreciation of the Chinese threat to India both on the frontier and to internal security.

b) An examination of military position and such redisposition of our forces as might be necessary, particularly with the idea of guarding important routes or areas which are likely to be the subject of dispute.

c) An appraisement of the strength of our forces and, if necessary, reconsideration of our retrenchment plans for the Army in the light of the new threat.

d) A long-term consideration of our defence needs. My own feeling is that, unless we assure our supplies of arms, ammunition and armour, we would be making our defence perpetually weak and we would not be able to stand up to the double threat of difficulties both from the west and north-west and north and north-east.

e) The question of China's entry into the UN. In view of the rebuff which China has given us and the method which it has followed in dealing with Tibet, I am doubtful whether we can advocate its claim any longer. There would probably be a threat in the UN virtually to outlaw China, in view of its active participation in the Korean war. We must determine our attitude on this question also.

f) The political and administrative steps which we should take to strengthen our northern and north-eastern frontier. This would include the whole of the border, ie. Nepal, Bhutan, Sikkim, Darjeeling and the tribal territory in Assam.

g) Measures of internal security in the border areas as well as the states flanking those areas such as Uttar Pradesh, Bihar, Bengal and Assam.

h) Improvement of our communication, road, rail, air and wireless, in these areas and with the frontier outposts.

i) The future of our mission at Lhasa and the trade posts at Gyangtse and Yatung and the forces which we have in operation in Tibet to guard the trade routes.

j) The policy in regard to the McMahon Line.

These are some of the questions which occur to my mind. It is possible that a consideration of these matters may lead us into wider question of our relationship with China, Russia, America, Britain and Burma. This, however, would be of a general nature, though some might be basically very important, e.g., we might have to consider whether we should not enter into closer association with Burma in order to strengthen the latter in its dealings with China. I do not rule out the possibility that, before applying pressure on us, China might apply pressure on Burma. With Burma, the frontier is entirely undefined and the Chinese territorial claims are more substantial. In its present position, Burma might offer an easier problem to China, and therefore, might claim its first attention.

I suggest that we meet early to have a general discussion on these problems and decide on such steps as we might think to be immediately necessary and direct, quick examination of other problems with a view to taking early measures to deal with them.

***Vallabhbhai Patel, The legacy of Nehru***

THE first months of independence were anything but easy. Often emotional, Jawaharlal was caught up in the human drama of the times. He was seen weeping at the sight of a victim one day, and erupting in rage at a would-be assailant hours later. Friends thought his physical health would be in danger as he stormed from city to village, ordering his personal bodyguards to shoot any Hindu who might attack a Muslim, providing refuge in his own home in Delhi for Muslims terrified for their lives, giving employment to young refugees who had lost everything. In one typical incident of the period, Jawaharlal emerged from a visit to a fasting Mahatma Gandhi in mid-January 1948 and confronted a demonstration of refugees chanting "Let Gandhi die!" He leapt from his car and dashed towards the demonstrators shouting, "How dare you say these words! Come and kill me first!" The demonstrators immediately ran away.

Affairs of state were just as draining. The new Prime Minister of India had to deal with the consequences of the carnage sweeping the country; preside over the integration of the princely states into the Indian Union; settle disputes with Pakistan on issues involving the division of finances, of the army, and of territory; cope with massive internal displacement, as refugees thronged Delhi and other cities; keep a fractious and divided nation together; and define both a national and an international agenda. On all issues but that of foreign policy, he relied heavily on Patel, who welded the new country into one with formidable political and administrative skills and a will of iron. A more surprising ally was the former Viceroy, now Governor-General of India, Lord Mountbatten.

For all his culpability in rushing India to an independence drenched in blood, Mountbatten made Nehru partial amends by staying on in India for just under a year. As heir to a British government whose sympathy for the League had helped it carve out a country from the collapse of the Raj, Mountbatten enjoyed a level of credibility with the rulers of Pakistan that no Indian Governor-General could have had. This made him a viable and impartial interlocutor with both sides at a time of great tension. Equally, as a Governor-General above the political fray, he played a crucial role in persuading maharajahs and nawabs distrustful of the socialist Nehru to accept that they had no choice but to merge their domains into the Indian Union.

When fighting broke out over Kashmir between the two Dominions (whose armies were still each commanded by a British general), Mountbatten helped prevent a deeper engagement by the Pakistani Army and brought about an end to the war. And the Governor-General and his wife distinguished themselves by their personal interest in and leadership of the emergency relief measures that saved millions of desperate refugees from misery and worse. In 1950, when India became a Republic with its own Constitution, Jawaharlal arranged for it to remain within the British

Commonwealth, acknowledging the British sovereign no longer as head of state but as the symbol of the free association of nations who wished to retain a British connection. Mountbatten's influence was decisive in prompting Jawaharlal to make this choice. Nehru's close relations with Edwina Mountbatten have been the stuff of much posthumous gossip, but his relationship with her husband was to have much more lasting impact on India's history.

As Prime Minister, Jawaharlal had ultimate responsibility for many of the decisions taken during the tense period 1947-49, but it is true to say he was still finding his feet as a governmental leader and that on many key issues he simply went along with what Patel and Mountbatten wanted. Nehru was the uncontested voice of Indian nationalism, the man who had "discovered" India in his own imagination, but he could not build the India of his vision without help. When the Muslim rulers of Hindu-majority Junagadh and Hyderabad, both principalities surrounded by Indian territory, flirted with independence (in Hyderabad's case) and accession to Pakistan (in Junagadh's), the Indian Army marched in and took over with scarcely a shot being fired. In both cases the decision was Patel's, with acquiescence from Nehru....

Apart from handling weighty matters of state, Jawaharlal had to deal with issues of domestic politics. He had surprised some of his most ardent supporters by his reluctance to embrace radical change, and his willingness to retain, and indeed rely on, the very civil servants and armed services personnel who had served the British Raj, the "steel frame" of which continued as the administrative superstructure of independent India. The Government proved its worth in handling the absorption of some seven million refugees from Pakistan, a colossal political and administrative feat. But the civil service continued in the traditions of colonial governance learned from their British masters; Nehru did little to instil in them a development orientation or a new ethic of service to the people. Continuity, not change, was the watchword. Many of the freedom fighters, who had gone to jail while these officials prospered under the British, were dismayed ...

Gandhi's assassination by a Hindu fanatic strengthened his hand on the communal issue. Even Patel agreed to the RSS being banned, though the ban was lifted after a year. On other questions, ranging from the grant of "privy purses" (or annual subventions to the erstwhile maharajahs to compensate for the loss of their princely states) to the clash between the right to property and the need for land reform, he found himself outmanoeuvered by the party's right wing. Patel ran his Home Ministry as firmly as he administered the country as a whole, and he brooked little interference from Nehru.

Lord Mountbatten left India for good on 21 June 1948, ten months after he had presided over its freedom—and its dismemberment. He was succeeded as Governor-General of the Dominion by the man who had once been thought more likely than Jawharlal to be Gandhi's heir, C. Rajagopalachari. Though temperamentally a conservative, "Rajaji" had no patience for the communal sympathies of the Congress right, and so in his own way complemented Jawaharlal as head of state. But when the time came for that position to be converted to that of President of the Republic (upon the adoption of independent India's new Constitution on the symbolic date of 26 January 1950, the old "Independence Day" becoming the new Republic Day), Patel engineered the election of his crony Rajendra Prasad as the Congress candidate. Jawaharlal had been completely bypassed; he was so surprised that he actually asked Prasad to withdraw and propose Rajagopalachari's name himself. Prasad cleverly suggested that he would do whatever Nehru and Patel agreed upon, at which point Nehru understood and threw in the towel. One of Prasad's first acts upon election was to ask that 26 January be changed to a date deemed more auspicious by his astrologers. Jawaharlal flatly turned him down, declaring that India would not be run by astrologers if he had anything to do with it. This time, Nehru won.

Nehru and Patel came dangerously close to a public clash only once. In 1950, under pressure from the right to intervene militarily in East Pakistan where a massacre of Hindus had begun, Jawaharlal first tried to work with his Pakistani counterpart, Liaquat Ali Khan, on a joint approach to communal disturbances and then, when this had been ignored, offered President Prasad his resignation. (Stanley Wolpert has speculated that Jawaharlal, exhausted and heartsick, was contemplating eloping with Edwina

Mountbatten, who had just been visiting him at the time.) But when Patel called a meeting of Congressmen at his home to criticize Jawaharlal's weakness on the issue, Nehru fought back, withdrawing his offer of resignation, challenging Patel to a public debate on Pakistan policy and even writing to express doubt as to whether the two of them could work together any more. The counter-assault was so ferocious that Patel backed off and affirmed his loyalty to Jawaharlal, supporting the pact Nehru signed with his Pakistani counterpart (which had even prompted the two Cabinet Ministers from Bengal to resign). The entire episode marked the closest the Congress would ever come to repudiating Nehru in his lifetime.

But in those early days Jawaharlal was not always a successful political infighter. His setback over Prasad's election was echoed in the elections to the Congress party presidency a few months later. Having withdrawn from the race himself on the grounds that it would not be proper for him as Prime Minister to also serve as party President, Jawaharlal supported his old rival Kripalani against the rightist Purushottamdas Tandon (the very man whose inability to win Muslim support for the chairmanship of the Allahabad municipality had given Jawaharlal his experience of mayoralty in 1923). But Tandon had Patel's backing, and despite Jawaharlal's open opposition, won handily, with over 50% of the votes in a three-man field. Nehru publicly grumbled that the result would only please communal and reactionary forces in the country, and refused to join Tandon's Working Committee.

When finally cajoled into doing so he made no secret of his reluctance. He spent the next year undermining Tandon much as his mentor Mahatma Gandhi had undermined Bose thirteen years earlier. In September 1951 Jawaharlal brought matters to a head by resigning his party positions and making it clear that he and Tandon could not co-exist: one of them had to go. Tandon did. Jawaharlal himself was elected Congress President, his earlier scruples about the Prime Minister serving in such a position completely forgotten. There was another reason for the decisiveness of his victory. By this time Nehru's greatest rival, Sardar Patel, was dead. He had suffered a heart attack a few months after the Mahatma's assassination; then stomach cancer struck, and in

December 1950, having fulfilled his historic role of consolidating India's fragile freedom, he passed away, aged 76. Patel and Nehru had also served as a check upon each other, and his passing away left Jawaharlal unchallenged.

If ever there was a moment when he might have been tempted by the prospect of near-dictatorial authority, this might have been it, but Jawaharlal remained a convinced democrat. He was not, however, a native one. He realized that the Home Ministry, with its control over the institutions of law and order, was a valuable tool for a potential competitor. He was therefore careful after the Sardar's death to appoint only trusted associates—with no competing political ambitions or agendas of their own—to the Home Ministry.

## Sardar Vallabhbhai Patel—Relations with Nehru

Sardar Patel's relationship with Nehru has always been a source of controversy and intense historical interest. But it's most important phase came between 1947 to 1950, India's first years as a free nation. Chakravarti Rajagopalachari, Nehru and Patel formed the *Triumvirate* which ruled India. Prime Minister Nehru was intensely popular with the masses, but did not enjoy the enormous loyalty and respect Patel had for his political judgment, leadership and integrity within the Congress Party and among most Indian nationalists. Even the British were forced to admit that Patel was the only leader capable of standing up to Gandhi, and the most dangerous as well. Patel was intensely loyal to Gandhi, and both he and Nehru looked to him to arbitrate disputes.

Nehru and Patel sparred intensely over national issues. Patel objected to Nehru overruling his Home Ministry's officials, such as sending his own representative to Ajmer, the scene of communal violence, despite a senior Ministry official having already gone there and Patel himself personally briefing Nehru. Nehru had not bothered to inform Patel of his intentions. Nehru felt offended by Patel making important decisions regarding the states integration without reference to him or the Cabinet. Beneath this lay core ideological differences. Patel was a Hindu who was proud of ancient traditions and Indian culture. He was from the sturdy peasantry of Gujarat, who proudly owned and worked their lands. Nehru was a socialist who despised rituals and religious dogma, who was rich and Westernized in thinking, attitude and mannerism.

An exasperated Patel did not want to battle Nehru, and asked Gandhi to relieve him. He did not have Nehru's youth and popularity, which would overtake him in time, and he knew that an open political battle would hurt India. After much personal deliberation and contrary to Patel's judgment, Gandhi on January 30, 1948 told Patel not to leave the Government, and to stay by Nehru's side. India, according to Gandhi, desperately needed the joint leadership, and Patel. He was assassinated just an hour afterwards. Patel was the last man to have had an intimate conversation with the Mahatma.

At Gandhi's wake, Nehru and Patel embraced each other, and addressed the nation together. However, criticism soon arose from the media and other politicians that Patel's Home Ministry had failed to protect Gandhi. An emotionally exhausted Patel wrote out a letter of resignation, offering to leave the Government despite Gandhi's word so that he may not embarrass Nehru's administration any further. Patel's secretary convinced him to withhold the letter, seeing it as fodder for Patel's enemies and political conflict in India.

Nehru sent Patel a personal letter dismissing any idea of personal differences and that he wanted Patel to leave. He reminded Patel of their 30 year partnership in the freedom struggle, and that after Gandhi's death, it was especially wrong for them to quarrel. Moved, Patel personally and publicly endorsed Nehru's leadership and refuted any suggestion of discord. Patel dispelled any notion that he would like to be India's Prime Minister. He recognized Nehru's importance, and his sacred word to Gandhi. The two committed themselves to joint leadership, and non-interference in Congress party affairs. However, the two would criticize each other in matters of policy. Nehru remained an opponent of Patel's plan to forcibly integrate Hyderabad, and against Patel's advice asked for the United Nations to arbitrate the Kashmir dispute. The former Nehru had to conceed in 1948, and the latter became a source of intense criticism in the years afterward.

Nehru also resisted Patel's counsel on sending assistance to Tibet, which had been invaded by China, and ejecting the Portuguese from Goa by military force. The former resulted in the 1962 Sino-Indian War and the latter was done by Nehru himself in 1961. Patel did not himself force the issue at the time. But Patel did not help Nehru when he had purposely bypassed him, only later to need his help.

Nehru attempted to oppose the will of a majority of Congressmen by suggesting that Governor General Chakravarti Rajgopalachari become India's first President. Nehru's arbitrariness and imposition angered the party, which backed its favorite, Dr. Rajendra Prasad. Patel did not help Nehru to win his way, and Prasad became the President of India in 1950. Nehru also opposed the 1950 Congress presidential candidacy of Purushottam Das Tandon, a Hindu conservative leader. Endorsing Jivatram Kripalani himself, Nehru attempted to thwart Tandon's bid, threatening to resign if he were elected. The party voted for Tandon, and Patel endorsed Tandon in Gujarat, where Kripalani received not one vote despite hailing from that state himself. Patel also personally encouraged Nehru and assured him that he should continue as Prime Minister after Prasad's election to the Presidency, which had made Nehru feel that the party was revolting.

## Nehru, Patel and Gandhi

The history of India would have been different had Sardar Patel not been the Deputy Prime Minister when India became independent in 1947. The triumvirate- Gandhiji, Nehru and Sardar Patel were responsible for giving direction to the destiny of the country. Sardar Patel consolidated the country into one united whole in a unique manner.

### *Formative Years*

Born on October 31, 1875 at Nadiad, in the Kaira district of Gujarat, Vallabh Bhai Patel was the son of Zaverbhai Galabhai Patel, a Leva Patidar. This class of cultivators was known for their simple character, industrious habits and straightforward dealings. Vallabh Bhai possessed an ingenous mind as a school boy. He was a rebel whose exceptional organisational abilities were recognised by his schoolmates and teachers. Patel passed the matriculation examination from the Nadiad High School in 1897. Patel had two ambitions to fulfil, first to become a pleader and later a barrister. During those days a matriculate could become a lawyer by taking the pleaders examination. He became a pleader in 1900, and started practising in Godhra.

In 1902 he shifted to Balsad, a taluka headquarter, where he practised as a criminal lawyer for nearly eight years, during which period he had built a name for himself as a most successful criminal lawyer. In 1910, he left for London and joined the Middle Temple, where he took an examination in Roman Law and stood first. He returned to India in 1913 and started practising as a barrister in Ahmedabad, fulfilling his second ambition.

### *Gandhiji's Disciple*

The impact of Gandhiji's personality on Vallabhbhai was tremendous. It gave him a new mission in life. The Champaran struggle waged by Gandhiji had a sweeping effect on Patel's mind. In Gandhiji's Champaran victory Patel saw the beginning of a new agrarian revolution. His interest in politics had been kindled, as became abundantly clear in the Provincial Political Conference organised by the Gujarat Sabha and presided by Gandhiji at Godhara. The conference appointed a permanent committee with Gandhiji as the President and Patel as one of the secretaries. He became a staunch follower of Gandhiji. From then on there was no looking back. Blessed with rare qualities of fortitude, integrity and an iron determination, Patel played an important role in the freedom movement.

### *Indomitable Personality*

It was due to his sterling leadership and practical vision that the peasant movement in Gujarat became a success. It was in this struggle that the organisational capacity for which Sardar Patel was famous in the whole country became visible. He took over as the nascent nation's Home Minister at a very crucial juncture in history and devoted himself whole heartedly to ensure that the country which was already partitioned, remained intact and united.

### *Building a Union*

On the eve of their departure, the British government announced that its paramountcy would lapse not only over the British territory but even over the native States. This meant that as many as 625 small and big native States would become independent like India and Pakistan. Consequently, the country would be divided into a number of small and big units.

Before embarking on this mammoth task, Sardar sought to ensure the stability of administration by forging a bridge of faith and confidence with the"Steel Frame". Most of the I.C.S. officers suspected that the Congress leaders, particularly Sardar in view of his past experiences with them, would have no faith in the I.C.S. But Sardar rose to the occasion and reposed total trust in their capability to serve the nation.

He was, thus, able to win their unstinted support in the endeavour of nation building. Attempts were afoot for finalising the standstill agreement with the States. It provided that the Central Government will be vested with powers of defence, foreign policy and communications even over the States. Travancore, Hyderabad and some other States declared themselves sovereign States and created hurdles in the agreement. On the other end, Jinnah with a view to tempt Jodhpur, Jaisalmer and other border States made them an unconditional offer to align with Pakistan on their terms.

### *Political Sagacity*

To find an amicable solution to this complicated situation, Sardar issued a statement to the princes wherein he appealed to their sense of patriotism and reiterated that the new States department in no way, desire to have supremacy over them. "If at all, any sense of supremacy is required, it would be with common understanding and for common good. We are at a momentous stage in the history of India. By common endeavour, we can raise the country to new greatness, while lack of unity will expose us to unexpected calamities. I hope the Indian States will realise fully that if we do not cooperate and work together in the general interest, anarchy and chaos will overwhelm us all great and small, and lead us to total ruin". The statement which amply reflected his statesmanship and political sagacity, removed whatever doubts lurked in the minds of the princes.

There was a popular agitation in Travancore and the State acceded to India. The Nawab of Bhopal could not take all this but when he realised that there was no alternative, he sent the instrument of accession duly signed to Sardar. A man of iron will and absolute fearlessness, Sardar Patel tackled the question of 550 and odd State territories and principalities in such a strategic manner which left even his wildest critics in complete amazement. Almost within a year he redrew the map of India with every princely State joining the Indian union and thus, forming part of the political stream of life that was endowed with cultural unity and harmony.

***Intricate Situation***

The intricacy of the situation can perhaps be gauged by the fact that there were 26 small States in Orissa and 15 in the Chattisgarh area of present Madhya Pradesh. It required skilful diplomacy on the part of Sardar Patel to persuade them to merge into bigger, more viable units. Even more ticklish was the case of Saurashtra where there were 14 big States, 119 small States and other units under different administrations totalling 860.

The herculean task of merging all of them into the Saurashtra union was also accomplished by Sardar Patel. Soon, State after State started acceding to the Indian Union. One after the other, Gwalior, Indore, Dhar, Dewas all accepted the advice of Sardar. Rajputana States followed the same. The Sikhs of Punjab also cooperated with the merger.

Even by August 15, Hyderabad kept aloof. Hence, Lord Mountbatten himself started negotiations. At one stage, it appeared that there was a settlement but Nizam found himself helpless against the pressures of Razakars. The Razakars started harassing the local public. Thus, when the situation went out of control, Sardar with the consent of the Governor General initiated police action. In 108 hours, the Nizam surrendered and Hyderabad acceded and merged with India. The Nawab of Junagadh accepted an accession with Pakistan. Sardar solved this complex problem in his own inimitable way and the Nawab and his Diwan left Junagadh for Pakistan.

Thus, the 'Yagna' for establishment of a united India undertaken by Sardar was completed with the merger of Hyderabad. Politically, India became one and united. In the history of India stretched over ages, India became one and united for the first time and that too without shedding a drop of blood. That was the marvel of the personality of Sardar. The sterling qualities of leadership he had shown as leader of Satyagraha, flowered in greater way in the administration of the country, maintenance of law and order and ensuring stability of the country and making it invulnerable.

# 7 Nehru and Indian Foreign Policy

### *Foreign Relations*

India's Foreign Relations reflect a traditional policy of nonalignment (see Glossary), the exigencies of domestic economic reform and development, and the changing post-Cold War international environment. India's relations with the world have evolved considerably since the British colonial period (1757-1947), when a foreign power monopolized external relations and defense relations. On independence in 1947, few Indians had experience in making or conducting foreign policy. However, the country's oldest political party, the Indian National Congress (the Congress—see Glossary), had established a small foreign department in 1925 to make overseas contacts and to publicize its freedom struggle. From the late 1920s on, Jawaharlal Nehru, who had the most long-standing interest in world affairs among independence leaders, formulated the Congress stance on international issues. As a member of the interim government in 1946, Nehru articulated India's approach to the world.

During Nehru's tenure as prime minister (1947-64), he achieved a domestic consensus on the definition of Indian national interests and foreign policy goals—building a unified and integrated nation-state based on secular, democratic principles; defending Indian territory and protecting its security interests; guaranteeing India's independence internationally through nonalignment; and promoting national economic development unencumbered by overreliance on any country or group of countries. These objectives were closely related to the determinants of India's foreign relations: the historical legacy of South Asia; India's geopolitical position and security requirements; and India's economic needs as a large developing nation.

From 1947 until the late 1980s, New Delhi's foreign policy goals enabled it to achieve some successes in carving out an independent international role. Regionally, India was the predominant power because of its size, its population (the world's second-largest after China), and its growing military strength. However, relations with its neighbors, Pakistan in particular, were often tense and fraught with conflict. In addition, globally India's nonaligned stance was not a viable substitute for the political and economic role it wished to play.

India's international influence varied over the years after independence. Indian prestige and moral authority were high in the 1950s and facilitated the acquisition of developmental assistance from both East and West. Although the prestige stemmed from India's nonaligned stance, the nation was unable to prevent Cold War politics from becoming intertwined with interstate relations in South Asia. In the 1960s and 1970s, New Delhi's international position among developed and developing countries faded in the course of wars with China and Pakistan, disputes with other countries in South Asia, and India's attempt to balance Pakistan's support from the United States and China by signing the Treaty of Peace, Friendship, and Cooperation with the Soviet Union in August 1971.

Although India obtained substantial Soviet military and economic aid, which helped to strengthen the nation, India's influence was undercut regionally and internationally by the perception that its friendship with the Soviet Union prevented a more forthright condemnation of the Soviet presence in Afghanistan. In the 1980s, New Delhi improved relations with the United States, other developed countries, and China while continuing close ties with the Soviet Union. Relations with its South Asian neighbors, especially Pakistan, Sri Lanka, and Nepal, occupied much of the energies of the Ministry of External Affairs.

In the 1990s, India's economic problems and the demise of the bipolar world political system have forced New Delhi to reassess its foreign policy and to adjust its foreign relations. Previous policies proved inadequate to cope with the serious domestic and international problems facing India. The end of the Cold War gutted the core meaning of nonalignment and left Indian foreign policy without significant direction.

The hard, pragmatic considerations of the early 1990s were still viewed within the nonaligned framework of the past, but the disintegration of the Soviet Union removed much of India's international leverage, for which relations with Russia and the other post-Soviet states could not compensate.

Pragmatic security, economic considerations, and domestic political influences have reinforced New Delhi's reliance on the United States and other developed countries; caused New Delhi to abandon its anti-Israeli policy in the Middle East; and resulted in the courtship of the Central Asian republics and the newly industrializing economies of East and Southeast Asia.

Although India shares the concerns of Russia, China, and many members of the Nonaligned Movement about the preeminent position of the United States and other developed countries, different national interests and perceptions make it improbable that India can turn cooperation with these countries to its advantage on most international issues. Furthermore, although Cold War politics have ceased to be a factor in South Asia, the most intractable problems in India's relations with Pakistan—conflict over Kashmir, support for separatists, and nuclear and ballistic missile programs—still face the two countries.

## Role of the Prime Minister

Nehru set the pattern for the formation of Indian foreign policy: a strong personal role for the prime minister but a weak institutional structure. Nehru served concurrently as prime minister and minister of external affairs; he made all major foreign policy decisions himself after consulting with his advisers and then entrusted the conduct of international affairs to senior members of the Indian Foreign Service. His successors continued to exercise considerable control over India's international dealings, although they generally appointed separate ministers of external affairs.

India's second prime minister, Lal Bahadur Shastri (1964-66), expanded the Office of Prime Minister (sometimes called the Prime Minister's Secretariat) and enlarged its powers (see The Executive, ch. 8). By the 1970s, the Office of the Prime Minister had become the de facto coordinator and supraministry of the Indian government. The enhanced role of the office strengthened the prime minister's control over foreign policy making at the expense of the Ministry of External Affairs. Advisers in the office provided channels of information and policy recommendations in addition to those offered by the Ministry of External Affairs. A subordinate part of the office—the Research and Analysis Wing—functioned in ways that significantly expanded the information available to the prime minister and his advisers. The Research and Analysis Wing gathered intelligence, provided intelligence analysis to the Office of the Prime Minister, and conducted covert operations abroad.

The prime minister's control and reliance on personal advisers in the Office of the Prime Minister was particularly strong under the tenures of Indira Gandhi (1966-77 and 1980-84) and her son, Rajiv (1984-89), who succeeded her, and weaker during the periods of coalition governments under Morarji Desai (1977-79), Viswanath Pratap (V.P.) Singh (1989-90), Chandra Shekhar (1990-91), and P.V. Narasimha Rao (starting in June 1991). Although observers find it difficult to determine whether the locus of decision-making authority on any particular issue lies with the Ministry of External Affairs, the Council of Ministers, the Office of the Prime Minister, or the prime minister himself, nevertheless in the 1990s India's prime ministers retain their dominance in the conduct of foreign relations.

## Ministry of External Affairs

The Ministry of External Affairs is the governmental body most concerned with foreign affairs, with responsibility for some aspects of foreign policy making, actual implementation of policy, and daily conduct of international relations. The ministry's duties include providing timely information and analysis to the prime minister and minister of external affairs, recommending specific measures when necessary, planning policy for the future, and maintaining communications with foreign missions in New Delhi. In 1994 the ministry administered 149 diplomatic missions abroad, which were staffed largely by members of the Indian Foreign Service. The ministry is headed by the minister of external affairs, who holds cabinet rank and is assisted by a deputy minister and a foreign secretary, and secretaries of state from the Indian Foreign Service.

In 1994 the total cadre strength of the Indian Foreign Service numbered 3,490, of which some 1,890 held posts abroad and 1,600 served at the Ministry of External Affairs headquarters in New Delhi. Members of the Indian Foreign Service are recruited through annual written and oral competitiive examinations and come from a great variety of regional, economic, and social backgrounds. The Foreign Service Training Institute provides a wide range of courses for foreign service officers, including a basic professional course, a comprehensive course in diplomacy and international relations for foreign service recruits, a refresher course for commercial representatives, and foreign language training.

The Ministry of External Affairs has thirteen territorial divisions, each covering a large area of the world, such as Eastern Europe and the post-Soviet states, or smaller areas on India's periphery, such as Afghanistan, Iran, and Pakistan. The ministry also has functional divisions dealing with external publicity, protocol, consular affairs, Indians abroad, the United Nations (UN) and other international organizations, and international conferences. Two of the eighteen specialized divisions and units of the ministry are of special note.

The Policy Planning and Research Division conducts research and prepares briefs and background papers for top policy makers and ministry officials. The briefs cover wide-ranging issues relating to India's foreign policy and role in the changing international environment, and background papers provide information on issues concerning international developments. The Economic Division has the important task of handling foreign economic relations. This division augments its activities to reflect changes in the government's economic policy and the international economic environment (see Liberalization in the Early 1990s, ch. 6). In 1990 the division established the Economic Coordination Unit to assess the impact on India of the Persian Gulf crisis arising from Iraq's invasion of Kuwait, changes in Eastern Europe and the Soviet Union, and formation of a single market in the European Economic Community (after 1993 the European Union), as well as to promote foreign investment.

The Economic Division also runs India's foreign aid programs, including the Indian Technical and Economic Cooperation Programme, the Special Commonwealth African Assistance Programme, and aid to individual developing countries in South Asia and elsewhere. The ministry runs the Indian Council for Cultural Relations, which arranges exhibits, visits, and cultural exchanges with other countries and oversees the activities of foreign cultural centers in India.

The Ministry of External Affairs had a budget of Rs8.8 billion (for value of the rupee—see Glossary) for fiscal year (FY—see Glossary) 1994. The largest single expense was the maintenance of missions abroad: Rs3.8 billion, or close to 44 percent of the ministry's expenditures. Foreign aid totaled Rs1.3 billion, or 15.1 percent of the ministry's expenditures. The single largest recipient—as in most previous years—was Bhutan (Rs690 million), whose government operations and development are heavily subsidized by India.

## Other Government Organizations

Besides the Office of the Prime Minister and the Ministry of External Affairs, there are other government agencies that have foreign policy-making roles. In theory, the ministers of defence, commerce, and finance provide input to foreign policy decisions discussed in cabinet meetings, but their influence in practical terms is overshadowed by the predominant position of the prime minister and his advisers. The armed forces are removed from policy making and have influence only through the minister of defence, to whom they are subordinate.

Only a limited role in foreign policy making is provided for India's bicameral Parliament. Negotiated treaties and international agreements become legally binding on the state but are not part of domestic law unless passed by an act of Parliament, which also has no say in the appointment of diplomats and other government representatives dealing with foreign affairs. For the most part, because of the widespread domestic support for India's foreign policy, Parliament has endorsed government actions or sought information. The most important official link between Parliament and the executive in the mid-1990s is the Committee on External Affairs of the Lok Sabha (House of the People), the lower chamber of Parliament. The committee meets regularly and draws its membership from many parties. Usually it has served either as a forum for government briefings or as a deliberative body.

## The Role of Political and Interest Groups

Institutional connections between public opinion and foreign policy making are tenuous in the mid-1990s, as they have been since independence. Although international issues receive considerable attention in the media and in academic circles, the views expressed by journalists and scholars in these publications have little impact on foreign policy making. Interest groups concerned with foreign relations exist inside and outside Parliament but are less organized or articulate than in most other democracies. These organizations include such business groups as the Federation of Indian Chambers of Commerce International; religious groups, especially among Muslims; and various friendship or cultural societies promoting closer ties with specific countries. Among the latter are informal groups known as the "Russian" and "American" lobbies.

Opposition political parties often have more effectively articulated differing views regarding foreign policy, but even these views had little impact on policy making until the 1990s. Other than the Congress (I)—(I for Indira), only the communist parties, the Janata Party, and the Jana Sangh and one of its successors, the Bharatiya Janata Party (BJP—Indian People's Party), developed coherent platforms on foreign policy. After the mid-1950s, the communist parties were broadly supportive of Indian foreign policy. At the beginning of Janata Party rule (1977-79), Prime Minister Desai promised to return to "genuine nonalignment." However, security considerations forced Desai and his minister of external affairs, Jana Sangh stalwart Atal Behari Vajpayee, to adhere to the foreign policy path carved out by the Congress (I) – nonalignment with a pro-Soviet orientation. BJP foreign policy positions differed most strongly from those of the Congress (I).

The BJP criticized nonalignment and advocated a more vigorous use of India's power to defend national interests from erosion at the hands of Pakistan and China. The BJP also favored the overt acquisition of nuclear weapons. By the early 1990s, the rising political fortunes of the BJP had an impact on the conduct of foreign policy, forcing the coalition government of V.P. Singh, which depended on BJP support, to take a hard line in the Kashmir crisis in 1990. Pressure from the Congress (I) also had an impact on India's response to the Persian Gulf crisis.

### *Nehru and India's Foreign Policy*

Jawaharlal Nehru, the first Prime Minister of India, has been under criticism from different quarters all through. The reasons of this have been diverse for different political streams. Currently a section of intellectuals is blaming him for forcing India into Socialist Russia's camp. Their argument comes in the backdrop of Left's pressure not to sign the nuclear deal with U.S. One of the inherent arguments of critics of left and others is that not signing it will keep us away from the deeper friendship of U.S., the land of wealth and prosperity, whose alliance will benefit us a lot. In the complex scenario, which our world is, to support or oppose a political line is not easy enough.

Also the left while opposing the nuclear deal has an attitude towards nuclear power, energy itself, which is not acceptable to most peace workers. While one will like that the left takes a stand which is totally against the nuclear energy and weapons, this is not the case. The major built in argument in their current stance in opposing the nuclear deal with U.S., is that this will push us in the camp of America, as its satellite ally and that will be the doom of India's foreign policy, which has been that of non alignment. There is a criticism that in the name of non-alignment India was tilted towards the Soviet block of yesteryears. Some also pose the question, is it possible in today's post 'Soviet regime' era to remain non-aligned, not to toe the singular pole of global power, America?

Critics of Nehru's foreign policy undermine the fact that India's foreign policy was aimed at minimizing the domination of imperial powers in the World in general and India in particular. Though U.S. and USSR both were the superpowers, there was some difference in their attitude. While opposing the concept of global poles, one also recognizes that most of the countries which were coming out from the slavery of colonial powers needed to develop their industrial infrastructure. U.S. and U.K. were not for helping these countries with the technological support for this infrastructure while USSR partly helped India in building the foundation of industries, which in turn laid the base for the major industrial growth in times to come.

The contrast is most visible, when India is compared to its major neighbor Pakistan, which allied with America, and the difference in the in the trajectory of two nations is there for all to see. Pakistan, happy with the short cut of supply of industrial goods, as a US ally, free market, no license permit raj, a free economy to begin with landed up as a puppet economy in due course. India seeing that the industrialists here cannot set up the base of industrial growth on their own opted for the mixed economy, public sector, many of which were supported by the USSR, for heavy industries and private sector for the rest. The public sector was labeled as Socialist by all and sundry, without givingmuch thought to the concept of socialism, and was strongly opposed by the right wing economists, communalists and western imperialist powers. U.S. pursued its policies of supporting its minor allies by giving them weapons and ready made goods in return for various things including their loyalty to its global designs.

This struggle between capitalist and socialist model was in turn also a shadow boxing between the upcoming economies in the third world countries and the domination of western ex-colonial powers. U.S. and its allies, with their economic interests being jeopardized by the independent attitude and policies of the third world nations, the success of Soviet block in various fields, stepped up their ideological campaign against socialist ideology. What the Western powers wanted was that the third world should not set up their own industrial base and shouldremain dependent on the U.S. and its allies.

The socialist policies in India meant essentially a public sector which will provide the base for growth of theindustries in general and lift up India's level from an economically dominated colony towards the possibility of an strong economy with own say. Interestingly as India began to chart its course after getting independence, the thinking of the big industrialists, which got reflected in the Bombay plan, and Nehru's fascination for growth model of the countries like USSR, which helped them come out fromthe clutches of feudal economic system, matched wellat this point of time. Industrialists did want the state to set up infrastructure industries. Here centralized planning and its accompaniments, which later became frozen and were unable to change with times and led to the demise of Soviet socialist economies.

India's charting independent path with the help of others, more particularly with USSR, in setting up theinfrastructure, helped it stand on its feet, while most of the countries which became independent at that time and opted for pro U.S. policies eventually marched towards banana republics, without the core, the base for their social and economic systems. Parallel to this economic path, India took the road of non alignment.

The major opposition to the nonalignment policy came from the BJP and its predecessor Bharatiya Jansangh, who have always advocated thick relations with U.S. Politically their ideologueGolwalkar had listed communists as a threat to Hindu nation. So far the policies of RSS-BJP had always been in parallel to those of US. In late 1940s America was following MaCarthism and hunting communists. Around that time in the aftermath of Gandhi murder, Golwalkar was writing to the Sardar Patel that RSS workers should be released from jails and in turn they will help the government to contain communists. And today when

U.S. is leading the global anti Muslim tirade, RSS is the lead organization spreading anti Muslim venom here in India.

USSR had no problems with the this non alignment course in foreign policy so it not only endorsed it but also kept giving core support to India for its indigenous growth. US annoyed with India's not accepting US patronage branded India's policies andnon alignment in general as the decoy for being proUSSR. India did keep supporting the national liberation struggles in Vietnam and many other nations to the annoyance of US. Today with the changed of World scenario, US is keen that India does not formanother block away from U.S., that's why its tilt towards India, away from its nurturing of Pakistan till date.

The basic dilemma which countries like India faced was weather to have 'ready made goods' or to produce the same the hard way. US wanted India to go on this readymade path, while India defied it and pursued independent path. The same got reflected in the foreign policy and attempt to stay clear of US-USSRblocks. It's another matter that USSR for its own strategic reasons was supportive of the non alignment. This had reflection in India's policy vis a vis Israel-Palestine. Israel, the hub of US interests, hand in glove with Western powers, dominated theregion, led to the exile of lakhs of Palestinians and installed an authoritarian state. Palestinians has been struggling for years to get back their own land. Here the aggressor-victim duel was clear and India did opt to keep away from Israel and kept supporting the cause of Palestine. US designs in the region wereprompted by the lust for oil, its policy is hegemonic, it theme, 'Oil is too important to be left to the Arabs'.

In this direction it overthrew the Government of Mossadeq in 1953, installed Raza Shah Pehlvi who in turn brought in superficial westernization notbothering to develop the country's infrastructure. The political rebellion against him was given a religious turn and so came in Ayatollah Khomeini. And with this began another chapter in World history. US projected it as signaling the rise of Islam as the 'new threat' to freedom and democracy and this slogan has been serving it in all its aggressions in the Middle East.

While condemning the foreign policy charted out by the builder of Modern India, Nehru, these ideologuesconveniently forget that it is important for the Worldas a whole to promote democratization amongst nationsand democratization within nations. The attempt tokeep India out of the stifling patronage of US is of paramount importance to ensure the building of democracy amongst nations, away from the hegemony of global bully. The current hegemonic, bullying policies of US, which are the major cause of violence in theworld, aggression on Afghanistan and Iraq was preceded by promotion of terrorist outfits, Al Qaeda and its clones, to fight Soviet occupation of Afghanistan. These need to be understood in their proper perspective. We do have to keep the goal that the world marches towards peace and harmony amongstnations and amongst people.

In the contemporary scenario it is easy and also fashionable enough to criticize Nehru's economic-foreign policy. It is difficult to see todaythat it is precisely these policies of public sectorand non alignment which resulted in India charting the course of democracy and economic growth. One is not saying that what has been achieved is satisfactory. The point is this was the comparatively better option, which did help us go some distance in the direction of industrialization-education in the givencircumstances. World is essentially global, how westrike a balance between external support and internal growth is a million rupee question. Blindly submittingto the wishes of super power number one, may land us up in the direction of many a banana republics or leadto the fate which our neighbor is seeing due toembracing the Uncle Sam.

Time that we build the non aligned movement again, time that we promote regional alliances, time that we see the vision of Nehru in its perspective of indigenous growth and global democracy away from thedomination of one or the other superpower. *India Foreign Relations*

India's Foreign Relations reflect a traditional policy of nonalignment, the exigencies of domestic economic reform and development, and the changing post-Cold War international environment. India's relations with the world have evolved considerably since the British colonial period (1757-1947), when a foreign power monopolized external relations and defense relations. On independence in 1947, few Indians had experience in making or conducting foreign policy. However, the country's oldest political party, the Indian National Congress (the Congress – see Glossary), had established a small foreign department in 1925 to make overseas contacts and to publicize its freedom struggle. From the late 1920s on, Jawaharlal Nehru, who had the most long-standing interest in world affairs among independence leaders, formulated the Congress stance on international issues. As a member of the interim government in 1946, Nehru articulated India's approach to the world.

During Nehru's tenure as prime minister of India (1947-64), he achieved a domestic consensus on the definition of Indian national interests and foreign policy goals – building a unified and integrated nation-state based on secular, democratic principles; defending Indian territory and protecting its security interests; guaranteeing India's independence internationally through nonalignment; and promoting national economic development unencumbered by overreliance on any country or group of countries. These objectives were closely related to the determinants of India's foreign relations: the historical legacy of South Asia; India's geopolitical position and security requirements; and India's economic needs as a large developing nation. From 1947 until the late 1980s, New Delhi's foreign policy goals enabled it to achieve some successes in carving out an independent international role. Regionally, India was the predominant power because of its size, its population (the world's second-largest after China), and its growing military strength. However, relations with its neighbors, Pakistan in particular, were often tense and fraught with conflict. In addition, globally India's nonaligned stance was not a viable substitute for the political and economic role it wished to play.

India's international influence varied over the years after independence. Indian prestige and moral authority were high in the 1950s and facilitated the acquisition of developmental assistance from both East and West. Although the prestige stemmed from India's nonaligned stance, the nation was unable to prevent Cold War politics from becoming intertwined with interstate relations in South Asia. In the 1960s and 1970s, New Delhi's international position among developed and developing countries faded in the course of wars with China and Pakistan, disputes with other countries in South Asia, and India's attempt to balance Pakistan's support from the United States and China by signing the Treaty of Peace, Friendship, and Cooperation with the Soviet Union in August 1971. Although India obtained substantial Soviet military and economic aid, which helped to strengthen the nation, India's influence was undercut regionally and internationally by the perception that its friendship with the Soviet Union prevented a more forthright condemnation of the Soviet presence in Afghanistan. In the 1980s, New Delhi improved relations with the United States, other developed countries, and China while continuing close ties with the Soviet Union. Relations with its South Asian neighbors, especially Pakistan, Sri Lanka, and Nepal, occupied much of the energies of the Ministry of External Affairs.

In the 1990s, India's economic problems and the demise of the bipolar world political system have forced New Delhi to reassess its foreign policy and to adjust its foreign relations. Previous policies proved inadequate to cope with the serious domestic and international problems facing India. The end of the Cold War gutted the core meaning of nonalignment and left Indian foreign policy without significant direction. The hard, pragmatic considerations of the early 1990s were still viewed within the nonaligned framework of the past, but the disintegration of the Soviet Union removed much of India's international leverage, for which relations with Russia and the other post-Soviet states could not compensate.

Pragmatic security, economic considerations, and domestic political influences have reinforced New Delhi's reliance on the United States and other developed countries; caused New Delhi to abandon its anti-Israeli policy in the Middle East; and resulted in the courtship of the Central Asian republics and the newly industrializing economies of East and Southeast Asia. Although India shares the concerns of Russia, China, and many members of the Nonaligned Movement (see Glossary) about the preeminent position of the United States and other developed countries, different national interests and perceptions make it improbable that India can turn cooperation with these countries to its advantage on most international issues. Furthermore, although Cold War politics have ceased to be a factor in South Asia, the most intractable problems in India's relations with Pakistan – conflict over Kashmir, support for separatists, and nuclear and ballistic missile programs – still face the two countries.

## Nehru's Bungling Foreign Policy

In one of the most incisive books written about the Tibetan situation, "The Fate of Tibet: When big insects eat small insects" by Claude Arpi, Mr. Arpi shows that not only did the Nehru government betray Tibet, but it also severely destabilized India's national security. In 1947, India had special rights in Tibet, a legacy of the British Raj. In 1949, though clearly aware of China's strategic interests in Tibet, Nehru failed to get any assurance from China that it would not invade the region. However, what is worse is the fact that he did nothing to prevent China from committing blatant aggression against a weak and peace loving Tibet, in 1950. Mr. Arpi provides proof in his book that argument that India was not in a position to halt Chinese aggression in Tibet in 1950 is erroneous and misleading. India had three trade agencies with military escorts within Tibet and with the support and help of the democratic world could have checked the communist aggression. Paying more attention to the Korean War than the happenings in Tibet, Nehru gave an open and clear invitation to China that she could unhesitatingly conquer the poor and helpless nation. In one stroke, Nehru's government was single-handedly responsible for converting the Indo-Tibet border into the Indo-China border. Nehru's reaction was expressed merely in words saying that the "Indian government was perplexed and disappointed by the Chinese Government's action".

Once Tibet was occupied, China undertook a gigantic road-building program between 1951-52. In 1959, Nehru said that it had taken his government over 2 years to notice that the Chinese had been building a road on the barren heights of Aksai-Chin plateau in Ladhak. In his book Mr. Arpi shows that Nehru and his associate Krishna Menon were fully aware of the Chinese encroachment in Aksai-Chin. In 1955, an English Mountaineer named Sydney

Wignall deputed by General Thimayya verified reports that the Chinese were building a road through Aksai-Chin. This basically shows that government did know about the encroachment but did nothing about it.

After the Chinese invasion, the Indian government was expected to spring to its feet and make an attempt to consolidate its borders with China. Instead Pandit Nehru started an era of false and pretentious friendship with the Chinese, which culminated in the famous Hindi-Chini-Bhai-Bhai campaign. The Chinese for one, never considered India as any friend, instead cleverly used Nehru's stupidity to further their interests. After having "gifted" Tibet to China, the fictitious fraternization concluded in the so-called "Panch-Sheel" Treaty.

Prime Minister Nehru and the Chinese counter part, Chou-En-Lai, signed this treaty on April 29, 1954. "Panch Sheel" literally meant five norms of good conduct, viz. mutual respect for each other's territorial integrity and sovereignty, mutual non- aggression, mutual non-interference in each other's internal affairs, equality and mutual benefit and peaceful co-existence. China very diplomatically signed the treaty but was never intent on following its norms. The treaty was aptly described in the Indian Parliament by the Late Acharaya J.B. Kripalani, a former President of the ruling Congress Party, as "born in sin".

## Fifty Years of Continuity in Nuclear Issues

If there is an area where tradition, continuity and a sprit of freedom have managed to prosper in the Indian policy, it is in the arena of Indian foreign policy. Through the five decades of Independence, a consensual approach to foreign policy making has been wide spread support for policies and initiatives that Congress and non-Congress governments alike have taken. The successful conduct of foreign policy has in large measure been the result of the strong foundation laid by the architect of India's foreign policy-Jawaharlal Nehru. It is entirely fitting that India's Prime Minister in its Golden Jubilee year is Inder Kumar Gujral, a self professed Nehru admirer, who has sought to conduct foreign policy in the Nehruvian vision.

Despite the presence of Prime Ministers who have taken personal interest in foreign policy, it has continued to remain insulated from any discernible personality cult enveloping it. While consensus cutting across party lines has been the dominant element of foreign policy in the past five decades, there is nevertheless an acceptance that it bears Nehru's stamp on its numerous facets. In many ways, Nehru represented the bridge between the emotional and social urges of the freedom movement and daunting task of governing an independent country in a world which has seen radical changes following the end of the second World War. The truly nationalist moorings of Indian foreign policy allowed Nehru to craft India's foreign policy in the context of its times. Admittedly, the genius of Nehru lay in giving Indian foreign policy a vision, which has continued to be its guiding star fifty years later.

The particular stress on anti-colonialism and the fight against racial discrimination were drawn from experiences gathered during the freedom struggle. Similarly, Nehru's advocacy for a world without nuclear weapons was rooted in the underlying philosophy of the Gandhian struggle-non violence. Taken together, this Nehruvian vision translated into a sort of natural leader of newly independent countries, which were seeking to find their feet in the post -World War II international system, that was driven by bloc politics and undergirded by a balance of terror which was predicated on an unprecedented nuclear arms race.

In India's fiftieth year of Independence, Nehru's deep concern for the threat humanity faced from nuclear weapons continues to remain a major concern for the Gujral government. Throughout the CTBT debate, the Narasimha Rao and later the Deve Gowda governments steadfastly held on to the Nehruvian vision that any effort to achieve nuclear disarmament must be non-discriminatory and global in its approach. I.K. Gujral as External Affairs Minister masterfully handled the end game of the CTBT negotiations, creating an unprecedented consensus within the political and intellectual spectra. This allowed India to stand on principled grounds in objecting to the flawed CTBT. It may have cost India in terms of a seat in the UN Security Council, but the decision not to endorse the CTBT in its present form made every Indian walk tall.

Even in the post-CTBT situation, the Gujral government's spirited defence of its nuclear policies and its refusal to be provoked into going overtly nuclear is another manifestation of the Nehruvian vision. While Nehru advocated the need for global nuclear disarmament, he was conscious to the underlying security needs of the country. By creating the Atomic Energy Commission (AEC) within a year of Independence, Nehru was seeking not only to harness the atom for peaceful purposes, but also to safeguard the country's security against all eventualities. The present government has been following this policy and it is a testament to Nehru that fifty years later, it continues to remain relevant.

## Congress Nationalism & the Decline of U.S.-India Relations

Congress foreign policy was shaped by India's first prime minister, Jawaharlal Nehru (1947-64). The nostalgia with which Americans have recently recalled the idealistic tenor of Nehru's foreign policy represents the most fundamental misperception of Indian politics. Educated in England, Nehru exemplified the ambivalence of Westernized Indians. Attracted to the West by training, alienated from it by the experience of prejudice, he was often more hostile to the United States than his more rustic colleagues. He was also a romantic, with visions of a broad coalition of former colonies transforming the world, and he considered himself a socialist, which caused as much friction as his nationalism or his calls for third world solidarity.

Nehru was an unabashed Indian nationalist. Although he insisted on tolerance for cultural minorities within India, he viewed the creation of Pakistan as illegitimate. And though he was an advocate of the rule of law internationally, he consistently refused to implement UN resolutions calling for a plebiscite in the disputed territory of Kashmir. Despite advocating third world solidarity, he viewed India as entitled to a special role in world affairs and as the natural leader of the third world.

Nehru the socialist and Nehru the nationalist had a single worldview that appeared contradictory to Americans. Nehru the socialist sought American food aid, so he could divert resources from agriculture to state-owned heavy industry, which Nehru the nationalist justified as necessary for developing the "power resources" (industrial base) to maintain sovereignty. If the U.S. became frustrated with feeding a country that made little effort to feed itself, Nehru saw the West's reluctance to fund steel mills as evidence of a desire to keep India backward.

India, Pakistan, and KashmirAt independence in 1947, British India was divided into a Hindu-majority Republic of India, containing eighty percent of the subcontinent's population, and a Muslim-majority Pakistan, established in two wings (East and West) separated by 1,000 miles of Indian territory. Although the two states absorbed most of the semi-independent princely states within their territories, mountainous Jammu and Kashmir—with a Hindu ruler, a majority Muslim population, and borders with both India and Pakistan—ended up as a disputed territory. A war between India and Pakistan in 1948 left a third of the province with Pakistan and the rest with India. India claims the entire province on the grounds that the ruler agreed to join India, while Pakistan, in accordance with a UN resolution, demands that a plebiscite be held to determine the wishes of the Kashmiris.

Economic conflicts have had a powerful effect on Indian attitudes toward the United States. Amendments to international trade rules in the 1950s allowed industrialized countries to use quotas to limit textile imports. India was one of the big losers and subsequently turned inward. Many Indians still point to textile quotas as evidence of both the West's protectionist impulses and its untrustworthiness generally.

Mistrust of the United States became pronounced with the Johnson administration's approach to food aid during a drought in India that threatened mass starvation. As a condition for food aid, Johnson insisted that India invest in agriculture, devalue its currency, and liberalize trade regulations. The changes in agricultural policy were consistent with the wishes of many in India and were negotiated in secret to avoid the impression of being adopted under pressure. However, Johnson insisted that the food aid be delivered one month's supply at a time to ensure compliance, a "short tether" policy Indians viewed as playing with lives to punish India for opposing the U.S. regarding Vietnam.

Even worse, the financial assistance that Washington had promised, in order to help implement a more liberal Indian trade policy, did not materialize.

The changes required of India in trade policy had little support within India. Prime Minister Indira Gandhi (1966-77, 1980-84), who devalued India's currency against the advice of her senior colleagues, felt betrayed. The period of most active U.S. assistance had included a successful trip to the U.S. by Indira Gandhi but left India deeply distrustful of U.S. intentions and embittered the woman who was to lead India for two decades.

Political and military relations also saw good intentions ending in mistrust. The romantic and nationalist in Nehru merged into the role of champion for newly independent countries in Asia and Africa. Formally, this meant leading a bloc of "nonaligned" countries that remained neutral in the cold war. To Americans, however, nonalignment meant a double standard on international norms. Both the Anglo-French invasion of the Suez and American policy in Vietnam were condemned harshly, yet Soviet crackdowns in Eastern Europe and Chinese repression in Tibet received muted criticism. When Nehru ordered the Indian army to annex Goa, Portugal's Indian enclave, Americans derided him for hypocrisy.

But Washington's perception reflects a misunderstanding. India's nonalignment always wed morality to self-interest through opposition to renewed European colonialism. Nehru's calls for the peaceful resolution of disputes reflected concerns about India's military weakness. Developing country solidarity was desirable emotionally but also essential on practical grounds. The Soviet suppression of Hungary, while deplorable, did not set a precedent that threatened non-European societies; the need to take Goa by force, while regrettable, was justified by the higher goal of ending European colonialism.

If American foreign policymakers had understood Nehru's logic, they might not have found India's nuclear position baffling. Although Nehru was an early advocate of universal nuclear disarmament and, failing that, of a complete ban on nuclear testing, his positions were aimed at eliminating the threat posed to India—and other non-nuclear powers—not merely of nuclear attack but of nuclear blackmail. India's objections to the Non-Proliferation Treaty (NPT), signed in 1970 and renewed in 1995, linked two concerns. Generations of resentment against colonial discrimination were focused on the NPT's creation of two classes of states, those allowed to possess nuclear weapons and those barred from doing so. India has consistently offered to join a global nonproliferation regime that would eliminate all nuclear weapons. Opposition to the NPT's "nuclear apartheid" dovetailed, though, with concerns about the threat from China, which did not initially sign the NPT.

India's relationship with China came to symbolize the tension between the emotional and the pragmatic in Congress foreign policy. Convinced that China shared his sentiments of pan-Asian solidarity, Nehru was taken by surprise when Beijing used force in 1962 to settle a long-simmering border dispute with India. Subsequently China refused to sign the 1963 partial test ban treaty (which permitted only underground nuclear tests), conducted a nuclear test in 1964, and began to develop ties to Pakistan after that country's war with India in 1965.

Neutralizing China became a central goal for India. In the NPT negotiations, after Nehru's death, India sought guarantees of protection from the U.S. and other nuclear powers to counter threats from China. The major powers (including the Soviet Union) refused, and some suggest that this was as much a cause of India's refusal to sign the NPT as was the treaty's discriminatory nature. If true, it means that just as the moral dimensions of nonalignment grew out of a self-interested concern over global inequities, so India's moral stance on the NPT also reflected regional geopolitical concerns.

The 1962 border dispute with China could have marked a turning point toward improved India-U.S. relations, but U.S. ties to Pakistan established in the context of the cold war prevented this. The U.S. dispatched the U.S.S. Enterprise to the Bay of Bengal in a symbolic show of support to India that may have led China to withdraw from most of its gains. Several years of U.S. military aid to India followed. However, U.S. aid to India was constrained by Pakistan, which had joined two U.S.-sponsored military alliances and received far more sophisticated aircraft and tanks than India possessed. The Johnson administration refused to sell India advanced aircraft, arguing that they were not needed to fight China in the Himalayas.

The U.S. had also long assured India that weapons provided to Pakistan would only be used against India in self-defense. However, the U.S. underestimated the chronic difficulties of determining who had attacked whom in disputes over Kashmir. In 1965 war broke out when armed guerrillas crossed from the Pakistani side of the cease-fire line in Kashmir, and India responded with regular troops. The U.S. remained neutral and imposed an arms embargo on both sides. Each accused the other of having started the war and blamed the United States for not living up to its commitments. India eventually turned to the Soviet Union for weapons and a counterweight against China, while Pakistan grew closer to China.

U.S. global concerns conflicted again with India's local concerns in the 1970s. When President Richard Nixon decided to establish ties with China, Pakistan played the intermediary. Pakistan's contribution to this diplomatic effort made the Nixon administration reluctant to pressure Pakistan into showing restraint against East Pakistani separatists in 1971. India eventually intervened militarily in the civil war after first signing a friendship treaty with the Soviet Union. Although the U.S. did not prevent India from breaking up Pakistan to create Bangladesh, Nixon dispatched the U.S.S. Enterprise to the Bay of Bengal. Although U.S. officials maintain that their intent was to prevent an Indian invasion of West Pakistan, the action has long been viewed in India as evidence of American hostility.

### *Nehru's Foreign Policy in a Sentence*

We are told Jawaharlal Nehru, our first prime minister, was a worldly man. He knew the vast history of India expressed in his *Discovery of India*. He understood the secular nature of our nation. He understood our neighbourhood. And he understood the importance of technology in a modern nation-the five IITs and government-owned monster steel and power plants are a testimony of his superior intellect. Sure he lost a war to China and let Pakistan keep occupied Jammu & Kashmir. But the general conclusion is, overall, his near two decades in power, leading a young nation, was positive force.

After reading one episode in a recent bock on the history of Indian foreign policy, I am not so sure. Thirty years before P.V. Narashima Rao's Look East Policy, Badruddin Tyabji, an IFS senior policy adviser to Nehru, proposed, in early 1961, in a meeting with Indian ambassadors posted to Southeast Asian countries, that India needs to create and nurture close relations with Southeast Asian countries. Historians and linguists have known for centuries about the close cultural and trade ties between former Indo-China region and India. And one would expect it to be natural that India pursue close ties with this region.

But Nehru's unbending closeness to Soviet Union, which he developed while living in an Utopian socialism period in England, early in his life, had a peremptory response, "Do you gentlemen want India to become friendly with Coca Cola governments?" Thus single handedly killing any initiation of significant diplomatic contacts with Southeast Asian countries making India blind to the amazing rise of Singapore, Taiwan, Thailand, Malaysia, and others from poor deprecate nations to rich to middle-income nations.

The significance of Nehru was not in his actions, while important at the time and now, but the precedents he set: 17 years in unquestioned power (by contrast, George Washington run for two terms, for a total of eight years, as US president, about 200 years prior, and was well aware of any precedent he was setting as a leader of a new country), path to economic socialism, non-response to Pakistani and Chinese aggression, and much more. We are, more than 40 years after his death, still unable to get out from under his shadow.

## Foreign Relations

India's Foreign Relations reflect a traditional policy of nonalignment (see Glossary), the exigencies of domestic economic reform and development, and the changing post-Cold War international environment. India's relations with the world have evolved considerably since the British colonial period (1757-1947), when a foreign power monopolized external relations and defense relations. On independence in 1947, few Indians had experience in making or conducting foreign policy. However, the country's oldest political party, the Indian National Congress (the Congress – see Glossary), had established a small foreign department in 1925 to make overseas contacts and to publicize its freedom struggle. From the late 1920s on, Jawaharlal Nehru, who had the most long-standing interest in world affairs among independence leaders, formulated the Congress stance on international issues. As a member of the interim government in 1946, Nehru articulated India's approach to the world.

During Nehru's tenure as prime minister (1947-64), he achieved a domestic consensus on the definition of Indian national interests and foreign policy goals – building a unified and integrated nation-state based on secular, democratic principles; defending Indian territory and protecting its security interests; guaranteeing India's independence internationally through nonalignment; and promoting national economic development unencumbered by overreliance on any country or group of countries. These objectives were closely related to the determinants of India's foreign relations: the historical legacy of South Asia; India's geopolitical position and security requirements; and India's economic needs as a large developing nation. From 1947 until the late 1980s, New Delhi's foreign policy goals enabled it to achieve some successes in carving out an independent international role. Regionally, India was the predominant power because of its size, its population (the world's second-largest after China), and its growing military strength. However, relations with its neighbors, Pakistan in particular, were often tense and fraught with conflict. In addition, globally India's nonaligned stance was not a viable substitute for the political and economic role it wished to play.

India's international influence varied over the years after independence. Indian prestige and moral authority were high in the 1950s and facilitated the acquisition of developmental assistance from both East and West. Although the prestige stemmed from India's nonaligned stance, the nation was unable to prevent Cold War politics from becoming intertwined with interstate relations in South Asia. In the 1960s and 1970s, New Delhi's international position among developed and developing countries faded in the course of wars with China and Pakistan, disputes with other countries in South Asia, and India's attempt to balance Pakistan's support from the United States and China by signing the Treaty of Peace, Friendship, and Cooperation with the Soviet Union in August 1971.

Although India obtained substantial Soviet military and economic aid, which helped to strengthen the nation, India's influence was undercut regionally and internationally by the perception that its friendship with the Soviet Union prevented a more forthright condemnation of the Soviet presence in Afghanistan. In the 1980s, New Delhi improved relations with the United States, other developed countries, and China while continuing close ties with the Soviet Union. Relations with its South Asian neighbors, especially Pakistan, Sri Lanka, and Nepal, occupied much of the energies of the Ministry of External Affairs.

In the 1990s, India's economic problems and the demise of the bipolar world political system have forced New Delhi to reassess its foreign policy and to adjust its foreign relations. Previous policies proved inadequate to cope with the serious domestic and international problems facing India. The end of the Cold War gutted the core meaning of nonalignment and left Indian foreign policy without significant direction. The hard, pragmatic considerations of the early 1990s were still viewed within the nonaligned framework of the past, but the disintegration of the Soviet Union removed much of India's international leverage, for which relations with Russia and the other post-Soviet states could not compensate.

Pragmatic security, economic considerations, and domestic political influences have reinforced New Delhi's reliance on the United States and other developed countries; caused New Delhi to abandon its anti-Israeli policy in the Middle East; and resulted in the courtship of the Central Asian republics and the newly industrializing economies of East and Southeast Asia. Although India shares the concerns of Russia, China, and many members of the Nonaligned Movement about the preeminent position of the United States and other developed countries, different national interests and perceptions make it improbable that India can turn cooperation with these countries to its advantage on most international issues. Furthermore, although Cold War politics have ceased to be a factor in South Asia, the most intractable problems in India's relations with Pakistan—conflict over Kashmir, support for separatists, and nuclear and ballistic missile programs—still face the two countries.

## Historical Legacy

During the British colonial period, India was a large political entity bordered by the buffer states of Afghanistan, Nepal, Sikkim, Bhutan, and Tibet to the north and Ceylon (as Sri Lanka was then called) to the south. The withdrawal of the British and partition in 1947, which created India and Pakistan, resulted in geographical boundaries that cut across regional religious, social, ethnic, and linguistic groups, and disrupted economic and cultural ties. A slice of eastern India and the westernmost part of India became the East Wing and West Wing of Pakistan, respectively, and in 1971 the East Wing became Bangladesh.

After independence India's leaders attempted to build a secular state in which national identity would supersede regional, religious, or cultural identities. They regarded the movements for regional autonomy or independence in Punjab, Jammu and Kashmir, Tamil Nadu, and Assam as threats to Indian unity, particularly because Indian leaders believed that their neighbors—Pakistan, later Bangladesh, and Sri Lanka—supported these movements. Furthermore, despite the commitment of Congress (I) leaders to the secular ideal, communal tensions and the rising influence of Hindu political parties pushed the Indian government increasingly to identify Indian greatness with Hinduism. The inability of Indian leaders to restrain anti-Muslim communal violence and the Kashmir policy of the Indian government resulted in continual tensions in relations with its Muslim neighbors. Thus, internal security and domestic political considerations, which stemmed from the perceived goals of building national identity and preserving national unity, permeated India's relations with its neighbors.

# 8 Relevance of Nehru Today

Any interest in the outstanding figure such as Jawaharlal Nehru does not diminish with time. More so, with his relevance which needs hardly to be overemphasized. It is mostly due to his charm coupled with far-sighted vision and statesmanship, his personality and concern for the masses and downtrodden that he remains ever fresh in the minds of the people. It is also due to fascination of not only those who were lucky to work with him personally but also those who came to know him through his rich literary works, numerous memoirs and several scholarly publications about him.

The other reason for the unflagging interest and relevance of him in the readers and researchers lies in the fact that as a thinker he touched upon a vast variety of problem which concern mankind today. As a matter of fact, Nehru does not belong only to India he belongs to all mankind. He was one of the architects of international peace and solidarity. He believed in a common destiny of mankind, in rapprochement between the West and the East. 'Panchsheel' became the beacon light for all peace loving countries in the world. Sino-Indian relations were built upon this idea in the hey day of Nehruvian politics.

Nehru was, in fact, a multifaceted personality. In him we have a happy blend of western scientific temper and modern Indian idealism. He accepted Gandhi's moral leadership and yet he retained his modern outlook. He was a great democrat and a true socialist. He was a nationalist of the first order, yet an internationalist of great repute. In short, must I say that Nehru was a rare phenomenon in the history of mankind?

**Relevance of Nehru:** With all these contributions in the background, can we today visualize any good reason to relegate Nehru's relevance? On the contrary the more world communities march ahead towards closer international co-operation and better understanding between countries, Nehru's relevance becomes not only relevant but increasingly becomes indispensable, particularly for the Third World countries who in their strive towards the goal of becoming developed nations follow a non-aligned path.

What appeals us most in his relevance to us today is his intense love for India and the Indian people. He loved his motherland more than anything else in his life. To keep alive his thoughts and ideals we have nowhere to go but study those clearly expressed views in his own writings that stand out today unparalleled in their range and variety.

In his writings are revealed his hopes and aspirations, struggles and the patterns on which he hoped and strongly expressed to shape the future of our country. He was indeed passionately devoted to his ideas that are being vigorously pursued even today. It is given cognizance by all international communities as an up-coming great power of the world. Can we dispense with his relevance today? Perhaps not.

We know that Nehru was a prolific writer and an acknowledged master of English prose. He corresponded with his friends, colleagues and admirers both in India and abroad. In his 'Autobiography', 'Glimpses of World History' and 'Discovery of India', are found his ideals and thoughts written in lucid and flawless language, which are frequently interspersed with rare beauty of thoughts. Indeed, such noble thoughts have seldom been enshrined in such a noble language. These three great works of Nehru encompass the inevitable relevance of him today. To illustrate let me discuss in brief about them.

## India Old and New

It is generally acclaimed as among the few truly great memorable autobiographies of the country. Nehru himself proclaimed it as having traces of his mental development which surveyed the courses of events in India prior to attainment of independence and revealed an insight into the blueprints of the 'New India' he cherished that was soon to emerge. In this work he reflected how greatly were his father, Motilal Nehru, Gandhiji and Rabindra Nath Tagore, influential upon him and who molded his life and the love for his country.

This May be summed up in his own words.

"And yet India with all her poverty and degradation had enough of nobility and greatness about her, and though she was overburdened with ancient tradition and present misery, and her eyelids were a little weary, we had a beauty wrought from within upon the flesh, the deposit little cell by cell, of strange thoughts and fantastic reveries and exquisite passions." Behind and within her battered body one could still glimpse a majesty of soul. Through long ages she had traveled and gathered much wisdom on the way, and trafficked with strangers and added them to her own family, and witnessed days of glory and of delay, and suffered humiliation and terrible sorrow, and seen many a strange sight; but throughout her long journey she had clung to her immemorial culture, drawn strength and vitality from it, and shared it with other lands. Like a pendulum she had swung up and down; she had ventured with the daring of her thought to reach up to the heavens and unravel their mystery, and she had also had bitter experience of the pit of hell. Despite the woeful accumulations of superstition and degrading custom that had clung to her and borne her down, she had never wholly forgotten the inspiration that some of the wisest of her children at the dawn of history, had given her in the Upanishads. Their keen minds, ever restless and ever striving and exploring, had not sought refuge in blind dogma or grown complacent in the routine observance of dead forms or ritual and creed. They had demanded not a personal relief from suffering in the present or a place in a paradise to come, but light and understanding: "Lead me from the unreal to the real, lead me from the darkness to light, lead me from the death to immortality". In the most famous of the prayers recited daily even to-day by millions, the 'Gayatri Mantra' the call is for knowledge, for enlightenment.

## The Variety and Unity of India

With such background as legacy, Nehru expressed his cherished dream to see a unified India despite multiple ethnic diversities with differing religious beliefs that were embraced by its multitude populace as expressed in his work, the 'Discovery of India'. This book is his last major work wherein he sets out to discover his own country. Coverage of the book ranges from the earliest days of Indian history to the dawn of independence. This survey provides clear interpretations of history and the complexity of contemporary problems as revealed through the mind and personality of one of the noble sons of India whose importance in the framing of policies is as ever more relevant in contemporary India than before. Instance of his vision is found in that:

"The Pathan and the Tamil are two extreme examples, the others lie somewhere in between. All of them have their distinctive features; all of them have still more the distinguishing mark of India. It is fascinating to find how the Bengalis, the Marathas, the Gujaratis, the Tamils, the Andhras, the Oriyas, the Assamese, the Canarese, the Malayalis, the Sindhis, the Punjabis, the Pathans, the Kashmiris, the Rajputs, and the great central block comprising the Hindustani-speaking people have retained their peculiar characteristics for hundreds of years, have still more or less the same virtues and failings of which old tradition or record tells us, and yet have been throughout these ages distinctively Indian, with the same national heritage and the same set of moral and mental qualities. There was something living and dynamic about this heritage which showed itself in ways of living and a philosophical attitude to life and its problems. Ancient India, like ancient China, was a world in itself, a culture and a civilization, which gave shape to all things. Foreign influences poured in and often influenced that culture and were absorbed. Disruptive tendencies gave rise immediately to an attempt to find a synthesis. Some kind of a dream of unity has occupied the mind of India since the dawn of civilization. That unity was not conceived as something imposed from outside, standardization of externals or even of beliefs. It was something deeper and, within its fold, the widest tolerance of belief and custom was practiced and every variety acknowledged and even encouraged.

"Differences, big or small can always be noticed even within a national group, however closely bour ᵈ together it may be. The essential unity of that group becomes apparent when it is compared to another national group, though often the differences between two adjoining groups fade out or intermingle near the frontiers, and modern developments are tending to produce certain uniformity everywhere. In ancient and medieval times, the idea of the modern nation was non-existent, and feudal, religious, racial, or cultural bonds had more importance. Yet I think that at almost any time in recorded history an Indian would have felt more or less at home in any part of India, and would have felt as a stranger and alien in any other country. He would certainly have felt less of a stranger in countries which had partly adopted his culture or religion.

Those who professed a religion of non-Indian origin or, coming to India, settled down there, became distinctively Indian in the course of a few generations, such as Christians, Jews, Parsees, Moslems. Indian converts to some of these religions never ceased to be Indian on account of a change of their faith. They were looked upon in other countries as Indians and foreigners, even though there might have been a community of faith between them.

"Today, when the conception of nationalism has developed much more, Indians in foreign countries inevitably from a national group and hang together for various purposes, in spite of their internal differences. An Indian Christian is looked upon as an Indian wherever he may go. An Indian Moslem is considered an Indian in Turkey or Arabia or Iran, or any other country where Islam is the dominant religion." It speaks volumes of his concept of Indian 'Unity in diversity' which still binds the people of India together.

## Old Civilization: India's Inheritance and Present Age

This work of Nehru is astonishing in its range and in projecting great sweeps of the mind-set of the author. It also reveals the breadth of Nehru's culture and his ability to write clearly in an interesting manner for the young. His comprehension of the old civilization and India's inheritance and of our present age was unique. He wrote, "Egypt, Knossos, Iraq and Greece - they have all gone. Their old civilizations, even as Babylon and Nineveh, have ceased to exist. What, then of the other two ancients in this company of these old civilizations? What of China and India?

As in other countries, they too have had empire after empire. There have been invasions and destruction and loot on a vast scale. Dynasties of kings have ruled for hundreds of years and have been replaced by others. All this has happened in India and China as elsewhere. But nowhere else, apart from India and China, has there been a real continuity of civilization. In spite of all the changes and battles and invasions, the thread of the ancient civilization has continued to run on in both these countries. But it is interesting and rather wonderful to think of this long range and continuity Indian culture and civilization right from the dawn of history, through long ages, down to us".

## Tribal Policy and Evolution of States in the North East

In addition, to mention an instance relating to Nehru's relevance in the North East is that of his policy on tribals which is a landmark in the evolution of States in the north east. Despite his advice not to take extreme step to adopt Assamese language, the then Congress Ministry did so. This hastened the process of formation of non-viable States in the region; particularly the hill districts of Khasi and Jaintia and Garo Hills, Naga Hills, Lushai Hills and North-Eastern Frontier Areas into separate States. With them, so were Manipur and Tripura, which were then already princely States.

Nehru wanted that tribals and their land should be left to themselves to develop their own genius. We may recall an instance wherein he spelled out part of his policy on tribals particularly of the North-East India in his public meeting in Shillong which ran as follows: "Tribal rights on land and forest should be respected. These hill people who love to have good communication in their areas have lost much of their enthusiasm with the apprehension that good communication means forfeiture of their lands, and economic and social exploitations on the other.

Thus, even good communication, instead of being an asset to the development of the hill people, works adversely to the interest of the said people. This is so, in as much as the rights to administer and govern to suit the peculiar nature of the people and along the lines of their own genius have been denied to the people".

**Nehru's Concern for Women Upliftment:** It goes without saying that Nehru's concern for the welfare and upliftment of status of women had manifested in more than one way right from his assumption of the office of the first Prime Minister of India. His letters to his daughter, Priyadarshni Indira Gandhi, gave enough witnesses to it. He inducted Padmaja Naidu to the high office of Governor, assigned Vijay Lakshmi Pandit as Indian Representative to the UNO and Ambassador of India and was instrumental in Indira Gandhi becoming the Prime Minister of India on her own merit.

He was fascinated with the womenfolk of Manipur for their active role in the fields of social, economic and political life that prompted him to call Manipur as the 'Jewel of India'. Similar is the case with his exceeding appreciation of the courage of young 'Gaidinliu' whom he saw in a Jail in Assam imprisoned by the British Indian Government for her spearheading the 'religio-cultural' movement of the Zeliangrong Kabui tribes of Manipur whom he decorated with the title of 'RANI' and a life-time pensionery benefits and accorded the status of a "Very- Very Important Person. These are few instances of his vision for the upliftment of women that had definitely paved the way for the present day politicians and the Government of India for intense desire to introduce a bill on women upliftment. He was also opinionated for setting aside a certain percentage of reservation of seats in Parliament and State Legislative Assemblies. Recent trend of introducing the bill on women is a reminder of the relevance of Nehruvian farsightedness and incisive understanding of the needs of our society.

**Legacy of Subverting Democracy:** In Constitutional matters written text of the Constitution, Constitutional conventions and judicial interpretations of various articles of the Constitution are equally important elements. These have not been given serious consideration and violated by the Congress Party since the days of Indian Freedom struggle despite the fact that the party had incorporated these elements which were framed by their legal stalwarts. It became more apparent during the regime of United Fronts. Sinha described it as follows:

"The United Front, a conglomeration of the rejects of the Congress, also wants to remain stuck to the chair till death doth them part. For this, they are bent upon wiping out all noble traditions of a democracy". The legacy is seen from the time when Jawaharlal Nehru was elected to the office of presidentship of Congress Party despite his getting support only from three Provincial Committees out of eighteen against Sardar Patel for two terms at the interference of Mahatma Gandhi in favor of Nehru who also superseded in becoming Prime Minister of India in preference to Chakravatty Rajagopalan, respectively in 1929, 1937 and 1946.

Brushing aside the majority vote, Gandhiji pleaded very strongly with the delegates of the Congress session in favor of Jawaharlal Nehru. He said: "Seniors had their innings. Future struggle to be carried on by young men and women... Jawaharlal has all the qualities for which he deserves to be recommended.... For his bravery, determination, behavior, honesty and patience, he is held in high esteem by the youth of this country. He has come in contact with farmers and workers. He is close to European politics... They (youth) would consider as an award to them if Jawaharlal is elected. And they would consider it as proof of belief of the nation in its youth. Give them an opportunity to prove themselves worthy of this trust". Gandhiji said this in consideration of the sacrifices made by Jawaharlal's family."

The circumstances thus highlighted above have simply manifested that in the Congress set-up, there has never been any respect for majority or democracy. Another argument put forward by Gandhiji in favor of Jawaharlal was that when negotiations were going on with the British for the independence of the country, Jawaharlal would be more suitable for the office, because Nehru and the Englishmen spoke in 'common idiom'.

Durga Das wrote in his book on India from Curzon to Nehru and after that the same year when Nehru took over as Prime

Minister of Interim Government "... most of the members of Working Committee were not altogether happy. They preferred Sardar Patel who was the "Iron man with his feet firmly planted on earth", and that he would be able to deal better with Jinnah than Nehru with the firm belief that even at that late stage could ensure the solidarity and integrity of the sub-continent. It was further argued that crucial hours lay ahead and the Sardar's rugged realism, would provide a 'safe-shield'.

Durga Das asked the reactions of Gandhi on the above contention of the Congress Working Committee, and Gandhi readily agreed that Patel would have proved a better negotiator and organizer as President of Congress Party, but added that Jawaharlal would not take the 'second place'. Thus despite the fact that Sardar Patel had more organizational capability and administrative efficiency, Nehru was made the Prime Minister in the interim Government because he 'spoke English better than others in the Congress and also because he was not prepared to take the 'second place'. Patel, unlike Nehru did not have Gandhi as 'Godfather'. Obviously, democracy did not have a place in the scheme of things; it was only of cosmetic value in the Congress.

It is written that Gandhiji wrote a confidential letter dated the 15th July, 1946, to Jawaharlal Nehru on his becoming President of the Congress Working Committee saying;

"You are in office, but you are not in power yet. To put you in the office was an attempt to find you in power, quicker than you would otherwise have been. Anyway that was at the back of my mind when I suggested your name for the crown of thorns. Keep it on though the head be bruised".

Nehru followed the advice in letter and spirit and bound them upon his neck. However, he refused to write them upon the table of his heart therefore, did not accept moral responsibility for the debacle in the wake of Chinese aggression in 1962, compelling VK Krishna Menon to be the sacrificial goat that resulted in the latter's resignation from his Ministership. Thus despite the fact that his head was seriously bruised and bleeding, keeping the advice of his Godfather - Gandhiji - Nehru refused to part with the crown of thorns, till he breathed his last.

## The Good Boatman Sidelined

Mohandas Karamchand, best known the world over as Mahatma Gandhi of the twentieth century, is best understood not so much in words as in his actions. His action speaks more than his word for he lived a full life of action from the time he went to South Africa to serve as a lawyer to a Muslim client to the day he was assassinated in Delhi on one cold day of January, 1948.

Many books have been written about him and many works have analyzed his life and work than one can remember. Yet, it is sad to say that his memory is fast receding in the minds of his own countrymen. Therefore, it is imperative that his memory should be revived not because we are important to Gandhi but because Gandhi is important to us. And he is important to us not because his image has been simplified as "Father of the Nation" and frozen in few statues of indifferent merit but because his life has a message. In much the same manner as Gandhi himself once said succinctly, his life was his message. The one cannot be separated from the other. And so, his message is best understood in his actions. This action-filled life has been discriminatingly described... consciously marginalized his relevance and deliberately sidelined his importance. It was true that among his disciples was Chakravarti Rajagopalachari, a rich lawyer from Madras who gave up his practice to join the National Movement, the man with whom Gandhi had best relationship, reposed highest confidence and had 'greatest hope' on him, but in the end he turned to Jawaharlal Nehru. In early 1942, he told the All India Congress Committee, "I have said for some years and say it now, that not Rajaji, not Sardar Vallabbhai Patel, but Jawaharlal Nehru will be my successor. You cannot divide water by repeatedly striking it with a stick. It is just as difficult to divide us. ... When, I am gone, he will speak my language..."

Rajmohan Gandhi recounted that when Nehru heard this, he, who till then was sitting cross-legged on the floor with a bolster behind his back "sprang from his seat and sat on top of his bolster". To complete the record, it must be stated that after Gandhi was gone, Nehru forgot to speak his Master's language. Gandhi was forgotten in deeds and remembered in words.

## Legacy of Corruption

The issue may be traced back to the period 1937- 38 before independence of India in the Congress regime in the then Central Provinces and Berar, now called Madhya Pradesh, when Dr. N.B. Khare was the Chief Minister (then called Prime Minister), he was forced to quit the office by the Congress High Command allegedly for asking action against a couple of his corrupt Ministers.

On being out of office, Khare published some letters from High Command members recommending appointments to some top positions, like Advocate General of the State. Later, after independence, while he was a Member of Lok Sabha in 1952-55, in reply to charges of rampant corruption in early fifties, Nehru stated that there was more corruption in the British time than in the free India Congress regime. Reacting to it, Khare claimed that as member of Viceroy's Advisory Council in 194346, he knew how the corrupt were pulled up quickly in British times, contrary to the lenient view of Nehru. He was followed by another Member of the Parliament, Dr. Harindranath Chattopadhyaya, the younger brother of Sarojini Naidu, composing a couplet, recited as follows:

*The expenditure on dams*
*is souring like rockets*

*It does not irrigate the lands,*
*it irrigates the pockets.*

In this context, it is pertinent to note of the serious concern of Gandhiji about the complaints received on rampant corruptions soon after independence as highlighted by Durga Das, the former Editor of Hindustan Times, in his book of personal reminiscences of 50 years of journalistic career, titled, India: From Curzon to Nehru as follows:

"But it was not only the communal situation that troubled Gandhi in those months following independence. He was also deeply concerned about the rot that was setting into the Congress party. He also received information that some Congress legislators were taking money from businessmen to get them licenses that they were indulging in black-marketing and subverting the judiciary and intimidating top officials to secure transfers and promotions for their protégés in the administration. Gandhi thought of a remedy for this alarming state of affairs..."

Earlier to this, Saratchandra Bose, elder brother of Netaji Subhash Chandra Bose complained of the corruption in Delhi even during interim Government of 1946. Durga Das continued to state that since the general election of 1952 Nehru started subverting the election processes by exploiting the State apparatus for the election campaign. The AIR blared out his election speeches million fold to drawn his opponent's voices as cries in wilderness. In any case, as Rajaji said, corruption like water flows from top to bottom. Verily, the system has become a 'Thieves' Kitchen. The dynastic dispensation has reduced Indian democracy to a Kloptocracy - rule by compulsive thieves. And Gandhiji is no less responsible for this state of affairs. Gandhi knew well that Nehru abhorred tenets of Gandhian austerity, and personal probity, and how he himself injected massive doses of hypocrisy in public life through tattered marks of truth and non-violence.

**Kashmir—The Legacy of Personal Likes and Dislikes:** August 15, 1947 was a historic day. On this day, partition of India on communal lines became a 'fait accompli' and a truncated India got freedom. At this point of time, Kashmir was under the rule of Maharaja Hari Singh. He was in a dilemma as to whether should he cede the State to India or Pakistani. Therefore, he did not accede to either of them, though he was inclined towards India. And as for Sheikh Abdullah and his National Conference Party, he wanted that the Dogra Maharaja should quit Kashmir so that he might be in control of the Kashmir Valley in 1946 before the British left for good for which he landed himself in jail. As against it, Pandit Ram Chander Kak, the Prime Minister of the Maharaja wanted the State to remain as sovereign State for which he sought the assistance of Sardar Patel and also requested both Pakistan and India for Stand-Still Agreements to gain time, which was readily accepted by Pakistan.

On the other hand, while all the Princely States of India were given to Sardar Patel as Home Minister to deal with, Nehru kept Jammu and Kashmir under his charge.

Nehru had a soft corner for Shiekh Abdullah and wanted him to be released from Jail and the power transferred to him as a pre-condition for acceptance of accession of Jammu and Kashmir to India. The Maharaja was not agreeable to it. Thus, the issue relating to accession of Jammu and Kashmir either to India or Pakistan was entangled into multiple issues of action and reaction that were associated with inevitable result of 'Indo-Pak tension', resulting in Indo-Pak War of 1947, 1965 and 1971. And without an inkling it must be said that the Indo-Pak tension will persist till such time as Pakistan exists that will thus remain a Nehru Legacy as constant reminder of his being relevant so long as India exists. Because, instead of learning from experience and history, Nehru allowed his personal likes and dislikes and his idealistic imagination to run riot, particularly in regard to Kashmir.

Now as we turn towards the North-East of India, particularly the Naga issue, it may be equated with that of Kashmir. It was generally considered that the opportunity to settle the Naga problem once and for all came when the Prime Ministers of India and Burma, Pandit Jawaharlal Nehru and U Nu respectively visited Kohima on March 30, 1953. But the then Deputy Commissioner of Kohima, for reasons best known to him, did not allow the Nagas to submit a Memorandum to the visiting Prime Ministers. The several thousand Nagas gathered at the venue to receive the VIPs turned and left the ground enmass when they learned they were not to make themselves heard before the Prime Ministers. Visibly disappointed with humiliation Nehru was reported to have murmured to his daughter, Indira Gandhi, that he would never visit Nagaland again in his life-time, and so did he live thus till he breathed his last, shelving all possible solution of the Naga problem till date.

**Conclusion:** And thus his relevance today is best said in the words of Reid Escott (Envoy to Nehru: 1952:57) 1981, Oxford University Press, Canadian High Commissioner to India which runs as follows:

"He will become even more conscious of his place in the history of India and of the world. He must already know that he will be ranked with India's two great rulers of the last 2500 years,

Ashok and Akbar, that if India succeeds he will be called the Creator of Modern India, and that whatever happens, he will go down in history as one of the great men of the world...".

Nehru was a vanguard for social change. He needed peace for development. He had therefore made no compromise on nuclear armament despite India's deep concern of the Chinese threat to its frontiers. His worst fear had come true. Sino-India relationships had never dived during his lifetime. India had been subjected to aggressive Chinese intrusions in NEFA and other areas. India's friendship stood shattered. Pained as he was he never recovered from that set back and we lost him, his statesmanship and the dynamism that his policies had displayed.

Relevance of Nehruvian policies remained much longer after he has died. His progenies carried on with his policies in frontiers of education, industries and foreign policy. His daughter Indira Gandhi and her son Rajiv Gandhi displayed Nehruvian acumen in politics and in understanding the needs of the country.

However, all said and done about Nehru's ideology at the end we cannot but conclude that some of the nagging problems like that of Kashmir and Sino-Indian relations has been the gifts of his prolonged inactive policies. In order to gain international accolades for being projected as apostles of peace Nehru had compromised India's interests for which several times questions had been raised in the Parliament. The other aspect was that of corruption. Though he was against corruption of his colleagues he sheltered them and sometimes interfered in the process of law to save them. This soft-pedaling made politicians of different times to follow more and more corrupt ways in public life. His soft attitudes had created more problems than solving them. This was a bane to our society. Today we are more corrupt because of the relevance of his policies.

# 9 Nehru's Legacy to India

The importance of this Series is in inverse proportion to the attention it receives from scholars, Indian and foreign, and from the media. Ivor Jenning's masterpieces *Parliament* and *Cabinet Government* are based on memoirs and correspondence from which he distils the conventions of the Constitution. Even the long text of our Constitution cannot lay down every norm or rule of governance. Who more qualified to opine on them than the foremost of the founding fathers, Jawaharlal Nehru? He drafted the Objectives Resolution on which the preamble to the Constitution is based. He was Chairman of the Constituent Assembly's committees on Union Powers as well as on the Union Constitution. He was the prime architect of the Union. As builder of the Indian state, history will rank him with Asoka and Akbar. For 17 years after Independence he kept up a steady stream of letters and notes of advice, instruction and admonition to all who mattered, concerning almost every facet of the country's affairs. No political scientist and no constitutional lawyer can ignore them.

The Indian National Congress adopted the credo of secularism in the 19th century. Nehru became its most eloquent and articulate exponent before and after the Partition. Judge him not by the ones who exploit his name. Judge him by those who hate him. The Bharatiya Janata Party (BJP) regime, under the National Democratic Alliance (NDA) mask, did its best to erase his impact on our polity- and failed.

In the realm of foreign affairs, likewise, Nehru laid down the law. Opposition was not only unorganised, but uninformed; in some quarters, viciously personal. Jaswant Singh accused him of seeking to wind up the Army, on the testimony of the first Commander-in-Chief of the Army, General Sir Robert Lockhard, whom Nehru had sacked, ignoring Nehru's admirable memo on the armed forces, dated February 3, 1947, published in Volume 2 of the *Selected Works* (page 363). Some recent writings on Nehru also neglect them.

This is a particularly noteworthy volume. The dust jacket is in a tasteful brown, not the gaudy blue of yore and it indicates on the spine and the cover the period covered by the volume. Professor Mushirul Hasan, Vice Chancellor of the Jamia Millia Islamia, has joined the team of editors, the veterans H.Y. Sharada Prasad and A.K. Damodaran, and has written the Editorial Note. *The volume contains documents of crucial importance on the two problems which continue to bedevil foreign policy, distort its thrust and warp the national outlook.* How many, rather how few, will care to peruse them? Fewer still, one fears, will "allow the facts to get into the way" of their thinking. British Foreign Secretary Sir John Simon received a report from the Ambassador in Berlin citing details of Hitler's arms build up. "A distributing document", Simon minuted on the margin and had it filed away; affected not a bit by the report. Given our hard, frozen mindset, both on the border dispute with China and the Kashmir dispute with Pakistan, will the document matter one bit to the foreign policy establishment or "the strategic community"?

The volume has a most "disturbing" one on each dispute plus related ones. The first, to begin with, is a Note by Nehru to Krishna Menon, Minister without Portfolio, dated May 6, 1956. It bears quotation *in extenso*, for it holds instruction for Nehru's detractors as well as apologists. He wrote: "You know that, in Chinese maps, quite a good part of Assam is shown as if it belonged to Tibet. Also, a bit of the U.P., bordering on Tibet. Some two or three years ago, we drew the attention of the Chinese government to this. Their reply was that these maps were old maps from Chiang Kai-shek's time and that they had had no time to revise them. Recently, a new set of maps has been printed. They are exactly as the old ones except for a note that they are reproductions of the old maps.

We have decided previously not to raise the question of our frontier with China because, so far as we were concerned, there was no dispute. The Tibet frontier ran along the McMahon Line and we consider it a firm frontier. I stated this more than once in Parliament.

Even when I went to China (in 1954) I casually mentioned Chinese maps to Zhou Enlai and, so far as I remember, he said something about the maps being old and that we can settle frontier questions in a friendly way later. *In effect, therefore, China never clearly accepted our frontier as it is.* All that they have said is that the old maps are not reliable. We have stated to them and in Parliament that our frontier is as given in our maps.

"At the time of the agreement with China about Tibetan questions (1954) it was *taken for granted by us* that all pending questions between India and China had been settled. In some of our communications too, stress was laid on this. *But, China has never admitted this clearly, though they did not deny it either* (emphasis added, throughout)."

Four features deserve note. First, Menon had emerged as the prime foreign policy adviser in residence; not that he was shy about offering advice from his perch in London earlier. Secondly, the note was confined to the McMahon line in the eastern sector. It was silent on the Aksai Chin in Ladakh in the western sector though it was also depicted as China's territory on its maps. Thirdly, it seems not to have occurred to Nehru that the decision he had taken in 1951-52 on the Ambassador to China K.M. Panikkar's advice had been proved to be unwise. Lastly, Nehru's unilateral alteration of India's maps in 1954 to show the Aksai Chin as Indian territory did not inhibit him from questioning China's maps. The Chinese were of course, well aware of the 1954 alteration.

On October 2, 1951, Nehru cabled to Panikkar: "Our provisional view; that, in first instance, conversations should take place between China and us regarding our interests in Tibet and *Common boundary between Tibet and India*" (SWJN; vol.16, Part 2, page 643). Incidentally, Sardar Patel's famous letter to Nehru, drafted by Girja Shankar Bajpai, Secretary-General in the MEA, dated

November 7, 1950, was also confined to "the policy in regard to the McMahon Line". Sarvapalli Gopal records: "In the instructions drawn up for Panikkar and approved by the Prime Minister and Panikkar himself it was stated that one of India's interests in the negotiations with China on Tibet was the affirmation of the McMahon Line and the rest of the frontier with Tibet.

But when, on return to Peking, Panikkar met Zhou, the latter confined the discussions to trade and cultural interests and appeared to the Ambassador anxious not to open up wider issues; and Panikkar, ignoring his instructions fell in line and did not refer to the frontier. Neither did he mention the subject in the note on India's interests in Tibet, which he formally presented to the Chinese Foreign Office" (*Jawaharlal Nehru*; vol. 2; pages 177-8). One wonders whether Bajpai's instructions covered the Aksai Chin at all. They should be published.

On June 16, Nehru wired to Panikkar. "We think it is rather odd that, in discussing Tibet with you, Zhou Enlai did not refer at all to our frontier. For our part, *we attach more importance to this than to other matters*. We are interested, as you know, not only in our direct frontier but also in the frontiers of Nepal, Bhutan and Sikkim, and we have made it perfectly clear in Parliament that these frontiers must remain. There is perhaps some advantage in our not ourselves raising this issue. On the other hand, I do not quite like Zhou Enlai's silence about it when discussing even minor matters...

We would naturally prefer a general and comprehensive settlement which includes the frontier. *In our instructions to you dated 25th January, you were asked to specify our interests including those on the frontier*. We presume you have done so. If so, we can presume that Zhou Enlai's silence means some kind of acquiescence. It is not for us to suggest any reconsideration. At the same time, I should like to be assured on this point. I leave it to you to exercise your discretion in this matter." But on June 18, Nehru wrote: "In view of what you say, it will be *desirable* not to raise the question of our frontier at this stage" (SWJN; pages 474-5). Nehru thus abandoned his own instruction to Panikkar on May 24, 1952, to seek China's "affirmation of the frontier". It was the familiar

Nehru style "on the one hand" and "on the other", "at the same time" - all the time. He sought always to keep his own options open.

However, on July 25, Nehru reversed his stand in a note to the Foreign Secretary: "*We should mention the frontier.* I appreciate the reasons which Panikkar advanced and it is because of these reasons that we have not brought up this subject. But I am beginning to feel that *our attempt at being clever might overreach itself. I think it is better to be absolutely straight and frank.* You might discuss this matter with Panikkar" who was in Delhi on transfer. The logic was impeccable.

Yet come July 29 Nehru informed the Foreign Secretary and Panikkar: "On reconsideration I accept Shri Panikkar's advice that we should not make specific mention about the frontiers" in the negotiations on the Tibet agreement (SWJN; vol. 19; pages 585 and 651). It was an unwise decision and not a "clever" one either.

To think that this was the very Panikkar whom Nehru had portrayed as an unscrupulous time-server in his very first talk with U.S. Ambassador Chester Bowles on November 6, 1951 (*Foreign relations of the United States*, 1951; Vol. VI, Part 2; page 2,188).

Nehru's note to Panikkar's successor, N. Raghavan, on December 10, 1952, did include "Ladakh and the rest of India" while speaking of "this entire frontier" (SWJN; vol. 20, page 488). A note of August 3, 1953, recorded "for the present, we need not raise the question of the frontier, *but this will have to be brought in a larger* settlement" (SWJN; vol. 23 page 484). In 1959, when an opportunity for precisely such "a larger settlement" on the boundary arose, Nehru simply refused to negotiate. He had decided as much in 1953, if not earlier. On December 3, 1953, he wrote to the Secretary-General of the MEA: "I agree about the attitude we should take up in regard to the frontier. *We should not raise this question.* If the Chinese raise it, we should express our surprise and point out that this is a settled issue" (SWJN; vol.24, page 598).

The Tibet (Panchsheel) agreement was signed on April 29, 1954. Nehru instructed the MEA on May 2: "We should establish check posts at all *disputed* points" - resolve a dispute unilaterally.

Zhou Enlai visited New Delhi from June 25 to 28, 1954, and had *five sessions of talks with Nehru*. Neither raised the boundary issue. Only three days after his departure, Nehru wrote the historic note of July 1, 1954 - all the old maps were to be "withdrawn". A firm line was to be shown "which is not open to discussion with anybody" (SWJN; vol. 26, pages 481-483). But, if Chinese maps claim "our territory", we should correct them.

A WORD about maps. The map attached to *Mountbatten's Report on the Last Royalty* to the King showed the McMahon Line as India's boundary but had the legend "boundary undefined" in respect of *the entire frontier from the Indo-Sino-Afghan trijunction in the West to the Indo-Sino-Nepalese trijunction*. This includes the boundary defined in the Sino-Pak agreement of March 2, 1963. Talk of Pakistan "ceding" territory to China is therefore, sheer nonsense. (Ed. by Lionel Carter; Manohar; Rs.850. A most useful document). The Surveyor-General's map attached to the White Paper on Indian States in 1948 did not even extend the colour wash to the Aksai Chin. The implication was clear. The map in the 1950 White Paper did extend the colour wash, but with the legend "boundary undefined". The 1954 map removed it after the Panchsheel accord.

(The maps are reproduced in the author's article "Negotiating with China", *Frontline*, August 14, 1998, pages 98 and 99). The 1954 unilateral alteration is devoid of legal or moral force.

In the 1956 Note, Nehru sought Krishna Menon's advice. "Should we definitely raise the question of the frontier with the Chinese government?" He was referring to the eastern sector. As with Panikkar, so with Menon. Nehru had grave reservations about the adviser. "Krishna, who himself is *often* a problem," he wrote to Vijayalakshmi Pandit on November 12, 1952 (SWJN; vol. 20, page 520). Nehru accepted Panikkar's advise in preference to that of a man he respected - Bajpai, who *consistently* urged that the boundary issue should be explicitly raised and resolved in the 1954 settlement. We do not know Menon's advice, however.

Nehru raised the maps issue in October 1954 during his visit to China and again in 1956 when Zhou came to Delhi. The visitor hinted at his acceptance of the McMahon Line, albeit called by another name. But nor did he raise with Nehru the new Indian map on the Aksai Chin. This had "far-reaching and malign consequences". Had he objected to the new delineation "it is highly probable that the dispute would have been avoided" (Neville Maxwell; *India's China War;* pages 94-5). China built the road in Aksai Chin in 1956. When Nehru finally brought matters to a head on December 14, 1958, Zhou replied by raising the issue of the western sector. Nehru cited the 1842 Treaty to contend that there was no dispute to resolve.

*On Kashmir, one finds the same tendency to assert the untenable and persist in the course with consequences as grave as on the border issue. And* the very same tendency to "resolve" a dispute unilaterally, ending up with denying that a "dispute even exists. Yet admirers and detractors alike describe the man as an "idealist" and "romanticist". This is particularly true of some former diplomats whose skills lay in providing enthusiastic rendering of the raag Darbari.

On Kashmir, this writer cited six pronouncements by persons of eminence, spread over 50 years from 1948 to 2003 on Kashmiris' feelings towards India. The first of them was Indira Gandhi's letter to Nehru, dated May 14, 1948, from Srinagar: "They say only Sheikh Saheb is confident of winning the plebiscite". (*Frontline,* August 15, 2003). To them add one more, Jayaprakash Narayan's letter to Nehru dated May 1, 1956. He warned Nehru that from all the information that he had "95 per cent of Kashmir Muslims do not wish to be or remain Indian citizens". He said it was unwise to keep people by force as it could have serious long-term political consequences "though immediately it may suit policy and please public opinion" but could prove disastrous for establishing a peaceful social order. He wished that "this question be considered more from a human, rather than a nationalist, point of view. All men have to live upon this earth as brothers, irrespective of what national frontiers divide them. World peace is possible upon no other hypothesis."

Nehru's prompt reply on May 3 was that Jayaprakash Narayan's information was "completely wrong. It is difficult for anyone to express a firm opinion about this matter. If one takes the population of the whole of the State, apart from the part occupied by Pakistan, I think, it is rather doubtful which way a majority would lie. I think, there is a fair possibility of the majority being in favour of India". He added, "Much depends on how this question is raised. If it is made a communal issue, then it is probable that a majority of Muslims might vote against India. If the issues are purely political, different voting would take place.

But all this is guess work and people's opinions vary from time to time and are affected by some occurrence." In the given situation, the distinction he drew was unreal. In 1957 and 1962 Nehru lauded the bogus polls staged by Bakshi Ghulam Mohammed just as he had lauded Sheikh Abdulla's bogus poll in 1951.

To another correspondent, Nehru wrote: "When Kashmir acceded to India in October 1947, there was no mention of plebiscite by India. What India said was that the people of Jammu and Kashmir would be *consulted*. The first mention of plebiscite *came long afterwards* in a resolution of the U.N. Commission, which we accepted. That resolution contained various conditions to be fulfilled before the question of plebiscite came up. Among these conditions was the withdrawal of the Pakistan forces."

Every one of these statements, now the staple of nationalist discourse, is manifestly, demonstrably untrue. Mountbatten's letter to the Maharaja dated October 27, 1947, did not say that the people of Kashmir would be a "consulted" but that the issue of accession "should be *settled* by a reference to the people". An earlier sentence enunciated India's policy on disputed accessions: "The question of accession should be *decided in accordance with the wishes of the people of the State.*"

On October 31, 1947, Nehru wired to Liaquat Ali Khan that this "is not merely a pledge to your government but also to the people of Kashmir and to the world". On November 2 and 3 he used the word "referendum" under U.N. auspices. On November 21 he promised "plebiscite or referendum" under U.N. auspices. All this was said immediately on Kashmir's accession, not "long afterwards". Under the U.N. Commission's resolution (August 13, 1948) the tribesmen were to withdraw first, unconditionally. Next,

Pakistan was to "begin" to withdraw its troops as part of a process that included withdrawal of "the bulk" of Indian troops. Nehru never agreed to "the bulk". When in July 1956 Michael Brecher asked him how he would respond if Pakistan's troops did withdraw unconditionally, Nehru evaded a direct reply (page 541). He sought a familiar excuse - even if Kashmir is solved "these basic conflicts would continue. We are given the full text of the interview. Nehru's pretext now forms a vital part of chauvinist discourse.

Nehru publicly offered settlement on the basis of the ceasefire line (now the Line of Control) on April 13, 1956. We now have (page 18) his amplification of the offer on May 4: "My justification for being in Kashmir primarily is because the people of Kashmir or a great majority of them, the national leaders, invited us and because I think that a very large section of them want us to be there. If nobody wants us there in Kashmir, we shall have no place there. We can't keep an army of occupation in place there. So that, both for practical reasons and other reasons, the natural result is that we should seek a settlement of the Kashmir issue as it is today in the ceasefire line, subject to some changes here and there." It was a *non sequitur*. The conclusion did not flow from the premises, which were factually wrong too. He had put Sheikh Abdullah in prison in August 1953 and further alienated the people.

In both cases, the border with China and the Kashmir question, Nehru left behind an unenviable legacy to the nation. He made assertions which none in the world accepted bar an exception or two. But he would make them emphatically, angrily. The U.S. endorsed the McMahon Line only on October 27, 1962; but never the Indian line on the Aksai Chin. Except the USSR and now Russia, the world - including the U.N. - still regards Kashmir as "disputed territory". Nehru's assertions - Aksai Chin is Indian territory and Kashmir's accession was ratified by polls to the State Assembly and is therefore no longer open to dispute - became conventional wisdom which mainstream media faithfully echoed. In this, academia did not lag far behind.

Time has resolved neither issue; but aggravated both. In each case, India's adversary used force, making matters worse, still. In each case India's position became weaker, China hardened its stand. On Kashmir India's position became stronger vis-a-vis Pakistan but since the alienation of the people deepened, it has made India's position far weaker, in the balance.

In each case, on the core of the dispute, India remains the only one in the world to propagate the myths Nehru fostered. A "great power" complex brings in its train rampant chauvinism. To this day none of Nehru's successors felt himself politically strong to tackle the two disputes. Nehru's writings enable us to learn the lessons from the past so that we can shape a different future.

The U.S. negotiator Dennis Ross identifies in his memoirs *The Missing Peace: The Inside story of the Fight for Middle East Peace* the "missing peaces" that "have perpetuated the conflict" as "the lack of public conditioning for peace, the reluctance to acknowledge the legitimacy of the other side's grievance and needs, the inability to confront comfortable myths, the difficulty of transforming behaviour and acknowledging mistakes, the inherent challenge of getting both sides ready to move at the same time, the unwillingness to make choices, and the absence of leadership.

This volume helps considerably to explain Nehru's psyche. It is to repeat an unenviable legacy he left behind on foreign policy. But not the only one; Many others, rooted in truth and wisdom, are ones we tend to take for granted. A biography which is honest and competent must reckon with *all* of them and help us understand the greatness of the man behind the apparent contradictions.

One has only to read Acharya J.B. Kripalani's autobiography (*My Times*; Rupa & Co.; pages 986; Rs.995) to realise how the very arguments he deployed in defence of his policy came to be used against him whenever he contemplated any initiative for conciliation. The book contains little that is not known. But it is a useful resume of events and an instructive record of the kind of opposition Nehru had to face within and outside the party.

Encounters are a half century old phenomenon. Nehru did not set an example of public accountability. He wrote to Home Minister G.B. Pant on the subject as far back as on May 2, 1956, about encounters in the Punjab ruled by Partap Singh Kairon. "Could we not have some kind of an informal inquiry without fuss by the Centre? It need not be a very elaborate inquiry. I do not want the

Punjab government to feel in any way that we are distrusting them or bypassing them. But the charges are too serious to be overlooked." To C.P.N. Singh, Nehru explained: "*Evidently, the police are afraid of even well known and dangerous dacoits getting off in the law courts because of some technical difficulty.*"

But when Nehru was pressed for some kind of an inquiry by independent persons from the Centre, he took the stand that "we were inquiring in our own way. I do not think any such formal inquiry is desirable." Nor were fake encounters "very uncommon in some other States".

In his interview to Michael Brecher, Nehru largely defended the police (page 521). He also defended preventive detention. "The Act being there and not being used much is itself a deterrent; both ways. And you see, of the 150 or so, I doubt if more than perhaps 10 were political people. The rest were just gangsters and goondas in big cities. It is very difficult to convict them. Everybody knows he is... he pulls the strings from behind."

Ergo, put them in prison without trial. Nehru *was* committed to democracy. But it is dishonest to hail him as a great democrat without reckoning with his lapses from democratic norms, a champion of press freedom, he also defended curbs on the press. "Again criticism was made about out dealing with the press here. You may have seen the press here. I don't know if you have seen the worst part of the press, in Hindi and Urdu and these languages?

Michael Brecher: "No, I am afraid not."

Nehru: "Terrible, something terrible and we found it did little good. *We put an end to it.*"

Brecher: "That gave rise to the Press Objectionable Matters Act?"

Nehru: "Yes, some say we are suppressing the press. It is absurd. You see the press here, how it functions." So impose illiberal curbs by law.

ON the Naga problem Nehru was equivocal: "There can be no doubt that an armed revolt has to be met by force and suppressed. There are no two opinions about that and we shall set about it as efficiently and effectively as possible. *But* our whole past and present outlook is based on force by itself being no remedy. We have repeated this in regard to the greater problems of the world.

Much more, must we remember this when dealing with our own countrymen who have to be won over and not merely suppressed." As ever, *lekin* (but) was adroitly deployed. Assert something and qualify it; all options securely preserved.

Nehru was appalled at the perks MPs enjoyed. Also he was strongly of the view that the President and the governors should exercise the power of clemency only on the advice, respectively of the Prime Minister or the Chief Minister (page 274). The Jan Sangh MP, U.M. Trivedi, was told "no government can tolerate this kind of violence. The continuance of this type of violence in an organised way indicates that the policy of the RSS [Rashtriya Swayamsewak Sangh] is based on violence and doing physical injury to those persons whom they dislike. It is for the RSS to consider if this can be called service to the country."

In one of the finest passages in the volume we have Nehru saying: "So far as the two-nation theory is concerned, we have never accepted the fact that Pakistan was a result of the two-nation theory. It may be so in the minds of the people of Pakistan but we did not agree to it even then. Our position has been that we cannot consider a nation and a religious community as the same thing. Nations contain more than one religious community. Even if all the Muslims in India believed in this theory, we would not accept it or even if all the Hindus believed in it."

## Tryst with Destiny

Tryst with Destiny was a speech made by Jawaharlal Nehru, the first Prime Minister of independent India. The speech was made to the Indian Constituent Assembly, on the eve of India's independence, towards midnight on August 14, 1947. It focuses on the aspects that transcend India's history. It is considered in modern India to be a landmark oration that captures the essence of the triumphant culmination of the hundred-year Indian freedom struggle against the British Empire in India.

***Text***

Long years ago we made a tryst with destiny, and now the time comes when we shall redeem our pledge, not wholly or in full measure, but very substantially. At the stroke of the midnight hour, when the world sleeps, India will awake to life and freedom. A moment comes, which comes but rarely in history, when we step out from the old to the new, when an age ends, and when the soul of a nation, long suppressed, finds utterance. It is fitting that at this solemn moment we take the pledge of dedication to the service of India and her people and to the still larger cause of humanity.

At the dawn of history India started on her unending quest, and trackless centuries are filled with her striving and the grandeur of her success and her failures. Through good and ill fortune alike she has never lost sight of that quest or forgotten the ideals which gave her strength. We end today a period of ill fortune and India discovers herself again. The achievement we celebrate today is but a step, an opening of opportunity, to the greater triumphs and achievements that await us. Are we brave enough and wise enough to grasp this opportunity and accept the challenge of the future?

Freedom and power bring responsibility. The responsibility rests upon this Assembly, a sovereign body representing the sovereign people of India. Before the birth of freedom we have endured all the pains of labour and our hearts are heavy with the memory of this sorrow. Some of those pains continue even now. Nevertheless, the past is over and it is the future that beckons to us now.

That future is not one of ease or resting but of incessant striving so that we may fulfil the pledges we have so often taken and the one we shall take today. The service of India means the service of the millions who suffer. It means the ending of poverty and ignorance and disease and inequality of opportunity. The ambition of the greatest man of our generation has been to wipe every tear from every eye. That may be beyond us, but as long as there are tears and suffering, so long our work will not be over.

And so we have to labour and to work, and work hard, to give reality to our dreams. Those dreams are for India, but they are also for the world, for all the nations and peoples are too closely knit together today for any one of them to imagine that it can live apart Peace has been said to be indivisible; so is freedom, so is prosperity now, and so also is disaster in this One World that can no longer be split into isolated fragments.

To the people of India, whose representatives we are, we make an appeal to join us with faith and confidence in this great adventure. This is no time for petty and destructive criticism, no time for ill-will or blaming others. We have to build the noble mansion of free India where all her children may dwell.

The appointed day has come-the day appointed by destiny-and India stands forth again, after long slumber and struggle, awake, vital, free and independent. The past clings on to us still in some measure and we have to do much before we redeem the pledges we have so often taken. Yet the turning-point is past, and history begins anew for us, the history which we shall live and act and others will write about.

It is a fateful moment for us in India, for all Asia and for the world. A new star rises, the star of freedom in the East, a new hope comes into being, a vision long cherished materializes. May the star never set and that hope never be betrayed!

We rejoice in that freedom, even though clouds surround us, and many of our people are sorrowstricken and difficult problems encompass us. But freedom brings responsibilities and burdens and we have to face them in the spirit of a free and disciplined people.

On this day our first thoughts go to the architect of this freedom, the Father of our Nation [Gandhi], who, embodying the old spirit of India, held aloft the torch of freedom and lighted up the darkness that surrounded us. We have often been unworthy followers of his and have strayed from his message, but not only we but succeeding generations will remember this message and bear the imprint in their hearts of this great son of India, magnificent in his faith and strength and courage and humility. We shall never allow that torch of freedom to be blown out, however high the wind or stormy the tempest.

Our next thoughts must be of the unknown volunteers and soldiers of freedom who, without praise or reward, have served India even unto death.

We think also of our brothers and sisters who have been cut off from us by political boundaries and who unhappily cannot share at present in the freedom that has come. They are of us and will remain of us whatever may happen, and we shall be sharers in their good and ill fortune alike.

The future beckons to us. Whither do we go and what shall be our endeavour? To bring freedom and opportunity to the common man, to the peasants and workers of India; to fight and end poverty and ignorance and disease; to build up a prosperous, democratic and progressive nation, and to create social, economic and political institutions which will ensure justice and fullness of life to every man and woman.

We have hard work ahead. There is no resting for any one of us till we redeem our pledge in full, till we make all the people of India what destiny intended them to be. We are citizens of a great country on the verge of bold advance, and we have to live up to that high standard. All of us, to whatever religion we may belong, are equally the children of India with equal rights, privileges and obligations. We cannot encourage communalism or narrow-mindedness, for no nation can be great whose people are narrow in thought or in action.

To the nations and peoples of the world we send greetings and pledge ourselves to cooperate with them in furthering peace, freedom and democracy.

And to India, our much-loved motherland, the ancient, the eternal and the ever-new, we pay our reverent homage and we bind ourselves afresh to her service.

# Bibliography


Ahmad, Imtiaz: *State and Foreign Policy: India's Role in South Asia*, New Delhi, Vikas, 1993.

Ashton, S.R.: *British Policy Towards the Indian States, 1905-1939*, London: Curzon, 1982.

B.N. Ganguli: *Indian Economic Thought: Nineteenth Century Perspectives*, New Delhi, 1977.

Balan, K. : *Mahatma Gandhi and Jawaharlal Nehru : The Two Stalwarts Who Shaped India*, Delhi, Authorspress, 2002.

Bhambhri, C.P. : *Indian Politics Since Independence*, 1999.

Bipan Chandra: *Modern India*, New Delhi, 1971.

Bourai, Himanshu : *Gandhi and Modern Indian Liberals*, Delhi, Abhijeet Pub., 2004.

Chakrabarti, Santosh : *Studies in Tagore : Critical Essays*, New Delhi, Atlantic, 2004.

Dan Nabudere: *The Political Economy of Imperialism*, London, 1977.

Dash, Nibedita : *Life and Thoughts of Gandhi and Nehru*, New Delhi, Dominant, 2004.

Gandhi, M. K. : *Satyagraha In South Africa* Navjivan Publishing House, 1922.

Gaur, Mahendra : *Indian Political Parties Annual*, Delhi, Kalpaz Pub., 2006.

Ghosh, Ila : *Rgvedic Rsikas : Life and Philosophy*, Eastern Book Linkers, Delhi, 2007.

Jain, U.C. and Jeevan Nair : *Encyclopaedia of Indian Government and Politics*, 2000.

Jawaharlal Nehru, *Towards A Socialistic Order*, New Delhi, 1956.

————————: *A Bunch of Old Letters*, Delhi, 1958.

————————: *An Autobiography,* New Delhi, 1962.

————————: *Discovery of India,* Calcutta, 1946.

————————: *Glimpses of World History,* Bombay, 1965.

————————: *Planning and Development,* Delhi, 1956.

Jha, Prem Shankar: *India: A Political Economy of Stagnation,* Bombay, Oxford University Press, 1980.

Kripalani, Krishna : *All Men are Brothers,* Navjivan Publishing House, 1937.

Kumarappa, Bharatan : *Nature Cure,* Navjivan Publishing House, 1944.

Maheshwari, Shriram: *Rural Development in India: A Public Policy Approach,* New Delhi, Sage, 1995.

Murthi, R.K. : *Discovery of Nehru,* Indian Pub., Delhi, 1993.

Noorani, A.G. : *Indian Political Trials : 1775-1947,* New Delhi, Oxford University Press, 2005.

Prasad, Lal Bahadur : *Indian Political System and Law,* New Delhi, Shree, 2005.

Pruthi, R.K. : *Indian Political Thought,* New Delhi, Mohit Pub., 2007.

Ram, S. and R. Kumar : *Encyclopaedia of Indian Freedom Struggle,* Commonwealth Pub., New Delhi, 2008.

Ray, B.N. : *Gandhigiri : Satyagraha After Hundred Years,* New Delhi, Kaveri Books, 2008.

S. Gopal: *Selected Works of Jawaharlal Nehru,* New Delhi, 1994.

Saksena, N.S.: *India: Towards Anarchy, 1967-1992,* New Delhi, Abhinav, 1993.

Sankar Ghose: *Congress Presidential Speeches,* New Delhi, 1975.

Sarvepalli Gopal: *Jawaharlal Nehru: An Anthology,* Delhi, 1980.

Sharma, P.R.P. : *Encyclopaedia of Hindu Religion and Ethics,* Anmol, New Delhi, 2008.

Stephen E. Ambrose and James Alden Barber: *The Military and American Society,* New York, 1972.

Trivedi, P.R. : *Concise Encyclopaedia of India,* Indian Pub., Delhi, 1998.

Yasin, Mohammad : *Indian Politics : Processes, Issues and Trends,* New Delhi, Kanishka, 2004.

# Index

□□□